Wilbur Samuel Jackman

Nature Study for the common Schools

Second Edition

Wilbur Samuel Jackman

Nature Study for the common Schools
Second Edition

ISBN/EAN: 9783337024949

Printed in Europe, USA, Canada, Australia, Japan

Cover: Foto ©Paul-Georg Meister /pixelio.de

More available books at **www.hansebooks.com**

NATURE STUDY

FOR

THE COMMON SCHOOLS

BY

WILBUR S. JACKMAN, A. B.

TEACHER OF NATURAL SCIENCE, COOK COUNTY NORMAL SCHOOL,
CHICAGO, ILL.

SECOND EDITION REVISED.

NEW YORK ·
HENRY HOLT AND COMPANY
1892

PREFACE.

In the preparation of this book it has been the aim to furnish a guide for teachers in the common schools who wish their pupils to pursue an adequate and symmetrical course in Natural Science. Science teaching for a few years past has been gradually working itself downward from the colleges and high schools into those of lower grades, but, in most cases, the plans followed, while fairly well adapted to the demands of advanced pupils, have been but poorly fitted to the needs of beginners. The plan here adopted is based upon what is believed to be the proper interpretation of the character of the knowledge that the child can acquire. This knowledge may be characterized as having great breadth but little depth. The forces of nature impinge upon the child from every side, and he responds at once to their touch. Animal, plant, mineral, river, cloud, sunbeam, mountain, physical and chemical changes are all matters of equal and absorbing interest to him, and if left to himself he will inquire as freely about one as another. It is a mistaken idea that the child's interest is best aroused by a " thorough " study of a few living things, animal or plant, such as form the chief stock in trade in many school-rooms. This specialization in elementary grades must result in one or both of two things : either the whole subject will become distasteful, or, at least, tiresome to the pupil, or his eyes will be closed to other sides of nature equally interesting and important. In either case the subject studied will be but poorly understood, because it has been isolated and its relations to other subjects not clearly seen. An attempt has here been made to get rid of the old linear arrangement of the different divisions of natural science in a course of study in which the various subjects were made to follow one another in an unnatural sequence.

The Unity of Science, with Life the central study, is the basal idea upon which the work has been prepared. Life, in the final analysis the individual's own life, is the center of all study, and the value of any particular subject must be ultimately estimated by what it contributes toward a better comprehension of it. This idea is embodied in the appended synopsis of the entire subject.

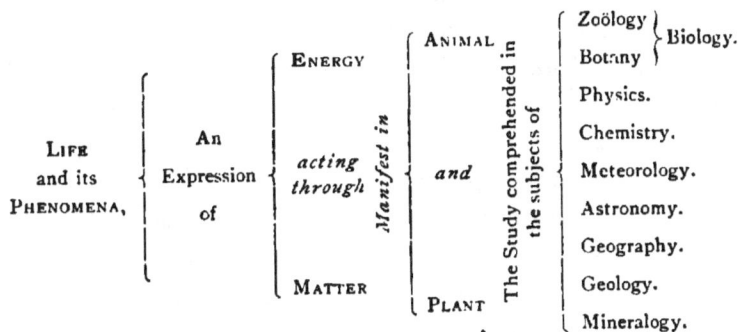

LIFE and its PHENOMENA, { An Expression of { ENERGY *acting through* MATTER { *Manifest in* { ANIMAL and PLANT { The Study comprehended in the subjects of { Zoölogy, Botany } Biology. Physics. Chemistry. Meteorology. Astronomy. Geography. Geology. Mineralogy.

It is not intended that the Science work outlined in the following pages should be incidental, as ordinarily understood, but that it shall be assigned a regular place in the daily programme with other lessons. Regularity and frequency of the exercises are of primary importance, while the absolute amount of time devoted to them is secondary. For a scheme of twenty exercises for a month the following division of the work is suggested : Zoölogy and Botany, one lesson each week ; Physics, Meteorology, Astronomy, Geography, and Geology, one lesson each in two weeks ; Chemistry and Mineralogy, one lesson each a month. This order and division should be modified so as to suit the character of the season, the grade, and the various minor conditions peculiar to the circumstances of the different teachers. By "lessons" it is meant that at regular times in general exercises the results of the pupils' observations will be gathered up and discussed and systematically arranged, and that at such times general experiments may be performed or other observatious made.

It may be thought that the results thus obtained will be disconnected and superficial ; but many thoughtful teachers who have tried the plan find the reverse to be true, and that the reasoning powers of the pupils are greatly quickened by their having at hand a large amount of data gathered in a varied experience. If the one lesson be of a *fruitful, stimulating* character, the pupils will be observant and thoughtful until the time for the next one arrives, which is all that is necessary to secure a healthy mind development.

The work assigned to each month has been selected because it will be most natural for the pupils in its proper season, and in many cases it can be better understood, and because at such times it is most convenient for the teacher to secure appropriate material and conditions. The division into different subjects is for the teacher's convenience alone, it not being necessary for the pupils to know even the approximate limitations of the subjects between which hard and fast lines do not exist.

It must not for a moment be supposed that it is the design for the teacher and pupils to *finish* the outlines prepared for any month or season. Science cannot be *finished* in a month, nor in a lifetime, though the study of it is too often most unfortunately finished by those teachers who put an end to their pupils' desire to know more about it. Certain lines have here been indicated, along which it is hoped that teachers may be able to awaken and foster observation and thought, and at the same time bring their pupils into fuller knowledge of themselves and of their duties and relations to the world around them.

The author desires to acknowledge his indebtedness for much that is contained in the chapter on Expression to the discussions which, under the leadership of Colonel F. W. Parker, have made the ever-to-be-remembered Monday evening Faculty meetings an unfailing source of inspiration in all the work.

W. S. J.

Cook County Normal School,
Chicago, Ill., *July* 1, 1891.

CONTENTS.

PAGE

PREFACE, ... III–VI
CHAPTER I. INTRODUCTORY: THE MOTIVE, . . . 1– 7
CHAPTER II. PRINCIPLES, ... 8–12
CHAPTER III. EXPRESSION, , ... 13–25
CHAPTER IV. PRACTICAL HINTS TO THE TEACHER, . 26–28

WORK FOR SEPTEMBER.

ZOÖLOGY:—Birds. Insects. Worms. Tadpoles. BOTANY:
—Fruits—Seeds. PHYSICS:—Light. Magnetism. CHEM-
ISTRY:—Fermentation. METEOROLOGY:—General Direc-
tions and Suggestions. Study of Signal Service Maps.
Charts I to VII. ASTRONOMY:—General Directions.
Equinox. Constellations. GEOGRAPHY:—Direction. Lati-
tude and Longitude. North America.—Position. GEOLOGY:
—Study of Immediate Vicinity. MINERALOGY:—Physical
Properties of Minerals. Mineralogical Record. Synopti-
cal Key for Analysis, ... 29–74

WORK FOR OCTOBER.

ZOÖLOGY:—General Observations. A Study of Tissues.
The Muscle. Connective Tissue. The Bone—Osseous
Tissue. Fat—Adipose Tissue. The Joint. BOTANY:
—Fall of Leaf. Distribution of Seeds. PHYSICS:—Evap-
oration. Ebullition. Condensation. Distillation. CHEM-
ISTRY:—Solution. Crystallization. METEOROLOGY:—Study
of Signal Service Maps. ASTRONOMY:—Change of Noon
Shadow. Full Moon. GEOGRAPHY:—Drainage—General
Conditions. North America. GEOLOGY:—Erosion and
Sedimentation. MINERALOGY:—Study of Sand, . 75–97

WORK FOR NOVEMBER.

PAGE

ZOÖLOGY:—General Observations. Animal Coverings and Warmth. The Skin of the Human Body. BOTANY:— Effects of Frost. Classes of Plants. PHYSICS:—Heat— Radiation—Absorption—Reflection. Temperature. Expansion—of Solids—of Liquids—of Gases. CHEMISTRY: —Chemical Change. METEOROLOGY:—Frost, etc. Study of Signal Service Maps. ASTRONOMY:—Variation of Length of Day. Seasons. GEOGRAPHY:—Climate of North America. Drainage of South America. GEOLOGY: —Pebbles. MINERALOGY:—Specific Gravity. Study of Coal, ... 98–134

WORK FOR DECEMBER.

ZOÖLOGY:—General Observations. Animal Movements. The Skeleton. BOTANY:—Effects of Freezing. PHYSICS: —The Lever. Equilibrium of Bodies. Heat—Liquefaction—Conduction—Convection. Capacity for Heat. Sources. CHEMISTRY:—Oxygen—Preparation—Experiments. METEOROLOGY:—Rainfall. Study of Signal Service Maps. ASTRONOMY:—Winter Solstice. GEOGRAPHY:—North America—Soil and Productions. Minerals. South America—Climate. GEOLOGY:—Atmospheric and Aqueous Agencies. MINERALOGY:—Iron Ore. Iron, 135–179

WORK FOR JANUARY.

ZOÖLOGY:—General Observations. Foods—Different Kinds. Cooking. Hunger and Appetite. BOTANY:—Effects of Freezing. PHYSICS:—Air—Elasticity—Pressure. The Pendulum. CHEMISTRY:—Hydrogen—Preparation and Experiments. METEOROLOGY:—Temperature. Study of Signal Service Maps. ASTRONOMY:—Rate of Change in Length of Day. Venus. GEOGRAPHY:—South America— Productions. GEOLOGY:—Fossil Plants. MINERALOGY: —Acid Tests, ... 180–220

WORK FOR FEBRUARY.

ZOÖLOGY:—General Observations. Prehension of Food. Mastication of Food. Insalivation and Swallowing.

PAGE

BOTANY:—Winter Condition of Plants. Pines. PHYSICS:
—Air—The Pump—The Siphon. Capillarity. Buoyancy
of Liquids. Pressure of Liquids. CHEMISTRY:—Carbon.
METEOROLOGY:—Snowfall. Study of Signal Service
Maps. ASTRONOMY:—Planets. Constellations. GEOGRA-
PHY:—Euro-Asia — Relief and Drainage. GEOLOGY:—
Fossil Animals. MINERALOGY:—Calcination, .   221–258

WORK FOR MARCH.

ZOÖLOGY:—Natural History Calendar. General Observa-
tions. The Circulation. BOTANY:—Tree Selected for
Special Study. PHYSICS:—Light. Images. Mirrors.
CHEMISTRY:—Nitrogen. Air. METEOROLOGY:—Extremes
in Weather. Study of Signal Service Maps. ASTRON-
OMY:—Vernal Equinox. Jupiter. Position of Planets.
GEOGRAPHY: —Euro-Asia—Climate. GEOLOGY:—Organic
Agencies. MINERALOGY:—Forms of Stones, .   259–302

WORK FOR APRIL.

ZOÖLOGY:—General Observations. Birds. Insects. Pond
Life. Respiration. BOTANY:—Germination. A Seed.
Development of Buds. Classification of Buds as to Posi-
tion, Activity, Covering, Arrangement. Underground
Forms of the Plant Axis. PHYSICS:—Light —Refraction.
Lenses. CHEMISTRY:—Water. METEOROLOGY:—Influ-
ences of the Month. Study of Signal Service Maps.
ASTRONOMY: — Function of Symbols. Constellations.
GEOGRAPHY:—Euro-Asia—Productions. GEOLOGY:—Study
of a Swamp. MINERALOGY:—Flame Tests, . .   303–344

WORK FOR MAY.

ZOÖLOGY:—Cruelty to Animals. Robbing Birds' Nests.
Preservation of Nests and Eggs. Birds' Nests and Eggs.
Parts of an Egg, and the Embryo. The Crawfish. Seeing.
BOTANY:—Use of Botanical Key. How to Study Flowers.
The Flower. Inflorescence. Buds. Ferns. Mosses.
PHYSICS:—Sound. CHEMISTRY:—Flame. METEOROLOGY:
—Influences of the Month. Study of the Signal Service

PAGE

Maps. ASTRONOMY:—Rate of Change in Length of Day and Night. Twilight. GEOGRAPHY:—Africa—Relief—Drainage—Climate and Productions. GEOLOGY:—Field Lessons. MINERALOGY:—Examination of Soils—Physical Constituents, ... 345-393

WORK FOR JUNE.

ZOÖLOGY:—General Remarks. Birds. Insects—Bees—Ants —Spiders—The House-fly — Beetles. Reptiles — Snakes —Turtles. BOTANY:—Plant Physiology. Water Culture. Plant Constituents. Leaves. Growth of Stem. The Grasses. PHYSICS:—Electricity. Magnetism and Frictional Electricity. Voltaic Electricity. CHEMISTRY:—Chlorine. METEOROLOGY:—Thunder-storms. Temperature. Study of Signal Service Maps. ASTRONOMY:—Importance of Searching for Causes. Summer Solstice. GEOGRAPHY:—Winds. Ocean Currents. GEOLOGY:—Springs and Wells. MINERALOGY:—Physical Properties of Soils, ... 394-438

INDEX 439-448

NATURE STUDY
FOR THE COMMON SCHOOLS.

INTRODUCTORY.

CHAPTER I.

THE MOTIVE.

It is of primary importance that the teacher who seeks to introduce elementary science into the common schools should make earnest study of the motive for doing such work, and at the same time carefully formulate intelligent methods for conducting it. It is under no other conditions that the undertaking can be successfully carried out, and, rather than attempt to do it blindly, the task had better not be begun.

Natural science, concerned largely with the earth and the living things it supports, affords the earliest and the only direct means of introducing the child to his earthly habitation. The life, health, and happiness of the individual is dependent upon his knowledge of the things about him, and upon the understanding that he has of their relations to each other and to himself. This knowledge and apprehension of relations can only be acquired by actual personal contact and experience with the things and forces which make up and govern the universe. It is true, the concept of a tree, gainéd from the study of the object itself, furnishes a starting point for a great deal of knowledge about trees in general, but that knowledge is weak and inaccurate so far as the objects described differ from that upon which the original concept is based. The avenues through which the elements of the concept must be gained are the senses, and therefore the very essence of science work, upon whatever plan conducted, must be direct, individual observation. The material selected should be of such character as will provide the mind with the most useful concepts. It will be a matter of profound surprise to any one who will take the trouble to investigate, to find how vague the ideas of very commonplace things are in the minds of many persons who are to be classed as intelligent and even educated. Critics make merry over patient endeavor to get pupils to do simple, easy things, which they say are self-evident from the very dawn of intelligence. Yet, the teacher will likely make a great mistake if he takes very many of even the simplest conceptions for granted. It is a proposition needing no demonstration that without these conceptions the reasoning faculty is powerless.

But true science work does not stop with mere seeing, hearing, or feeling ; it not only furnishes a mental picture as a basis for reasoning, but it includes an interpretation of what has been received through the senses. A child and a goat may see the same thing, with the advantage of vision on the side of the goat ; but the latter has no power to interpret what he sees, and is, therefore, essentially non-scientific. In these early interpretations, lie the beginnings of the reasoning power, and with its development comes self-reliance, independence of thought, and a general strength of character which marks a man among men. If a pupil be permitted to carefully examine an object or a set of conditions, and then be required to interpret what he sees, he is from that moment ever after stronger than he was before. By that act, no matter how trivial, he begins the great work of self-emancipation from the rule of chance in so far as his interpretation has taught him how the forces about him may be resisted, guided, and controlled.

A great work is to be done by inculcating living truth ; but one equally important must be accomplished in rooting out the influence of inherited errors. We are not yet free from the dominion of some super-stitions as dark as any that ever existed. There is a pressing need that the pupils be taught the truth about the laws of nature and about common things that, at least, they may not hereafter become the prey of the unscrupulous. It is by no means uncommon to find an advertisement of goodly proportions in daily papers, setting forth that Madame ——, seventh daughter of the seventh son, of necessity possessing occult power, will, for a very small consideration, reveal much that is of the highest importance to those in trouble, or otherwise in need of such information. Such advertisements throw strong side lights upon the present condition of the popular mind, from a scientific point of view. Properly interpreted, they mean that there are enough people about us, so grossly ignorant of natural laws, that they are the willing victims of a base fraud to the extent of supporting it in idleness at a handsome income, no doubt, after paying all expenses for advertisements and an establishment. But there is a larger class, perhaps, who will only plant their seeds in the light of the moon, who never begin anything on Friday, who dislike to be called number thirteen, and for whom a broken looking-glass bodes disaster.

The people of the present time over fifty years of age, who are absolutely free from such superstition, are the exception. And still further interpreting, in the r... ist narrow manner, Pope's dictum, "The proper study of mankind is man," pupils are actually taught to despise a great many creatures and things which probably play as important a part in the economy of the universe as do the lords of creation. In these times of indiscriminate pistol practice, nothing should be done which would tend to lower the value of human life in the estimation of the pupils ; but, in view of the ruthless and utterly purposeless slaughter of the harmless members of the so-called brute creation, the regard for human life seems almost exaggerated. The average boy may be tracked through the woods by the blood of the innocent creatures he destroys—a wanton destruction, based upon utter ignorance of the function of these creatures and upon groundless fears. From earliest childhood the notion is implanted that in most living things about him, of the brute creation, there is a hidden danger to his life or comfort. Then through the maxim that self-preservation is the first law of nature, he logically reaches his watchword, "kill." But if the truth were known, it is hardly an exaggeration to say that not one person in a thousand meets one thing in a thousand in the whole course of a year, which would do him the least harm. On the other hand, how many that are thoughtlessly destroyed do incalculable good? The notion, too, that fear of certain things and horror of others is instinctive and natural, is totally false, as any one may prove for himself by observing a little child. He is as much interested in a snake as in a kitten, and fondles one as freely as the other.

Ignorance of natural law is no less marked in its effects upon us than ignorance of living objects. Too many people still see in the lowering thunder cloud little else than the chariot of a great avenger ; who regard the lightning's stroke, the flood, and the fire chiefly as expressions of vindictive power. Speed the happy day when the general diffusion of scientific knowledge shall remove from the mind of man the last vestige of that feeling that he is being hunted off the face of the earth, the victim of a mighty wrath. Then, for the first time in the evolution of the race, will he be in the perfect attitude of a true student of nature.

While the motives for instruction in science here given may seem valid and of sufficient importance to warrant a place for it in the common schools, there is yet one thing lacking. The " Enacting Clause," to give positive character and vitality to the work, must be added. " For what good" must have an answer in a motive, which makes science instruction something more than a merely pleasant or fashionable pastime for both pupil and teacher. The true incentive will make scientific knowledge a necessity, and will do more than rouse simply a kind of adventitious interest in the works of nature. If it go no farther than this, then the teacher will be utterly unable to reach the pupil who says by word and action that he cares nothing for nature. The final motive for the study of science is to bring the pupil by degrees to a strong personal realization that he is the focus of innumerable forces about him which so bear upon him, and so limit his life and comfort, as to render the knowledge of how they may be resisted,

guided, and controlled, an absolute necessity.   Life, ultimately his own life, is the great center of all his interest
in the world ; and this motive will co-ordinate his interest
in nature exactly with his interest in his own existence.
This will give him life in the broadest and best sense,
which is the ultimate aim of all education.   Thus science
instruction takes its place in the common schools with a
motive at once pure and beneficent, and with an irre-
sistible appeal to all to become life-long students.
Many a boy who little cares whether, by the laws of
gravitation, a stone is pulled downward or pushed upward, will become interested intensely, when he realizes
that he is under its constant operation until it finally
pulls him downward into his grave.   The mechanics of
the lever is only so much "stuff and nonsense" to him,
until he finds that this knowledge will render possible an
economy of his energy, and thereby immensely prolong
his mortal existence.   In short, all phenomena of earth
and air are pregnant with the deepest interest when he
finds himself threatened through his ignorance and his
inability to interpret them.   When we for a moment consider how important this knowledge is, and how little of
what we possess was obtained in the schools, need we be
amazed to find that the average duration of human life
is but one-third of its possible length ?

No one has more clearly shown this point than Prof.
Huxley, who says : "Suppose it were perfectly certain
that the life and fortune of every one of us would, one
day or other, depend upon his winning or losing a
game of chess.   Don't you think that we should all consider it to be a primary duty to learn at least the names
and moves of the pieces ; to have a notion of a gambit,
and a keen eye for all the means of giving and getting

out of check? Do you not think that we should look
with disapprobation, amounting to scorn, upon the father
who allowed his son, or the state which allowed its members, to grow up without knowing a pawn from a knight?
Yet it is a very plain and elementary truth that the life,
fortune, and the happiness of every one of us, and more
or less of those who are connected with us, do depend
upon our knowing something of the rules of a game in-
finitely more difficult and complicated than chess. It is
a game which has been played for untold ages, every
man and every woman of us being one of the two players
in a game of his or her own. The chess-board is the
world, the pieces are the phenomena of the universe, the
rules of the game are what we call the laws of nature.
The player on the other side is hidden from us. We
know that his play is always fair, just, and patient. But
also we know to our cost that he never overlooks a mistake or makes the smallest allowance for ignorance.
To the man who plays well, the highest stakes are paid
with that sort of overflowing generosity with which the
strong shows delight in strength, and one who plays ill
is checkmated, without haste, but without remorse. My
metaphor will remind some of you of the famous picture
in which Retzsch has depicted Satan playing at chess
with a man for his soul. Substitute for the mocking
fiend in that picture a calm, strong angel, who is playing
for love, as we say, and would rather lose than win, and
I should accept it as an image of human life."

CHAPTER II.

PRINCIPLES.

IT is obvious that the methods of instruction adopted by the teacher in any subject should be those which suit themselves to the natural conditions of the pupil. The proper clew which will enable the teacher to determine upon the principles which must guide him in his methods of instruction in elementary science, must come, therefore, from a close study of the child. The normal child himself will tell by his actions what things appeal earliest and most strongly to him, and will thus indicate to the teacher the lines along which it is best to guide him. The time has come for teachers when "a little child shall lead them."

If it is perfectly safe to take the spontaneous development of the child's mind under the influence of his natural environment as a guide in instructing him, it is necessary for the teacher to carefully study the child's methods and to critically scan both the kind and the character of the knowledge he acquires. With this in mind, turn him loose for a time upon the world and give him rein. He will return by and by, in his realm a discoverer and a conquerer. He will tell of the flowers that he finds in his pathway; of the trees, and of the birds which sing in their branches. He tells of the shining pebble and sparkling sand beneath his feet, and of the great clouds rolling through the heavens overhead. He has found the tiny insect in its hidden home, and the remotest star whose radiance strikes his eye. He has watched the wonderful journey of the sun from the earliest morning ray, till the last golden shaft at night, and feels anew his delight at the appearance of the silver moon. He has been startled by the lightning's flash and awed into silence by the roar of thunder. He has seen the stream winding its way to the river, now peaceful, and again as a roaring torrent tearing its banks and building bars, and he has seen the fog lifting itself from the valleys. He has been fanned by the soft winds of summer, and chilled by the blasts of winter. He has tried to bathe himself in the glories of the rainbow and he has coveted the diamonds of the dew. He has been drenched by the pelting rainstorm and he has rolled himself in the blanket of snow. He has witnessed that great resurrection in spring-time, and has seen the living world grow, mature, and die, almost as he rouses himself from slumber in the morning, and sinks to rest again at night. He has tested his own strength and feels something of his own possibilities and limitations. In short, the great universe of God has been spread before him and he has scanned the whole as an open page.

This observation illustrates two important points—the only ones, it may be said, necessary to consider, in formulating a course of study. First, it gives a true idea of the scope of a child's observations, and second it indicates the character of the knowledge he can acquire. It is amazing to find what a field of observation is open for a child but two years of age. Every nook and corner of the house is explored and becomes part of the known. He ranges through the door-yard, garden, and farm, and learns the names of fruits, animals, and places. He takes up everything with such avidity and so rapidly that it would seem, if he could be kept growing at the same rate until he has lived through the years allotted to the common school course only, he would be a

renowned scientist. That this marvelous interest does
flag, however, is painfully evident, and the question that
pressess itself home is, Who is reponsible for it ?   Who,
indeed, can be but the teacher ?   The child comes to
him with an expanding soul, even as all have felt
their souls expanding once, under the genial influences of nature, and the school proceeds to deliber-
ately squeeze the life out of him with the same modes
of instruction which squeezed the life out of the generations before him.   He comes to the teacher with his
eyes filled with a thousand pictures, but they are ignored,
and he is robbod of them one by one until at last the
beauty of this world fades from his sight and it is changed
to a vale of tears.   In the beginning of science instruction and to the end, the fact must be recognized that the
child stands at the center of the universe, and from first
to last is touched by everything in it.   A complete and
symmetrical course of instruction must proceed outward
from this center though the phenomena that surround
it to the laws that lie beyond them.   By such a course
only can the teacher hope to impress upon the pupil his
true relations to the things and forces about him.

It remains to make more specific inquiry as to how the
teacher shall proceed in order to attain this end.   Turn
again to the child in direct contact with nature, and
look into the character of the knowledge he acquires.
If he tells about a flower, it will probably be something
of its color ; if about a bird, its song or its plumage ; if
about a pebble, its smoothness or roundness, and so on·
The character is unmistakable.   It is all breadth and no
depth.

This interpretation of the action of the child-mind
meets with opposition because it seems to encourage su-

perficiality. But the clew thus obtained from the child himself gives unmistakable evidence as to the course the teacher should pursue. It is a radical error to attempt to make specialists of the pupils from the beginning. Undue prominence given to any particular branch of science in the common schools will lead to one-sided development, and in the end to superficial work. Early specialization leads inevitably to a certain linear arrangement of the different branches of science which is radically wrong in its conception and misleading and confusing in its effects.

The arrangement of the subjects so that one shall, in turn, succeed another in regular order (this not being the same in any two schools), is a device which has done the most to obscure the relations of the so-called branches of science to each other and to the child. However necessary such an arrangement may be for an advanced course, in elementary work there is not the slightest foundation for it, either in nature as it presents itself for study, or in the conditions under which the child's mind develops. Nor is it so important as many teachers suppose to use the material afforded by any particular subject in a fixed order. In zoölogy, for example, it matters not the least whether the child begins with a vertebrate or an invertebrate, provided, in that particular thing there is something which he wishes to study. In botany, it matters not whether it be a fungus or a flower that opens up this great kingdom of life to him. The mistake made on this point by teachers is a fundamental one, and it lies in supposing that those objects which are physically near to the child are the only ones which have a psychic nearness. A bright butterfly, or even an oyster, is much nearer, psychically, to the child than a horse.

In disposing of this difficult question of arranging a course of study and selecting suitable material, the teacher must take his cue from nature and from his own immediate surroundings. Science teaching indoors will be vastly enhanced if it be supplemented and reinforced by nature outside.   The work should therefore be planned to suit the changing and recurring seasons. This is best because it is most natural, for the child is placed in contact with nature under normal conditions, and it is much more easy for the teacher and pupils to obtain appropriate material.   It is true, flowers may be studied in winter time ; but to the child they are freaks, and such a study is a distortion of the subject to his mind, and it gives the teacher endless trouble. A study of the plant, with its buds housed in their winter quarters or with its seeds buried in frozen soil, is an appropriate subject for the season, and the supply of material is natural and abundant.

The most serious obstacle in the way of science work is the teacher's own lack of faith in his ability to do anything useful or creditable.   He should without hesitation begin with the simple things around him, and grow with the pupils.   The crude and scanty appliances at hand, well used, will open the way for better ones which will surely come, for, in the end, the schools are not to suffer from the want of any really good thing.

CHAPTER III.

EXPRESSION.

THE value of science work to the pupil is very greatly enhanced by a complete and clear but concise expression. Success in teaching the subject depends so largely upon the teacher's judgment in using the appropriate modes of expression at the proper stage of each particular kind of work, that it becomes necessary to give the subject careful attention. Teachers usually lay much stress upon oral and written language ; but valuable as they may be, they are inadequate to the demands which a study of science makes upon the pupil for thought expression.

In order that the subject of expression may be understood, it is necessary to consider it in its relation to the means by which knowledge is gained. The various modes of expression have a natural basis in the different modes of study. By a mode of study is meant the means and the process by which the mind receives data from the world without. These modes may be included under three heads, as follows : First, the study of the object ; second, the study of the object by some means which partially symbolize it, and third, the study by means of symbols only.

The first mode mentioned, ordinarily termed direct observation, may call into play any or all the senses, touch, sight, hearing, taste, smell, and the muscular sense. On the other hand, the real object under observation presents all the attributes which can be cognized by the mind. As a result, having received one or more elementary ideas through one or more of the senses, the mind forms for itself a mental product which has the closest possible correspondence to the real object without. This is the concept of the object.

The second mode of study makes use of pictures or models, and to a limited extent of onomatopoetic words, which cannot present directly all the attributes of the real object, but may partially or wholly symbolize them. Fewer of the senses may therefore be engaged in this, and an imperfect concept is the necessary result.

The third mode of study is by means of hearing language and reading, and consequently has to do with pure symbols only. With the exception of an occasional onomatopoetic word, before mentioned, whatever may have been the origin of the symbols, they cannot now be properly considered the attributes of any object. Their function is simply to arouse in the mind certain activities which form the concept from data already there.

In its broad sense, the function of expression is to produce an external thing which corresponds to the internal concept. The motive for expression is, subjective, to intensify the thought of the one expressing it, and, objective, to convey that thought to others. Ethically considered, expression may be either selfish or unselfish, but there is naturally no conflict between the two ends. The more clearly defined and intense the thought becomes to the individual, the better can he convey it to others, and there is a naturally increasing desire to do so.

The modes of expression have a natural correspondence to the modes of study above outlined. They may be included under the heads of gesture (including facial expression, and attitude), music without words (including the different tones of voice used in oral language, and all moans and cries), making, modeling, painting, drawing, oral language and written language. Each mode of expression is peculiar in this, that it has a special function of its own which cannot be perfectly performed by any other one or more modes, though of course they do supplement each other in almost every expression of thought.

Closely associated with oral language, and from which it may have arisen, are the two modes above classed under gesture and music. The peculiar function of these most subtle forms, the one appealing to the eye and the other to the ear, is to convey directly from mind to mind the idea of emotion. No other mode has the adequacy of either of these for this purpose. They each convey an idea of something which is absolutely beyond the domain of material representation. They place man in immediate touch with his fellow-man, and form the universal soul-bond of humanity—nay, of all animate creation, for by them we even understand the brutes, and they us and each other. Originally of objective value chiefly, now all training in attitude, gesture, and modulation of voice, takes advantage of the power which these have to intensify the thought in the one giving it expression. The data for the thoughts which find expression by these means may be gathered through any or all of the senses.

The difficulties encountered by the teacher in dealing with these two modes are different from those which arise in teaching any of the others. Whereas the others are more or less arbitrary, these are perfectly natural, and they are the result, not of teaching, but of heredity. The difficulty lies in co-ordinating the more arbitrary forms with them. To make the word exactly correspond to the look, gesture, or tone is the thing to be sought. The naturalness of these modes is, unfortunately, very early lost, in most

cases through a soul-consuming self-consciousness, and it
is regained with the greatest difficulty. Upon its proper
co-ordination with these modes, the general intelligibility
of oral expression depends, and by them the teacher has
an almost exact measure of the intensity of the pupil's
thought and of his interest and comprehension of the
subject in hand.

Making is the most definite and complete mode of
expression where material representation is possible.
This is because the maker becomes acquainted not
only with the object in all of its parts and as a whole,
but also with the nature of the substances with which he
works. As it is only by a study of the real object
that all of its attributes appeal to the mind, so it is
only by making, that the exact external correspondence
to the concept of these can be reproduced. It is the
peculiar function of making to give this external correspondence material form. It is the simplest and lowest
mode because there are no mental pictures involved that
do not have a concrete basis in the material before the
maker. It is a universal mode because the idea, that of a
certain box, for example, will be expressed by all in the
same way. This allies it closely with the two preceding
forms.

The data for this mode of expression are gathered
through all of the senses, and it therefore follows that in
the outward material representation of the idea, each
sense may act as a corrective upon all of the others and
thus making becomes one of the easiest modes. Great
difficulties arise, however, due to the peculiar and various
properties of the materials employed, such as wood, stone,
iron, and glass. This is further enhanced by the inability
to properly estimate the value of solid angles and lines and

by the lack of skill necessary to form flat and curved surfaces.

Science work offers great opportunities for this mode of expression. Throughout the whole of physics and chemistry there are almost numberless pieces of apparatus and devices which should be made by the pupil. The difficulties peculiar to this mode are more than balanced by the intense interest which the pupil always has in making something. It brings him to the joy of a new creation in which he plays the rôle of creator, and, in the cultivation of self-reliance, this can hardly be overestimated. And when still further, as in the Sloyd, it is the thought, "This is for some one I love—for father or mother," that drives the plane or handsaw, it makes it, in its reflex upon character, second to no other moral influence.

Modeling, in itself, has to do entirely with form, both external and internal, and so far, it is identical with making. As a mode of expression, though, it is differentiated from making in regard to size. An object may be modeled many times as large or small as that of which it is intended to give the idea. The data for the model are gathered through the senses of sight and touch, and while, therefore, the judgment lacks some of the safeguards thrown around it in making, this is offset by the fact that there is less of the complete idea to be expressed by it. The difficulty to be overcome in modeling, as in making, is in the estimation of solid angles and in the formation of curves and plane surfaces. The material used may be of such character as to reduce the difficulty of its manipulation to the minimum.

The use of this mode in science work is varied. In zoölogy, clay modeling may be used with great advantage in the study of the larger animals and in the study of the skeleton. In botany, early study of roots, the various forms of underground stems and fruits will necessitate its use. In geography, geology, and mineralogy either sand or clay may be used to show the relief of any given area covered by an excursion or a field-lesson, and the latter is specially fitted for showing rock strata, dip, and forms of crystals.

Painting as a mode of expression is unique. Its peculiar function is to give the idea of color—something which cannot be even approximated by any other mode. It stands in contrast with both making and modeling, because it is primarily independent of volume, size, and substance. It can, it is true, be made to suggest solidity of form after the idea has been gained by other means.

The data for painting are gathered through the sense of sight alone. The chief difficulty which besets the judgment is due to the fact that there is no corrective sense; if the eye fails to give the proper datum there is no other means by which the mistake may be discovered.

In a large part of elementary science work the value of painting can hardly be overestimated. Primary pupils can tell far more with their brushes and colors, and can tell it much better than they can with either tongue, pen, or pencil. It will greatly enhance interest in the study of birds, insects, fruits, flowers, leaves, and minerals.

In drawing, the chief thing to be expressed is outline, not only of the whole, but, also that of the parts of an object. This mode of expression, closely related to painting on one side and to making and modeling on the other, is independent of solidity of form and size. It is allied to modeling and more remotely to making because it deals with form, but only so far as it can be expressed in outline without giving the idea primarily of volume. The chief difficulty in cultivating this form of expression with beginners lies in a lack of muscular control which is necessary in drawing straight and curved lines, and in the errors of judgment in the measurement of angles and estimation of distances. The judgment is, in this form of expression, dependent upon sight alone, and in this respect it is allied to painting.

In science, drawing may be employed with great advantage in all subjects. Its earliest application is found in the representation of apparatus used in physics and chemistry, and all material where sharpness of outline and detail of structure are required.

Between written language and the forms of expression already considered, there is a wide difference. It is wholly an arbitrary means of expressing thought, and can intensify it subjectively only in this way : by means of the device of which this mode of expression makes use —that is the written sentence—a relation is expressed which by the aid of this visible sign, is held more steadily before the mind as an object of study. In function, it is distinguished from the preceding modes by the fact that certain relations may be directly expressed by it which lie wholly beyond their domain. "Man should help his fellow-man," expresses an obligation ; by the written sentence, this idea is conveyed to others—something which could not be accomplished by any other single mode.

The judgment expressed by the written sentence rests upon data that may be gathered through every avenue of sense. The chief difficulty is in the lack of muscular control which is necessary to guide the pen, and in mak-

ing the arbitrary association of certain letters with definite sounds which the former represents.

In science work, written language is of universal application as a mode of expression. Too often, however,
its use is demanded when some other mode would be
more appropriate.

Closely allied to written expression is that by oral
language. It is related to written language, and differs
from all the other modes because ideas can be expressed
by it which are beyond the reach of material representation by any other single form. Its peculiarity is found in
the tone of voice which, independently of the words ut-
tered, intensifies or diminishes the strength and clearness
of expression. In developing this form, the chief obstacle
is encountered in the difficulty which the child finds in
associating his thoughts and feelings with the jingle of
sounds which represents them in the spoken sentence,
and in the training of the organs concerned in articulate
speech.

All of the senses may be concerned in completing the
thought which finds expression in oral language. Prac·
tice with this form of expression is frequently pushed
too far. Teachers are naturally ambitious to hear
their pupils talk, and feel disappointed when they fail
to so express themselves. Yet with children, that
it is wholly inadequate, sometimes, for the full
expression of the thought, is a fact which should be
recognized.

While expression may admit of the foregoing analysis,
and it would seem that each mode has its own peculiar
function, it will be observed that usually two or more
may be combined in the expression of any thought, the

fullness and clearness of which are greatly enhanced thereby.

It remains now to consider the natural order of their development. The different modes are not developed entirely *seriatim*, but something of the serial order is enforced, in practice, by certain difficulties before mentioned in connection with each. Expression is primarily dependent upon external stimuli, and it follows that the mode will be determined somewhat by the character of the stimulus of which the organism is susceptible, and for a like reason, the order of development will also be somewhat fixed.

The earliest kind of stimuli which the child receives are those producing bodily pleasure or pain, and the expression corresponds. The smile of the young babe in its cradle is the earliest expression of that light which through its new-born soul is destined, it may be, to make luminous the dark places of earth. The frown flitting like a shadow across its smooth brow is the earliest prophecy of a spirit which is born, perhaps, to crush a tyrant and emancipate a people. This mode, coming to the child by heredity alone, has no conscious relation at this time to the thought or feeling beneath it.

The next stimuli are received through the sense of sight, derived from the mere presence of an object and through the sense of touch, from its smoothness, roughness, hardness, or softness and so on. The appropriate form of expression is by oral sounds leading to articulate speech. After the mere presence of the object is made known the next stimulus comes from its most striking peculiarity. This is most frequently received through the sense of sight, and comes usually

from the color of the object. The natural and appropriate form of expression is by use of brush and paint in
color work. The pupil constantly compares the color he
uses with that of the object, and thus supplies the only
corrective to his judgment possible in this case. Associated closely with the idea of color is that of form. This
demand for an additional mode of expression is met by
exercises in modeling. This order, however, should often
be reversed, since peculiarity of form is sometimes more
conspicuous than brilliancy of color.

Developing considerably later than the ideas of color
and form is the idea of the outline of an object. The
natural expression for this is by drawing. Observation
confirms the fact that drawing with the pencil should not
begin much below the fourth grade. Previous to that it
may be practiced on the black-board in much broader
outlines and with less details than that required by the
pencil. This is not only because detail of figure does not
appear early to the pupil, but because his muscles are not
yet sufficiently under control. The arm moves the hand
chiefly from the shoulder ; individual muscles that move
the hand and fingers, absolutely necessary to fineness of
detail, are not yet separated one from another in their
functions. This difficulty is rapidly and completely
overcome by giving opportunities for blackboard drawing when the full arm may at first be used in drawing
large-sized figures.

Making as a mode of expression may be commenced
very early, but the difficulties, arising from a lack of
knowledge respecting the nature of the materials, somewhat limit its range. Its use is further diminished by the
fact that many things studied cannot be made. This is
offset by the intensely practical character of the work·

There may be those who do not wish to paint, who cannot draw, who fear to speak, or are too lazy to write, but
a pupil is rarely to be found who will not be interested
in *making* something. Most boys are in a continual
state of perplexity in trying to decide whether they will
be blacksmiths, carpenters, or shoemakers when they
grow up, and, for all such, making is the mode of expression *par excellence.*

The development of expression by means of written language should be coincident with that of the other modes.
Through its peculiar function, it acts as a corrective and
check upon all of the others. It is very important that it
should stand in proper relation as to amount with the
other modes and to the actual demand for it. Teachers
frequently err by trying to force their pupils to write beyond what they really have to express. Some pupils appear to talk well, but write poorly ; yet it may be that the
sum total of all their "talk" actually expresses no more
than the little they write. Again, too high an estimate
is often placed upon what the pupil really sees, and consequently there is a feeling of disappointment at the
amount of the written work. Rationally employed, written
expression is the most valuable adjunct to science work.

Although there seems to be a somewhat definite order
of development for the different modes of expression, yet
when once properly begun they should all be carried
forward in due proportion throughout the entire course.
If faithfully done, the so-called crudities and blotches of
the first grade will become tasteful products in the eighth.

The subject matter in science work presents itself
broadly under three heads: the study of *function*, the study
of *form*, and the study of the *mutual relations* between
function and form. These divisions at once suggest to

the thoughtful teacher a proper grouping of the modes
of expression. Evidently, those which best accompany
the study of function are oral language and written language, and to a less important extent what has been included under gesture. The other modes are not barred,
however, since one may, by a drawing, or in a clay model,
show how a squirrel holds a nut; but they are hardly to
be considered the initial modes of expression for such a
fact.

In the study of form almost any of the remaining
modes are more appropriate in the beginning than either
oral or written language. The particular form must be
determined by the one who makes the study—not by the
teacher. It is a fundamental mistake for a teacher to
say to his class, "We will model this," or "We will paint
that," or "We will draw the other." The substance of
the real question which should be proposed is, "What
do you see about this, or what can you find out about it,
and how will you tell it?" When the teacher dictates
"Draw," "Paint," or "Model," he must run the risk
either of telling the pupil to represent what he does not
see or understand, or else he is forced into the contra-
dictory position of pointing out to him the very thing he
should discover for himself in order that he may represent it. This logically and actually destroys the real
point of the lesson, so far as science is concerned, and
reduces it to the level of a lesson in dead color and
dumb form. The pupil cannot express what he does not
see, and he must express what he does see through what
is to him the most natural and appropriate channel. For
example, in beginning the study, to ask a child to model
a brightly colored butterfly is to outrage his every sense
of fitness ; while to expect him to either paint or model

with great enthusiasm a long-legged, angular grasshopper, is vanity of vanities. Full expression of thought will naturally involve more than one mode, but there is decidedly a right and a wrong place at which to begin.

The thoughts which come into the mind as it contemplates the mutual adaptations of the different parts of nature to each other, and their relations to the whole are, in their suggestions of infinite law, the loftiest that can possess the human soul. The full expression of these conceptions, involving the highest relations of man to man, rises to the plane of fine art. Embalmed in verse, or picture, or song, or chiseled stone, it will to future generations mirror forth the best and purest thoughts of this age.

PRACTICAL HINTS TO THE TEACHER.

In acting upon the suggestions in the following lessons, it is essential that the teacher should understand the spirit and purpose of the book. Recognizing the fact that most teachers find themselves unprepared in the subject matter of elementary science, the book has been written with a view to guiding them in their study so that they may acquire some of the necessary knowledge by actual work, and not with the intention of pouring out a mass of so-called facts for them to memorize. Teachers can never equip themselves for this work by reading alone ; if that were possible, the requisite preparation could be quickly made and, with a market well supplied with interesting reading books, it would have been done long ago. The main trouble is, not that the teacher's mind is so barren of facts, but that he lacks the scientific habit and methods of study. These can only be acquired by the exercise of the greatest patience, on the teacher's part, in solving for himself some of the simple problems presented so profusely by nature on every hand. Under every division of the subject it has been the aim to present two or three, sometimes more, leading topics which the teacher should assist the pupils to work out to the limits of their capacity by careful observation. Every recitation in the school-room must be preceded by lessons in actual observations, enough of which must be demanded from every pupil to give him a basis for his reasoning. A most pernicious habit, and one very easily acquired, is that of asking a pupil a question which will start him to guessing, thus deceiving himself into the belief that he is actually reasoning. As a mere " Question and Answer Book," this book must inevitably fail, since that is at utter variance with its purpose. The interrogative rather than the declarative form has been adopted because it has been found a little easier, by the former means, to carry the thread of a thought through several suggestions. In some cases one question suggests the thought of a topic ; in others several questions are asked for the same purpose.

The teacher's ingenuity will be continually taxed to furnish new devices adapted to the correct development of a topic, which will also be properly subject to his own peculiar circumstances and conditions. The latter are not the same for any two teachers ; and the fact that this will modify the treatment of any question is one that, first of all, must be recognized and acted upon.

In approximating what the teacher should have in mind in the preparation for each lesson to be given, the following outline is submitted as a guide :

I. PLAN FOR EACH LESSON.

   A. Knowledge of Subject-Matter.

    1. By direct observation.

     (*a*) What can be seen in a field-lesson ?

     (*b*) What can be collected by individual pupils ?

     (*c*) What can the pupils make ?

    2. What reading belongs legitimately to the preparation ?

    3. The adaptation to the pupils' and teachers' conditions.

    4. The adaptation to the age and capabilities of the pupils, *i. e.*, to the grade.

5. What is the length of time which should be devoted to the preparation of the lesson?

B. *What modes of expression should be used?*

1. Oral language? ⎫
2. Written language? ⎬ What suggestive reading?
                     ⎭
3. Painting.
4. Modeling.
5. Drawing.
6. Making.

C. *How is the lesson related to other subjects?*

1. Reading.
2. Number.
3. History and literature.
4. Language.

II. HINTS TO BE OBSERVED IN GIVING THE LESSON?

1. Have a reason clearly in mind for giving every
lesson. *Seek for this in the relation of the subject to the child.*

2. Have a reason clearly in mind for the way in
which the lesson is presented. *Seek for this
in a study of the laws which govern the growth
of the child's mind.*

3. Plan only for such work as the pupils can do
for themselves, or, at least, take the leading
part in doing.

4. Place the child directly in contact with nature
under normal conditions.

5. Begin with something which is really a part of
the pupil's experience—*not with something
which you have to tell him.*

6. Accept, as good, only such results as indicate
honesty of purpose and growth of mind.

7. Be faithful, and bide your time.

Zoölogy.

Each season of the year has its own peculiar influence upon living things, animal and plant. It is therefore most convenient and certainly most interesting to study each phase of life in the appropriate season, inasmuch as one may then more easily trace the various phenomena observed in living things to the forces in nature which cause them. As the sun rises later and later, and sets earlier, sinking still lower in the southern sky, and the air now and then steals down upon us with an edge acquired in northern snow-fields, animal creation takes the hint and prepares for the inevitable and impending change. The birds, the young ones that have never seen a flake of snow, as well as the veterans of experience, in good time gather themselves together, and within a few hours are safe in another zone. Their luckless relatives, the reptiles, appear with less and less frequency, and, finally, in the lowest depths of their burrows give themselves up to a stupor that seems more like death than sleep. The winged insect hosts, battered and bedraggled, demoralized by the gayeties of the season, until mere wrecks of their former selves, for most part stiffen and die where they are, rather than give up one moment of present pleasure to thoughts for the future, or desert the fields that may have seemed to them to promise endless enjoyment. Others, apparently as much by chance as through design, are saved from such fate by finding a lodgment in cracks in old walls, in decaying logs, under stones, and in holes in the ground. Other creatures, too plucky to leave, and refusing to waste the winter in sleep, seek to cut down living expenses in the time of dearth by taking on an extra thickness of fur or hair, and by packing away great layers of fat in times of plenty. In the streams the changes are not less marked. Chilled, and deprived of their insect food, the fishes seek the bottom and hide in recesses among the rocks. The " craws " withdraw themselves into their dens in the mingled sand and gravel, while the tadpoles wriggle themselves under leaves and grass on the sides and in the bottom of the ponds, and for a time their froggish ambition is stayed. Nor are these influences unfelt among human kind. Despite the fact that our natural appetites are becoming somewhat depraved by the fruits and various vegetables which modern means of rapid transit make possible for us in January, we still are in a measure moved by instincts similar to those which control our humble brethren, the brutes. The gradual change in color, texture, and thickness of clothing, and the modification in our appetites, are signs the youngest school-child may note, and which he will be interested to understand. These changes, in the total amounting to a revolution in a living creature's mode of life, take place every year so silently and almost imperceptibly as to scarcely attract attention of people in general ; nor does even the keenest observer yet fully understand the causes by which they have been wrought. To lead to a careful study of these phenomena, in which we ourselves are involved more deeply than might at first be suspected, by teaching the child to live in close and loving communion with nature about him, is the highest duty of the teacher. Not by set lessons in the recitation-room, nor by dissections in the laboratory alone, can this be accomplished ; before these can reveal the depths of their meaning he must study LIFE in at least some of its myriad forms, and know something of the forces that produce it, and conditions under which it exists.

The teacher should select from the following topics a few of those which are best suited to the conditions for study that environ the pupils. A thicket, or even a single tree, will generally enable the pupils to study the topics on birds.

To collect insects, the pupils should be provided with small nets. Make these by bending a wire, about No. 8 or No. 9, into a hoop six inches in diameter, and then twisting the ends together for two or three inches to form a handle. This may be thrust into a hole made in the end of an old broom-stick for a longer handle, if desired. Make the net about eighteen inches deep, using mosquito-netting or cheese-cloth. A little practice will enable the pupils to get the insect and transfer it from the net to the poison bottle (see Zoölogy for April, under Insects) with-out marring them. Collect not only those insects which are to be seen flying about, but also those that may be obtained by jarring the branches of a shrub or tree over the open net. A great number may also be easily obtained by placing in convenient places shallow vessels containing sweetened water or vinegar. Naturalists sometimes smear tree trunks with a mixture of beer and molasses for the same purpose.

In the lower grades, one or two poison bottles will suf-fice for each room. In the grammar grades each pupil should be encouraged to place a poison bottle among the material, which he should be expected to collect and keep for his own use during the year. The primary pupils will make far more use of the living insects than of the dead ones ; but in the upper grades the study will naturally be more detailed, and dead insects will be required.

In order to observe the work of earthworms in plugging their burrows, select some place where they may easily obtain leaves as they fall from the trees. It is astonishing to find how many leaf-stalks are sometimes pulled into one burrow.

BIRDS.

1. Are any birds nest-building or laying eggs at present?

2. Can you distinguish the young from the old? Which parent do they most resemble?

3. Do the young ones sing? Are they still under the care of the old birds after they have learned to fly?

4. Have any disappeared that were noticed during the summer?

The times of migration vary somewhat with the season, within rather narrow limits. The birds should be watched closely during this month and the next.

5. What influences can you discover at this season which would cause the birds to migrate?

INSECTS.

Nothing is more wonderful and interesting than the great variety of insect life which may be studied at this time. Some one has remarked that no region on the globe has proven so inhospitable that some insect cannot adapt itself to it ; nor has any other living creature succeeded in doing anything which the insects do not imitate.

1. In what different places have you found insects? Look on the leaves of plants, under boards, logs, stones,

etc., in old walls, in cellars, in cupboards, in the grass, on the flowers, and in holes in the ground.

2. What are the chief differences between those that spend their time in the open air and those that live under stones, etc., as, for example, between butterflies and beetles ?

3. What insects can you find that must have liquid food ? What ones take solid food ?

4. Where do butterflies get their food ? Can you tell certainly if they get it from flowers ?

5. Do they visit all kinds of flowers ? Is their food solid or liquid ?

6. If the flower furnishes their food where is it stored ?

7. What means does the butterfly employ in examining the flower ? What does it do with the organ when not in use ?

8. Does the butterfly store food for the future ?

9. How does it cling to the plant ?

10. How does it dispose of its wings when at rest ?

11. Compare the upper and under surfaces of the wings ; which render it more conspicuous.

12. Compare the color of butterflies with that of the flowers they visit.

13. How does the character of a butterfly's flight differ from that of a bird ? How can you account for it ?

14. Is the peculiar flight of advantage or disadvantage to it ?

15. Which has relatively the greater wing surface, the butterfly or bird ? Which is the stronger flyer ?

16. Compare the fore and hind wings ; is the venation the same in both ? Is it the same in the right and left wings of the same pair ?

17. Of what use are the legs? Compare and contrast the different pairs.

18. In what order do they move when walking? What way do they bend at the joints? Why are so many joints needed?

19. How are they arranged during flight?

20. In what directions can the butterfly see you approach?

21. Where are its eyes? Can it turn its head?

22. Can it move its eyes without moving its head?

23. Are the eyes sensitive? Can you tell if it has the sense of feeling?

24. Has it the sense of smell and of hearing? Does it make any sound? Does it breathe?

25. Are they social? Do they build nests?

26. Do they prefer sunlight or shade? Where do they stay during the night?

27. Are any eggs to be found at this season?

28. Can you tell the male from the female? Can you see any reason for difference in color?

Collect larvæ (caterpillars) of different kinds and put them in small boxes covered with light netting. Feed them with the leaves of the plant upon which they were found.

In a way similar to the above outline, study grasshoppers, beetles, bees, and flies.

WORMS.

1. Note the manner in which worms plug their burrows with leaves, etc. Do they eat them?

2. Are the castings as numerous as in the summer months?

3. Can you find sticks or straws or other material that has been drawn into their burrows during the season?

TADPOLES.

1. In what stages of development are tadpoles to be found?

2. How do they breathe? Look sharply for a small hole on one side behind the mouth. Is it always on the same side?

3. What is their food?

4. Do they venture out on the land?

5. What enemies do they have?

BOOKS FOR REFERENCE. Humboldt Library: Nos. 115 and 116. No. 99, Nature Studies, chapter on Birds of Passage. No. 33, Vignettes from Nature, chapters iv, xiv. No. 64, Distribution of Life. No. 92, Formation of Vegetable Mold. No. 26, The Evolutionist at Large, chapters x, xiv.

Botany.

Introduce the lessons on plants with outdoor observations both with the class as a whole, if possible, and by requiring individual work out of school hours. Indicate the points of a lesson a sufficient length of time before the recitation to give the pupils opportunity to make the proper observations. Only a small part of a plant's life-history is revealed to us in a single month, but in many cases the entire cycle of its life is shown in the course of a year. The study should so proceed, therefore, as to reveal the history as a connected whole when the year is ended. Facts are rarely interesting unless seen in their proper relations to each other. All drawings, paintings, models in clay as far as possible, and written work, should be carefully preserved so that additions may be made to them in the different seasons. Sheets of paper of a size 8½x11 inches, both for writing and drawing, will be found convenient for pupils of grammar-school age, while such sheets cut in two crosswise will suit those in the primary grades. These may be preserved by the pupil in a portfolio, which he can easily construct for himself out of cardboard. Drawing paper of the above-mentioned size is large enough to admit of the representation of the most prominent features of a plant's history. The drawings and paintings made in the fall, of leaf, twig, fruit, etc., should be so placed as to admit representations of the germinating seed and young plant to be placed beside them in the spring. Each sheet will thus present a *whole*, and the pupil will almost unconsciously acquire the habit of bringing all individual facts observed into proper relation with each other.

It will be a revelation to those botanists who are book-bred, as well as to the children, to find that there is not a day of the whole growing season in which some seeds, belated for one reason or another, are not trying to germinate. Germination of seeds is associated mostly with spring-time, because the seeds that do get a fair start at that time are the ones that become so conspicuous later in the season as to almost obscure the luckless ones that failed to make an early beginning. Still, the latter do not cease trying, and at the first favorable opportunity they put forth their energies, only to have a useless growth, nipped by an untimely frost, or smothered out by their hardier companions. One finds it difficult to make this lavish extravagance, and apparent waste of vital force, conform to human ideas of economy.

Make the *function* the central thought in the study of fruits, and introduce the study of the parts with their names as needed to explain it. With the child, the function of fruit has been fulfilled when it becomes an article of food for himself. There are, indeed, older people who see no further. Yet with the proper suggestive instruction, the colors, the edibility, the hooks and prickles, and the various sails and wings with which fruits are provided will reveal such a refinement of means to an end that it seems almost impossible, at first, to account for them except on the supposition of intelligence in the plant. Still further study gives the pupil a glimpse of the final conflict of the year in the great struggle among the plants for supremacy. Observation will show the effect of the strong early growth upon the maturing seeds; they are

usually better equipped in every way than the unfortu-
nates of later growth. From such studies the pupil's
notions of how the world's life has come to be what it is,
and of the enormous length of time involved, will be
broadened and strengthened.

1. Can you find any seeds germinating at this time?
Are they of this year or last year's growth? Can you
find any seeds in the ground that have lain there during
the summer without germinating? If so, can you account
for it?

2. Have plants finished their growth for this season?
How can you tell? Make measurements for at least two
weeks before deciding as to the growth of the plants.

3. What do these growths consist in? What ones are
permanent, what probably for the season only?

4. Compare by measurement the lengths added to the
twigs of different trees. Have the old ones added as
much as the young ones?

5. On what part of the tree have the longest twigs
grown?

6. Can you notice any difference in this respect between the north and south sides of a tree?

Do not trust to single observations for the answer to
these questions. Take the mean or average of at least
ten.

7. Are the new twigs undergoing any change at this
time?

8. Examine closely the leaves; on a branch bearing
fifty. How many do you find free from insect depredations?
In how many ways have they been used by animals?

9. Do any plants appear to be the especial prey of insects?

10. What ones seem to be freest from them? Can you

see any reason for it ? Give at least two weeks for observations.

11. In what way, if any, can you see the effects of the weather of this month upon vegetation ? Is it promoting growth or retarding it ? Is it tending to mature the young parts or to prevent their maturing?

12. What fruits are ripening this month ? Write a list of all you have seen.

Make a number of envelopes about 3x4 inches out of manilla paper, and collect and preserve in them seeds of all the different kinds of plants as they ripen. These will be used in the spring when studying germination. A great variety is then desirable, and cannot at that time be easily obtained.

13. How do you account for the brilliant colors of some fruits, as in the case of the berries ?

14. What color is most common amongst ripened fruits ? Why is it so ? What color is next ?

15. Are there any plants whose fruits do not change color in ripening ? What other changes take place while ripening?

16. What color prevails in unripe fruit ? Can you see a reason for it ?

17. What parts of the flower become the fruit ? Compare as many different kinds as can be found.

18. Do they all have any one thing in common ?

In a strict botanical sense a fruit is a " ripened ovary and its contents." In addition to this there are frequently present other parts of the flower, which are so modified as to assist directly or indirectly in the distribution of the seed. Sometimes these accessory parts are the most prominent features and are commonly regarded as the fruit itself. The typical ovary wall, as a whole known as the pericarp, is made up of three layers ; an outer, called the exocarp or epicarp, an inner, called the endocarp, and one between called the mesocarp. When the latter is fleshy, it is called the sarcocarp. The seed has, besides, its own coverings or coats, which closely invest the embryo. The chamber containing the seed is the cell ; often there are several of these in one ovary, in which case the partitions are called dissepiments. The part of the ovary to which the seeds are attached is called the placenta. This is axial if passing through the ovary as an axis, central if standing stalk-like in the middle of the ovary, basal when the seeds are clustered about a point in the bottom of the ovary, and parietal when the seeds are attached to the ovary wall. The classification of fruits is based upon the different development of these parts.

19. Select a number of fleshy fruits for study, such as the grape, tomato, cucumber, melon, squash, and apple. In what respects are these all alike ? By drawings or paintings, represent the different parts of these fruits, together with the leaf and twig of the plant.

20. Can you see any reason for the different colors ?

21. Why is purple a good color for grapes when ripe ? How would red or yellow do ?

Keep in mind the wild state of the fruits in trying to account for their characteristics.

22. On what part of the plant are the fruits most highly colored ? Are they equally colored on all sides ?

23. Of what advantage is it to certain fruits to acquire a hard or tough rind when ripening ?

24. What parts of these fruits have been most developed by cultivation ?

25. Select and in the same way study the stone fruits, such as the peach, plum, and apricot.

26. What parts of the flower form the fruit in each case? Make drawings and paintings of the structure.

27. How has cultivation affected the plants bearing these fruits? Does it tend to make them more or less hardy?

28. Where do these fruits grow in their wild state?

29. Are the locations where they flourish under cultivation similar to those where they grow wild?

30. Which of the fruits studied are most preyed upon by insects? Which the least?

31. What animals eat the ripened fruit in its wild state?

BOOKS FOR REFERENCE. Humboldt Library : Nos. 115 and 116, Darwinism, by Alfred Russel Wallace ; chapters on Variation and Colors of Plants. No. 26, The Evolutionist at Large, chapters ii and ix. No. 64, The Distribution of Life. Origin of Cultivated Plants (International Scientific Series). Field and Forest Botany ; Gray.

Physics.

In the study of Physics the most important conception for the child to gain is that concerning the nature of the forces, exclusive of those termed chemical, which act about him and upon him, in a great measure conditioning his existence. Experiments illustrating the action of these forces, as exhibited in the many varied natural phenomena of rain, snow, frost, dew, clouds, heat, light, magnetism, etc., together with the general principles underlying mechanics, may be performed by the children, under careful supervision, with comparative ease. The idea which prevails to some extent, that work of this kind does not possess the interest for young pupils that the study of animals and plants does, is a mistaken one. If the experiments are properly selected they will not fail to absorb the attention, for the reason that the children will be able to see the cause of certain vital phenomena that otherwise could not be understood. An error often made is the failure to impress the fact that an experiment is not an end in itself, but is valuable only as it throws light upon some phase of nature. Expensive apparatus is unnecessary ; for elementary work it is more often a hindrance than a help, in that it tends to distract attention. A little ingenuity on the part of teacher and pupil will readily supply nearly all that is needed.

LIGHT.

1. Place in a window where the direct sunlight will strike it a small glass prism. Near it on the side next

the sun place a piece of cardboard in which there is cut a small slit. Let the sunlight pass through the opening and strike the prism.

A prism may be made by taking three strips of clear glass of equal length and width, and placing them together so as to form a triangular prism. Cut a triangular piece of tin half an inch larger than the end of the prism and bend up outside so as to form a bottom. Seal all the seams with common sealing wax, and fill with clear water. Place on a support in the window and turn it until the spectrum falls upon the opposite wall or some other suitable screen.

2. What changes does the prism make in the sunlight?

3. Are the colored rays in a straight line with the sunlight that enters the prism?

4. Which rays are nearest to a straight line with it? Which are farthest from it?

5. How many colors can be distinguished?

6. Place a piece of white paper in the different rays; what color does it appear to be?

7. Make use of these colors in describing the tints of fruits, insects, and autumn leaves.

MAGNETISM.

Magnetize a large knitting needle by rubbing it over the poles of a magnet, and thrust it through a cube of wood or small cork half an inch in diameter, so that the needle will balance upon it. Attach a strong silk thread to this and suspend it from the ceiling or other support, where it will not be disturbed by air currents. Each pupil may make his own magnetic needle, using a sewing needle for the purpose.

1. When suspended, what direction does the needle assume ?

2. Will it remain in any other position ?

3. Find, before magnetizing, the exact point at which the needle balances ; when magnetized and suspended from the point, is the needle horizontal?

The variation from the horizontal is known as the dip of the needle. This increases gradually northward to a point near Boothia Gulf, when it stands vertical. This is called the North Magnetic Pole.

4. Is each end of the needle attracted by both poles of the magnet ? The north end of the needle is called its positive pole, the south end the negative pole.

5. Which pole of the needle does the north pole of the magnet (usually marked N) attract ? Which does the south pole attract ?

A compass consists of a needle magnetized and delicately poised on a pivot, so as to turn freely, and protected by a case provided with a glass top. Small magnets may now be purchased for one cent each.

6. How many useful purposes can you think of to which the compass may be devoted ?

7. When would the needle in the room be the most use to you ? What two directions does it give directly? What two, indirectly ?

8. Make use of this needle in determining the direction of the wind ; of the road home ; the direction toward different places, buildings, etc., in the neighborhood, etc.

Use the magnets in testing for iron and steel amongst metals.

In most places the needle does not point toward the true north ; east of a line running through Wilmington,

N. C., Charlottesville, Va., and Pittsburgh, Pa., the declination from the true north is toward the west ; west of it the declination is toward the east.

BOOKS FOR REFERENCES. Humboldt Library : No 1, The Earth a Magnet. No. 18, Appendix. An elementary lecture on Magnetism.

Chemistry.

FERMENTATION.

By means of a large-sized grater reduce a considerable quantity of the different fruits to a pulp. Press the juice through muslin or cheese cloth and bottle it. When the pupils have tested the juice so obtained by taste and have learned how it is obtained, a quart of sweet cider divided up into four or five bottles, and allowed to stand, will illustrate the changes which take place during fermentation. The different conditions under which they are placed will reveal those most favorable to the change.

The formation of hard cider is due to what is called alcoholic fermentation. The source of this is the yeast plant, which in its growth breaks up the sugar which the juice contains into alcohol, carbonic acid gas, and small amounts of other substances. After the alcoholic fermentation, the souring or change to vinegar is due to the formation of acetic acid in acetic fermentation. These changes may be followed and noted as they occur. The teacher should be particular to have the children do this work in a neat and cleanly manner ; otherwise they should not do it at all.

1. Note carefully the taste and color when freshly prepared.

2. Place different bottles under different conditions :

some corked, others open ; some in a cool, others in a warm place, etc.

3. Under what conditions do the changes occur most rapidly ?

4. Add a little yeast to some of the juice, and when fermentation has taken place it will be ready for distillation. (See Physics for October.)

5. Do the bubbles which rise contain air ?

6. Test by lowering into a half-filled jar a lighted match or taper. Does it behave as it does when lowered into air ?

7. By means of a bent glass tube through the cork of a bottle, force some of the gas into some lime water. Note the change. The tests with the flame and lime water indicate carbonic acid gas.

8. Can you account for the cork being blown from a tightly corked bottle while fermentation is taking place ?

9. Is the liquid remaining in the bottle after fermentation the same substance that was there before it took place ? How can you tell ?

10. The change which has taken place is called a *chemical change.*

Meteorology

GENERAL DIRECTIONS AND SUGGESTIONS.

In order to carry out successfully the work under this head, it is necessary that the pupils make daily observations for themselves, and that these be recorded neatly in some systematic manner, so that summaries can be readily made from which correct inferences may be drawn. For this purpose a blank form has been prepared, a model of which is given on another page. This may be prepared by each pupil himself, and should be on a sheet about 8½ by 11 inches. One such sheet will contain, without crowding, a month's observations and summaries.* An enlarged form of the blank, sufficient for a week's record, should be drawn upon the blackboard, and the daily observations written thereon by the pupils. To save time and avoid the confusion naturally arising from the varying accuracy in different observers, it is better to assign the work to a different pupil each day. This places him subject to the criticism of the entire class, and will promote carefulness in observation. His record, however, should not be changed simply because it does not agree with that of some one else, or with even a majority. Each pupil's work must stand for itself.

---

* Printed blank forms of this Meteorological record have been prepared by the author, and have been embodied in a notebook for general science work.

Select a time when it will be most convenient each day to make the record, and adhere strictly to it. It may, of course, vary within certain limits ; as, for example, between 2 and 3 P. M. To get data of greater general value, divide the school into three divisions and assign to the first, the time, say, between 9 and 10 A. M.; to the second, an hour near the middle of the day, and to the third the last hour. The average for each day can then be found when making up the summary for the week.

Teachers sometimes make the serious mistake of demanding strict uniformity in the records made by the pupils. Such uniformity could hardly be expected from a trained body of scientific observers, much less must it be looked for among children who are beginning. It is absolutely fatal to the good which may come of the work to the individual pupil, if the teacher falls into the very common habit of deferring to two or three of the brightest ones respecting certain observations, and then requiring the rest to abide by their decision. Better far let each pupil record his own observation, without discussion or reference to what his neighbor is doing, though you may know at the time it is entirely wrong. It is not a mistake which will immediately endanger his life, and he will have abundant opportunity to correct himself in future observations and in the discussions which follow, and thus his own blunders will tend to make him more acute in observing. In most cases the pupil's work will have enough of accuracy about it to give him self-reliance, and his mistakes will continually admonish him to be cautious.

If for any reason a day is missed during the week, let the space remain blank. Do the work at the proper time or not at all. No one should be permitted to copy any part of the work from another under any circumstances.

In the column under " Frost or Dew " write " Frost," " Dew," or " Neither," as the case may be.

If the wind is changing it may be denoted, for example, thus : S—W, indicating a south wind is becoming a west wind. Pupils may learn its direction by watching the drifting smoke from chimneys.

The kinds of clouds should be named, and, with the sufficiently advanced pupils, the amount of cloudiness expressed in tenths, indicating the area above the horizon that is covered.

The thermometer should hang on the north side of the building, free from it, but somewhat protected. Hang the barometer where freely accessible, and so that the upper end of the column of mercury will be on a level with the pupil's eye ; but it must not be too much exposed.

Rainfall may be expressed as light, heavy, or none, and the number of hours and time when it fell may be recorded. Example, Light, 1:00—4:30 P. M.

The records for the remaining columns may be taken from an almanac, inasmuch as the pupils will hardly be able to gather the data themselves with an accuracy sufficient for the purpose required. Much of the material here tabulated will be used under the lessons in Astronomy, and it is of great advantage to have it so that a month's record may be scanned at a glance. The pupils will soon begin to find out in these columns a series of causes whose effects appear in the others.

Represent the moon's phases by small drawings of the new moon, first quarter, half full moon, and last quarter, making the horns of the waxing moon to the left and of the waning moon to the right. The new moon may be represented by an open circle, and full moon by one that is shaded.

Both weekly and monthly summaries should be made out at the proper time. The character and fullness of these will depend upon the age of the pupils, but may include the following points : (1) Number of dews or frosts, indicated thus : 3 D. 2 F. 2 N.; (2) prevailing wind ; (3) number of cloudy days, and number of clear days ; (4) number of days on which rain fell ; (5) mean temperature ; (6) mean barometer; (7) length of day ; (8) total increase or decrease in day's length ; (9) total variation in time of rising or setting of moon.

In the consideration of the questions and suggestions which follow there should be a constant search for the causes underlying the phenomena observed. It is not expected that each set of questions will be "finished" before taking the next. Many of the questions are of such character as to require the data which may be collected during several months' observation before they can be satisfactorily answered. The teacher must carefully note the ability of the pupils to think, and thus determine to what extent the questions should be pursued, being careful to go no farther than the pupils' knowledge of geography and physics will warrant. The aim is twofold—to make him intelligent respecting the forces about him, and to train him in the habit of studying a subject for himself in its relations to other subjects. The teacher is too apt to try to push the pupil faster than he should go by simply *telling* him facts, instead of patiently giving him intelligent assistance in gathering them for himself.

If it is desired to measure the amount of rainfall, a rain gauge can be made by a tinsmith at small cost. For description and drawing of one, as well as for valuable hints regarding meteorological observations, see " Instructions to Voluntary Observers of the Signal Service," a pamphlet which may be obtained free by sending to the Chief of Weather Bureau, Washington, D. C. Daily Weather Bureau maps may be obtained, also, by applying to the officer in charge of the nearest station. They will be found to be interesting and useful in making comparisons, and in enabling one to trace the great storms across the country.

Most of the following questions may be used in studying both the weekly and monthly summaries.

The following charts show how the pupils may be taught to represent graphically many of the summaries which they should be required to make of their meteorological and astronomical observations. In each chart, part, or in some cases the entire record for the year from September, 1890, to September, 1891, is represented for the purpose of illustrating their use.

In Chart I the record begins September 25, the date when the day and night are equal. At that time the slant of the sun's rays at noon at Chicago as found by the shadow-stick is 43°. At the equator the slant is 0° which is shown to the left of the chart. At about the same time in October the slant is found to be 54°, or 11° more than in September. Since each space between the horizontal lines represents 4°, by measuring down the October line the point for 54° is readily found. These two points are now connected by a straight line, and the work is thus continued from month to month.

In Chart II, it will be seen that while in Chart I the line moved downward indicating the increasing slant of the sun's rays, here the line moves upward, showing a corresponding decrease in the length of day. The downward line representing in the left hand side the increasing length of night in the same time. Chart I indicates a cause and Chart II represents a very closely corresponding effect in the length of day and night. It will be noticed that the figure representing the *short* days and *long* nights, (the one on the left) is smaller than the one representing the *long* days and *short* nights. Also that the longest day is 15 hrs. 5 min. long while the longest night is but 14 hrs. 45 min. long ; that the shortest day is 9 hrs. 15 min. and the shortest night 8 hrs. 55 min. long. Also, that from September 25 to March 17 there are but 173 days ; while from March 17 to September 25 there are 192 days. These are only a few of the many problems which a comparison of the charts will suggest.

In Chart III each horizontal space represents one-tenth of an inch, and the column of figures to the left enables the pupils to readily find the points on the vertical lines which represent the mean height of the barometric column. The reduction to sea level need not be made by the pupils, but tables and formulæ showing how it is done are given in "Instructions to Voluntary Observers of the Signal Service."

In Chart IV the column of figures to the left represents degrees of temperature. By means of these, the point which will represent the mean temperature for each month on the vertical line will be easily found. Why is it that the line on this chart corresponds less closely to that on Chart I ?

Chart V needs no explanation, the name of the month being written at the end of the arrow which indicates the direction of its prevailing wind.

Chart VI shows at a glance the total rainfall for each month and for the year, each horizontal space representing one-half an inch.

Chart VII shows the number of rainy days in each
month and for the year. This chart was prepared from
the Weather Bureau Reports, in which not less than one-
hundredth of an inch is considered. The pupils may easily
make the record without any measurements, merely keeping count of the days on which rain falls.

As these charts are being made from month to month
they should be constantly compared with each other for
the purpose of tracing points of correspondence and difference. Lead the pupils to find out which of the charts
represent causes and which represent effects of those
causes, and which ones, if any, appear to be independent
of the others. Compare the three representing the mean
barometer, rainfall, and direction of wind. Note the extremes shown during each season and for the entire year.
The study may be pursued with almost endless variation
and will be found useful in working out the problems
and suggestions given in the Outlines under the heads
of Meteorology and Astronomy.*

1. What wind was accompanied by the lowest temperature ? The highest temperature ? Can you give a good
reason for this ?

2. Is the temperature increasing or diminishing ?

3. Did the prevailing wind accompany a cloudy or
a clear sky ?

---

* These charts are prepared in book form by the author, of suitable
size for school use, in the SCIENCE RECORD for the common schools.
This record also contains twelve pages of blank Meteorological Records, one for each month, twelve pages of blank records for minerals,
with a synoptical key to the terms used in description, twelve pages
for notes on the regular science work for the year, twelve pages for
notes on miscellaneous observations, and twelve pages of drawing
paper for drawings and paintings. The size of the page is 8½x11
inches.

4. What direction was the wind on cloudy days? What wind prevailed on clear days?

5. Was the prevailing wind accompanied by wet or dry weather? Consult maps and globe in looking for a reason.

6. What was the character of the weather when the barometer was lowest? Note temperature and direction of wind.

7. What was the weather like when the barometer was highest?

8. What were the indications of the thermometer and barometer when the heaviest rain fell?

9. What change followed with clearing weather?

10. Watch closely the indications of the thermometer and barometer, before, during, and after rainfall; are they uniform?

11. At what time of the day is the temperature highest? What reason can you see for this?

12. What kind of weather has prevailed on the days on which there was no dew? Has there been any uniformity in the weather on days when there was dew?

13. What was the character of the nights when there was no dew? When there was dew?

14. Is dew to be found everywhere and upon all kinds of objects?

STUDY OF THE WEATHER BUREAU MAPS.

Learn well the meaning of the various lines and symbols used on the map, and explained in the margin.

15. Note the *general* direction of the isotherms. In what region do they vary most from this direction?

16. What effect do the mountain ranges have upon the

lines? The Great Lakes? The coast lines? The river valleys and basins?

17. Note the regions marked "Low" and "High." Which marks a storm center? Where have most of these entered the United States during September?

18. How does the wind blow about these centers? Can you discover any uniformity in this regard?

19. What has been the direction of storm movement during September?

20. Has the movement been visibly influenced by mountains, river valleys, or coast lines?

BOOKS FOR REFERENCE. Light Science for Leisure Hours. Hum boldt Library, No. 1, chapter on Tornadoes.

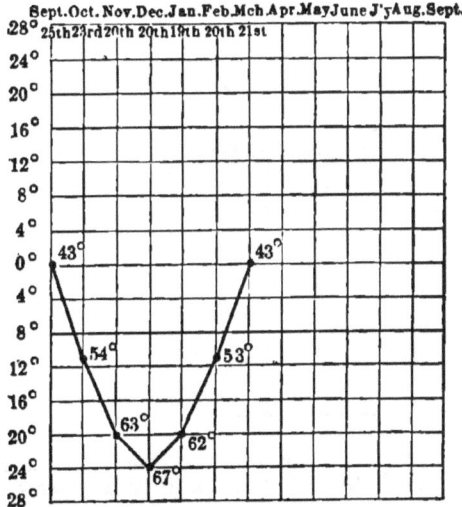

CHART I.—Showing variation in the slant of the sun's rays at Chicago from September to March inclusive. Record taken from the shadow-stick of the eighth grade, Cook County Normal Practice School. (Not absolutely correct.)

Sept. Oct. Nov. Dec. Jan. Feb. Mch. Apr. May June July Aug. Sept.

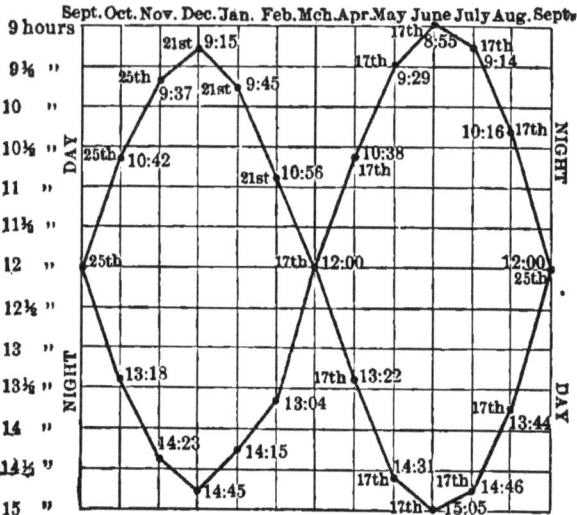

CHART II.—Showing the variation in the length of day and night during the year at Chicago.

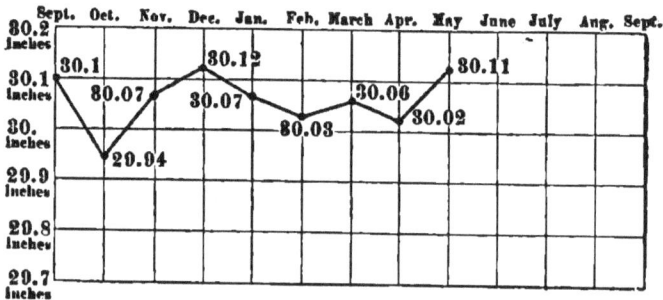

CHART III.—Showing mean height of barometric column at Chicago for each month from September to May inclusive, 1890–91. (Reduced to sea level.)

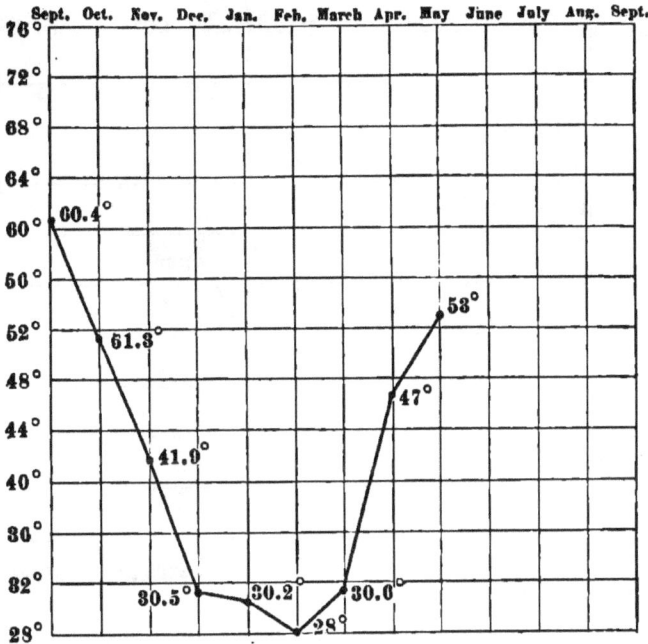

CHART IV.—Line showing mean temperature of each month at Chicago from September to May inclusive, 1890-91.

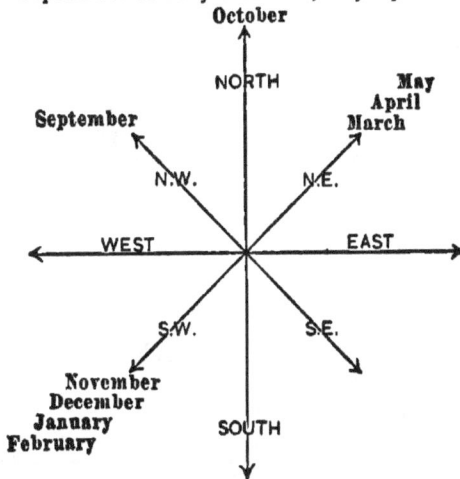

CHART V.—Showing prevailing winds at Chicago for each month from September to May inclusive, 1890-91.

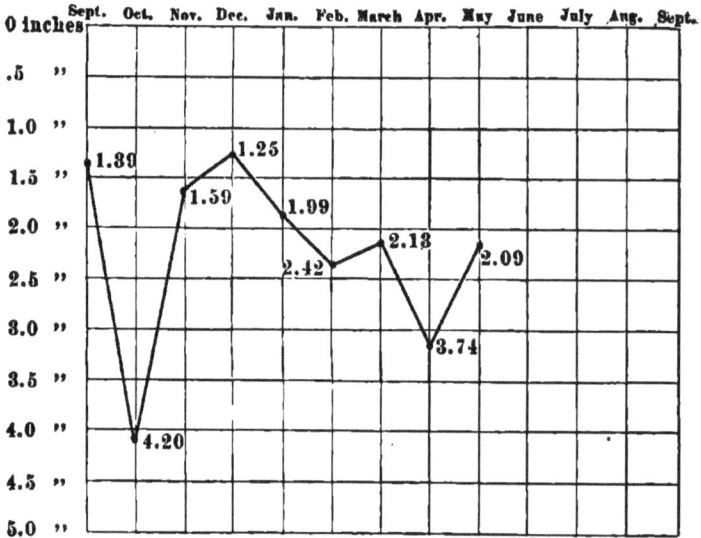

CHART VI. —Showing rainfall at Chicago for each month from September to May inclusive, 1890–91.

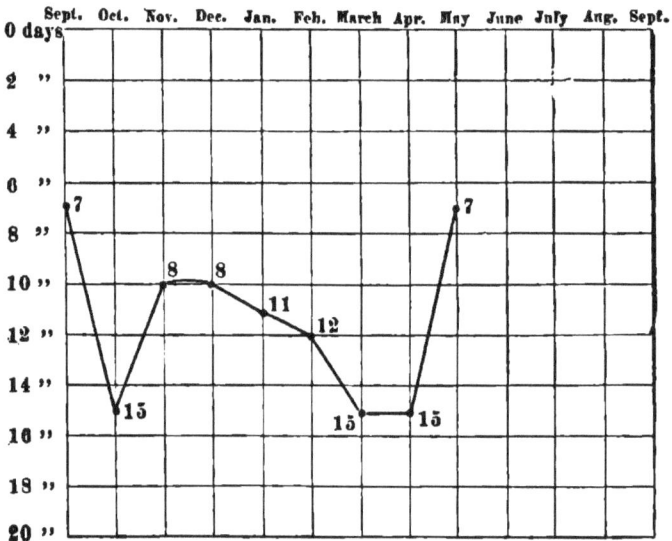

CHART VII.—Showing the number of days on which at least .01 inch of rain fell at Chicago in each month from September to May inclusive, 1890–91.

METEOROLOGICAL RECORD FOR _____189___

Time of Observation _____ By _____ Grade _____

Copyright, 1890, by W. S. Jackman.

DAY	DATE	Frost or Dew	Direction of Wind	Cloudiness Fogs	Rainfall	Temperature	Barometer	Sun Rises	Sun Sets	Moon's Phases	Moon Rises	Moon Sets	Morning Star	Evening Star
WEEKLY SUMMARY														

Astronomy.

In following up these observations with explanations, it is necessary to be provided with a globe, or a good substitute, and objects to represent the sun, moon, and planets.

If an open space on the floor, a few feet square, is available, a spot in the middle should be selected to represent the position of the sun, and ellipses drawn around it with light lines of paint to represent the orbits of the planets. The surface of a large table may be used if floor room cannot be obtained. Representing the distance of the earth from the sun by 1, the distance of the planets may be approximately represented as follows : Mercury $\frac{1}{4}$; Venus $\frac{2}{3}$; Earth 1 ; Mars $\frac{5}{3}$; Jupiter 5 ; Saturn 9 ; Uranus 20 ; Neptune 30. For the purposes of illustration in the following lessons it will be more convenient to represent the earth's distance on a larger scale than that on which it would be practicable to represent the whole solar system. The varying length of shadow should be observed throughout the year. To do this, take a strip of wood two feet long and two inches in width, and to one end nail an upright strip of same width and four inches high. At noon place the long strip in a horizontal position on a north and south line with the upright toward the south. With a pencil and ruler draw a line across the horizontal strip marking the limit of the shadow cast by the upright. Note the date each time. The angle made by the sun's rays may be found thus : Take a stiff piece of cardboard six inches square, describe upon it a semicircle, and if a protractor be at hand, lay off the semi-circumference in degrées. Tack or paste this to a piece of wood of same size as the cardboard and one-half inch thick ; along the edge of this, which is opposite to the diameter of the semicircle and parallel with it, tack a straight strip of wood half an inch square and one foot long. Cut from a piece of tin or thin brass a pointer three inches long, and swing it on an axis or pivot fastened at the center of the circle. The pointer will always hang down when the dial is upright. To number the degrees on the dial, place it so that the stick which is fastened to the base will be horizontal, with the dial uppermost. The pointer will then be vertical, and zero degrees may be marked at this point. As either end of the stick is raised the pointer will still remain vertical, and indicate the number of degrees it is raised from the horizontal. To get the angle of the sun's rays, place one end of the stick at the extreme edge of the shadow and allow the other to rest on the top of the upright which casts it. The pointer will give the number of degrees the sun is above the horizon.

The most important conception for the children to get in this study is that of *time*, and a conception of space is next. When necessary, daily practice should be given the children in telling the exact time of day by clock or watch, until they can do so without hesitation. Of course, merely telling the time of day will not in itself give a conception of time, and such exercises as will enable them to grasp brief periods must be given in connection with it. As for example, let them find out how long it takes them to walk home ; or, the length of the recitation period, or of the morning and afternoon sessions of school, the recess and noon periods, etc., and they will soon fix in their minds a stock of time units which will be of great service.

1. What do you notice about the relative length of day and night at the beginning of the month ?

2. With a globe and some object to represent the sun, find out the relative positions of the two bodies when day and night are thus related in length.

3. How does the length of each vary during the month?

4. Using the globe as before, explain this change.

5. How has the length of the noon shadow changed ? By using the globe explain this.

6. Observe as accurately as possible the two points on the horizon where the sun rises and sets on that date in this month when day and night are equal. Fix these points with respect to yourself by means of a tree, post, or some permanent mark, and keep in mind for reference in future observations. A line connecting these two points runs east and west. Compare the length of day and night. This date is the time of the Autumnal Equinox.

7. Make a brief note of the condition of animal and plant life at this time and preserve for future reference.

Among the interesting constellations that may be observed during this month are : Great Bear, Little Bear, Draco, Cassiopeia, Cepheus, Pegasus, Sagittarius, Lyra, Cygnus, Dolphin, Hercules, Corona, Berenice's Hair.

BOOKS FOR REFERENCE. Science Primer, Astronomy, Lockyer. The Wonders of the Heavens, Humboldt Library, No. 14.

Geography.

Geography is defined as a description of the earth. This embraces everything that may be said of the earth, but it is usually understood to have a more limited meaning. It is sometimes said to be a study of the earth as a finished product; that cannot be strictly true, for it is no more a finished product to-day, in the sense that it is in a fixed condition, than it ever was. It has been constantly changing from the remotest periods of time under the operation of certain laws, and those laws are still affecting it. The changes in the earth itself, and in its relations to the other portions of the universe, have produced corresponding modifications in living things ever since mundane life began to exist. They are so gradual as to have had but the most trifling import in the time spanned by human history, yet it is believed that by them the earth has been brought out of a nebulous condition to its present state. Life, both animal and plant, by its amazing plasticity adapting itself to almost every corner of the globe, has managed to survive and perpetuate itself throughout countless ages of a vast period, in which the changes have been almost incredible.

Geography, as it is to be understood here, is the study of the earth in its present condition as a cause, of which life upon it is the effect. It comprehends a study of the earth in its present relation to life, and a study of life, as it now exists in its adaptation to the earth.

DIRECTION.

Teach the cardinal points and apply in giving the direction of the wind, movement of clouds, etc. (see Meteorology), and in the location of articles in the room, school-yard, and vicinity.

Countless problems may be proposed by both teacher and pupils which will give zest to the work and cultivate a habit in the children of keeping their bearings when moving about from place to place. The unpleasant experience which most people have had of being " turned round," when in a strange place, as to the points of the compass, is probably due chiefly to the fact that they do not habitually observe fixed landmarks with respect to the cardinal points on the horizon while traveling. The pupils should be practiced in this until it becomes a fixed habit, and they are able to hold the different directions in mind without conscious effort.

With this work, map making properly begins. If one pupil says that in going home he travels three blocks east and two north, let him show how the path looks on the blackboard. Let him locate his home and the school-house with respect to each other. This will necessitate the teaching of direction as applied to maps.

LATITUDE AND LONGITUDE.

In beginning with pupils to use latitude and longitude in the location of places, if it can be avoided, never use a flat map. A globe is the only thing that can give a correct idea of the parallels and meridians as they are related to each other.

1. Locate the equator and the poles on the globe. What is the position of the equator between the poles ?

2. How far from the equator to the poles? Teach the number of degrees in a circle, half circle, and quadrant.

3. When the rays of the sun just reach either pole, where are the vertical rays? On what date is this the case?

4. What do you notice about the length of day and night at this time?

5. When the sun is vertical at the equator, what is the angle of the rays in our latitude at noon? (See Astronomy for September.)

6. What determines the size of the angle at this time?

7. How would the angle change if we moved north? If we moved south? If we moved east or west?

8. If you know the angle of the sun's rays at noon at a given place when the sun is vertical at the equator, how can you find the latitude of that place?

9. In what latitude have the severest storms originated in the United States this month? (See Weather Bureau Map Studies for September.)

10. How many degrees of longitude has the heaviest storm passed over?

11. In what latitude have the heaviest rains fallen?

12. What latitude has been least visited by storms?

13. In what latitude do the isotherms vary most widely from their general course? In what latitude do they vary least?

14. Since the earth rotates once in twenty-four hours, through how many degrees does each point on the earth's surface pass in that time?·

15. Upon what circles are the degrees measured? Are the degrees of the same size on different circles?

16. Through how many degrees will any given point pass in one hour of time? On what circle would a point pass through the greatest number of miles?

Longitude is reckoned east and west from an established meridian, usually that passing through Greenwich, near London, or the meridian passing through Washington.

17. How many degrees of east or west longitude can be reckoned ? Where will there be no longitude ? Where no latitude ?

NORTH AMERICA.

1. Between what parallels does North America lie? Between what meridians ?

2. What contrasts between the northern and southern parts, due to difference in latitude, are found in animal life, vegetation, habits, character, and occupations of the people ?

3. What are some of the advantages of a country that extends through many degrees of latitude ?

4. What are the greatest disadvantages due to the same conditions ?

5. How did difference of latitude, as a cause, enter into the questions involved in the great civil war in the United States ?

6. When it is sunrise at New York City, how long before sunrise at San Francisco ?

7. When it is sunset at St. Louis, how long after sunset at Washington ?

To make the pupils familiar with maps and their use, they should begin by modeling and drawing maps of the school-room, school grounds, and surroundings. Mark the natural features of surface, and locate the buildings, etc., that are to be found upon it. Locate on map and globe all places mentioned in history and other subjects studied. This should be as much a matter of habit as it is to look for the meaning of a word in a dictionary.

Geology.

The conception of space is of first importance in this study, and that of time is second. Means should be provided in the beginning to enable the pupil to train himself accurately in judging distances, horizontal and vertical, and areas. The deficiency of pupils, even of high school age, in this respect is generally very great. This is almost wholly due to lack of actual practice ; they have talked a great deal about rods and acres, but have never measured them.

The units must be adapted to the age and comprehension of the children, but, as needed, one-fourth, one-half, and, if possible, one mile should be laid off, so that the limits may be plainly seen and the distances well fixed in mind. There should be similar opportunities given to study one foot, one yard, one rod, and one hundred yards. For the study of heights, units of ten, twenty-five, and, if possible, fifty and one hundred feet should be marked off on the side of the school-house or some tree. The square foot, square yard, square rod, acre, and later the square mile, will be needed in the estimation of areas.

It is well to give much attention from the start to the collection of specimens. Every region will furnish an abundance of many different kinds, and they possess an immense advantage over collections in some other branches of natural history, from the fact that they require little care, except an occasional dusting, and are practically imperishable. Fragments of different rocks, various kinds and forms of pebbles, and fossils of all kinds, should, when possible, be gathered and neatly arranged. There can hardly be a stronger stimulus for the imagination than that which one receives from the proper study of a fossil, and there is certainly nothing which will so broaden one's conceptions regarding the vast ages that make up the earth's history. Arrange in a tray or box certain typical specimens of those belonging to the immediate neighborhood, with which the pupils may compare their specimens as they find them. Among these may be granite, marble, limestone, sandstone, slate, coal, etc. The name should not be given to them by the teacher until they have compared their specimen with the types and learned some of its characters. None the less, however, should the pupils be led to study the dynamical side of the subject. There are everywhere plenty of excellent examples of either building or wearing away,—perhaps both,—which possess an abiding interest. Whatever it may be, whether a crumbling cliff, a building beach, a deepening gulch, or a slowly filling marsh, it makes but little difference. There to-day the Titans may be seen making and unmaking the world, as they have been doing it for unnumbered ages in the past.

1. In looking over the country about you, can you tell what has been the most important agent in its formation ?

2. Is the same force still at work ? Is it working rapidly or slowly ?

3. What other forces have left their impress upon the country ? Are they still acting ?

4. Are there any evidences as to whether these forces ever worked more rapidly or more powerfully than now ?

5. Can you find any place where the land is being torn

down? What is doing it? What becomes of the material when torn away?

6. Are there any forces which oppose the tearing
away?

7. Are there any marshes, large or small, in the vicinity? How much of their history can you read in them?

8. What was their relation originally to the nearest lake
or stream?

9. Are they now filling up with earth, or being hollowed
out?

10. What is vegetation doing for the marsh? The
water?

11. How does a sod affect the wearing forces of any
region? What are the effects of forests?

12. Is the cultivation of the soil in any way changing
the formation of the country?

13. What kind of rock underlies the surface? Do you
find more than one kind?

14. Are they in layers, *i. e.,* stratified, or in masses that
show no stratification?

15. If stratified, are the strata horizontal or inclined?
When inclined the rock is said to *dip.* The line along
which the edge of the rock cuts the surface is called the
strike. It always runs at right angles with the dip.

16. What is the angle of dip measured from the horizontal?

17. Does the dip have the same angle in all places?
Does it have the same direction?

Books for Reference. Humboldt Library, No. 6, Town Geology. Shaler's First Book in Geology.

Mineralogy.

Give special attention to the collection and arrangement of different metals and minerals. Provide a small tray with compartments, in which there should be placed typical specimens of such, at least, as are likely to be found in the vicinity. Place with each one a label bearing its degree of hardness, its luster, color, diaphaneity, streak, taste or odor, and name. The scale of hardness consists of ten minerals, showing a regular gradation in hardness from talc, one of the softest, to diamond, one of the hardest minerals. It is as follows: *Very soft*—1, talc ; 2, gypsum ; can be scratched with finger-nail, or very easily with a knife. *Soft*—3, calcite ; 4, fluorite ; cannot be scratched with the nail, but easily scratched with a knife. *Hard*—5, apatite ; 6, orthoclase ; not easily scratched with a knife ; scratches glass. *Very hard*— 7, quartz ; cannot be scratched by a knife, scratches glass ; 8, topaz, scratches quartz. *Adamantine*—9, corundum ; scratched by the diamond and itself. 10, *diamond ;* not scratched by any other mineral.

Luster or glance refers to the light, both as to quality and quantity, which is reflected from the surface. The *metallic* luster is that of the metals. All the other kinds of luster are embraced under the general division nonmetallic. The chief varieties are : *Vitreous*, like glass ; *pearly*, as in mica or pearl ; *resinous*, as in resins, sulphur and sphalerite ; *silky* or *satiny*, as in satin-spar ; *greasy* or *waxy*, as in serpentine.

The degrees of diaphaneity are expressed as *transparent, translucent,* and *opaque.* The streak is obtained by powdering a little of the mineral by means of a file, or by drawing it over a piece of ground glass.

Use the magnet in the examination of metals, and find out which are magnetic and which are not. When a mineral is found by a pupil he should prepare a written description of it, including the characteristics above given, by comparing it with the specimens labeled in the tray. The teacher may then add the name. The collecting should be encouraged throughout the year.

From the beginning the pupils should be taught, in the grammar grades, at least, the best means by which a complete but concise record of their observations may be kept. Although it may appear a little tedious at first, its value will be more and more apparent as the record grows. The irksomeness of the task is usually chiefly due to the fact that the pupil is urged to record observations which he has not really made, and, being no part of his experience, he naturally has no interest in them. He should record briefly only what he can find out for himself. The blank form for a mineralogical record, here appended, may be prepared upon the sheet, eight and one-half by eleven inches, which was recommended on a previous page for science work. This will give space enough for ten minerals, and will be of uniform size with the sheets upon which his other written work is prepared.

BOOKS FOR REFERENCE. Crosby's Tables for the Determination of Common Minerals, Guttenburg's Course in Mineralogy for Young People (Agassiz Association Course), Crosby's Common Minerals and Rocks.

MINERALOGICAL RECORD

OF THE

COMMON SCHOOLS.

Grade ....

No. ....

By 189

	Name	H	G	Form	Tenacity	Lustre	Color	Streak	Diaphaneity	Acid Test	Flame Test
1											
2											
3											
4											
5											
6											
7											
8											
9											
10											

Suggestions to Teachers for Using the Mineralogical Record.

Each pupil should have a blank record. When he finds a mineral, its description is to be written in the blank form under the proper heads — the appended outline being used as a guide. Render the pupil as little assistance as possible ; he must be self-reliant. Do not hurry. When the pupil has done his best, the amount varying with age and practice, the teacher may give him the name of the mineral. Crosby's Tables for the Determination of Common Minerals is a most valuable manual for teachers.

I. SCALE OF HARDNESS.
1. Talc,   VERY SOFT ; can be scratched with finger nail, or very easily with a
2. Gypsum,   knife.
3. Calcite,   SOFT ; cannot be scratched with finger nail, but easily scratched
4. Fluorite,   with a knife.
5. Apatite,   HARD : not easily scratched with a knife ; scratches glass.
6. Orthoclase,
7. Quartz,   VERY HARD ; { Cannot be scratched with a knife ; scratches glass.
8. Topaz,   { Scratches quartz.
9. Corundum,   ADAMANTINE ; { Scratched by the diamond and itself.
10. Diamond,   { Not scratched by any other mineral.

II. SPECIFIC GRAVITY.
1. Weigh in air.
2. Weigh in water.
3. Specific Gravity = weight in air + loss of weight in water.

III. FORM.
1. External. {
Botryoidal—Surface grape-like.
Mammillary—Same, but larger.
Tufaceous—Porous, mineral incrustations formed from solutions.
Concretionary—Rounded masses.
Geode—Hollow concretion.
Stalactitic—Hanging from under surface of a rock, cone-shaped.
Stalagmitic—Formed on floors of caverns from dripping water.
Stratified—Deposited in layers.

2. Internal. {
Granular, coarse or fine—Small crystals.
Compact - Crystals invisible to unaided eye.
Foliated—In layers.
Fibrous—Thread-like.
Columnar—Stout, fibrous.
Amorphous—Without crystallization.

IV. TENACITY.
1. Brittle—Breaks easily.
2. Malleable—Flattens into thin sheets under hammer.
3. Sectile—May be cut into thin slices.
4. Flexible—Retains its form when bent.
5. Elastic—Comes back to original form when bent.

V. LUSTER.
1. Metallic, as in metals.
2. Non-Metallic. {
Vitreous, as in glass.
Pearly, as in pearl and mica.
Resinous, as in sulphur, sphalerite, resins.
Pitchy, as in cannel coal.
Silky or satiny, as in satin spar.
Greasy or waxy, as in serpentine.
Dull, as in chalk.

VI. STREAK.
Color obtained by rubbing the mineral over the surface of a piece of ground glass or over a file.

VII. DIAPHANEITY.
1. Transparent. Semi-transparent.
2. Translucent. Sub-translucent.
3. Opaque.

VIII. ACID TESTS. Use H Cl (hydrochloric acid), or dilute H₂ S O₄ (sulphuric acid), or both. Use a little of the mineral in a test tube.
1. Insoluble.
2. Soluble. {
With effervescence ; with or without heat.
Without effervescence ; with or without heat.
Gelatinizes—Becomes jelly-like.

IX. FLAME TESTS. N. B. Use a fine splinter of the mineral, or a thin edge in the flame of an alcohol lamp or bunsen burner. Note the color imparted to the flame.
1. Fusible—Melts.
2. Infusible—Does not melt.
3. Decrepitates—Breaks into small pieces with crackling sound.
4. Intumesces—Swells up without fusion.

Zoölogy.

The larvæ of several different species of moths (large green and brown worms) are usually abundant at this time, and should be collected. Put them in small boxes covered with mosquito netting, and feed with fresh leaves of the plant upon which they were found. They will soon spin a cocoon and enter upon a new stage of existence. Carefully preserve these through the winter, and in the spring the moth will appear. There is not a more fruitful series of observations possible in the school-room for children than that of watching the wonderful transformation of insects. Ants may be kept under observation during the entire year in glass jars filled with fine damp earth. A better method, however, is as follows : Get a tinsmith to fasten a small moat, an inch deep and one and a half inches wide, around a smooth piece of inch board, one foot square. On this board, equidistant from the moat on all sides, lay a pane of glass, ten inches square. On each edge of this, glue a strip of glass, leaving small passage ways at opposite corners. Fill the shallow vessel thus formed with finely sifted earth, and cover it with another pane of glass of same size as the lower one. Fill the moat with water. Take from an ant-hill a small box of earth and ants all together, and place them in a little heap on the top of the glass. By thrusting a small stick into the den through the passage-ways left at the corners, to give them a place for a beginning, with a little care the ants can be induced to enter and go

to work. Gradually remove the earth from the top of
the glass, wipe clean and keep in the dark by covering
the whole with a pasteboard lid, about two inches high.
Food—crumbs, sugar, and bits of meat—can be placed
under this on the glass. The changes made from day to
day in the earth, and the management of the larvæ,
visible through the glass, are sources of unfailing interest.

If a common mud or snapping turtle can be procured,
place it in a box of wet sand with a loose lid over it, and
in a few weeks it will disappear and remain out of sight
till spring, and furnish a text for the interesting subject
of hibernation.

1. What birds have disappeared within the past few
weeks? Note the date when last seen.

2. Can you tell which leave first, the old ones or young
ones?

3. Watch for migrating flocks of geese from the north.

4. What becomes of the insects during the cold nights?
Do any of them migrate?

5. What becomes of the butterflies? Of the bees?
Of the grasshoppers? Of the flies?

6. Can you find any preparing to live over winter?

7. Examine the burrows of earthworms; are the worms
as active as they were last month?

8. Gather a number of snails from the bottoms of ponds
and preserve in glass jars.

A STUDY OF TISSUES.

It is of fundamental importance that pupils should have
in the outset of the study of physiology correct conceptions as to the more important tissues of the animal body.
The following outline is intended to be used as a guide in
making them acquainted with these tissues, and to give

an idea of their uses. Procure a sheep's leg cut off so as to include what is commonly called the knee joint and the attached muscles a few inches above it. Each pupil should have a specimen which must be perfectly fresh and clean. The distaste that many pupils acquire for this kind of work, in the majority of cases, arises from carelessness of the teacher on this point. The use of good specimens gives the teacher a perfect right to require each pupil to do the work, and, feeling this, but few will raise any objection.

THE MUSCLE.

1. Note the reddish flesh forming the *body* of the muscle.

2. The slender cord attaching the body to the bone is the *tendon* of the muscle. Is it elastic or inelastic? Can it be pulled loose? Try pulling in different directions.

3. Note how it is attached to the bone. The point of attachment of the tendon which moves least in any motion of the part is called the origin of the muscle ; the other attachment is its insertion. Locate the origin and insertion of the muscle which flexes the forearm.

4. Note the thin sheath covering the body ; it is called the *perimysium*.

5. Cut the body crosswise and note the parts which compose it. They are best seen in boiled meat. The bundles thus shown are called fasciculi.

6. Follow out toward the tendons the white threads, and note the formation of the tendon.

7. Find tendons in your own body ; find the bodies of the muscles to which they are attached.

8. What advantage in the tendon ?

9. What is the advantage of its inelasticity ?

10. What uses can you discover for muscle ?

CONNECTIVE TISSUE.

1. Examine the white, thin tissue surrounding the muscle.

2. What are its characteristics? Is it elastic? This tissue is very abundant in the specimen, as well as in the whole body. It is called *connective tissue.* It is to be found almost everywhere, binding the different parts together. What characteristics especially adapt it to this end?

3. In how many forms does it appear in this specimen? Note the *tendons*, the *perimysium*, and the threads which ramify the muscle body.

THE BONE. OSSEOUS TISSUE.

1. Note the slender *shaft* and its enlarged *extremities.*

2. What advantage in the enlargement of the extremities?

3. Look for the sheath closely surrounding the shaft. What kind of tissue is it? The sheath is called the *periosteum.*

4. Look for the cavity in the shaft called the medullary cavity. Note the contents, called the *marrow.*

5. Split the bone; note the difference in the character of the bone at the extremities and in the shaft.

6. In the extremities it is called spongy or cancellated; in the shaft, compact bone.

7. Note the red marrow in the spongy bone.

8. What advantage is gained by the tubular form of the bone?

9. What advantage in the spongy character of the bones at the ends?

10. Can you see any means by which the bone is nourished ?

11. Place a piece of bone in the fire and thoroughly burn it. Put it on live coals, and let it remain over night.

12. How does the burnt bone differ from the fresh bone?

13. After the burning is completed, what must be the nature of the substance remaining?

14. Place another small bone in a mixture of one ounce of hydrochloric acid to a pint of water. Note the changes that occur.

15. How does the part which remains unaffected after a day or two differ from what remains after burning? This is the animal matter that is in bone.

16. What properties of bone are derived from the mineral matter it contains? What from the animal matter?

17. Animal matter is most abundant in bones in early life, and mineral matter is most abundant in old age.

18. When are bones most likely to be distorted ? When most easily broken ?

19. Why will bones, distorted for some time, assume permanently this new form ?

20. What school habits are most likely to distort bones?

21. What bones most frequently suffer distortion ?

22. How many in every ten people that you know are free from these distortions ?

FAT—ADIPOSE TISSUE.

1. Look for this about the joint and muscle.

2. Squeeze a small piece between the fingers. What is obtained ?

3. Can you think of any use for it ?

THE JOINT.

1. What motions are possible at this joint? Locate those joints in your body which have this motion only.

2. Such are called hinge joints. Define a hinge joint.

3. Find the cords which bind the bones together. These are called ligaments. How do they resemble tendons? How do they differ from them?

4. What tissue in the ligaments? How many can you find at this joint?

5. Open the joint with a knife. Note the sticky fluid found inside. It is called *Synovia*, or the *Synovial Fluid*. What use can you discover for it?

6. With your knife carefully separate the ends of the bones in the joint.

7. The two surfaces which rub over each other are called the articular surfaces. The soft translucent tissue covering these surfaces is *cartilage*. When found on the ends of bones in a joint, it is called *articular cartilage*. The meeting of two bones, as in a joint, is called an articulation.

8. Why should the ligament be inelastic?

9. What causes a sprained joint? How is the joint injured when sprained?

10. What must take place in a dislocation?

11. What occurs in a stiffened joint?

12. Review these lessons, and note the use of the word tissue. Can you write a definition of it?

Botany.

Watch the plants as a whole as the season changes. Note the disappearance of the sap, the drying of the leaf, the maturing fruit, the hardening of the new wood in the twig, and the newly-formed bud, in which is carefully packed away the destiny of the plant. Animals may hide in the earth or flee away to a milder clime, but the plant must face the blasts of winter where it stands, and it prepares itself accordingly. It is a most interesting phase of life. Continue to collect seeds and nuts of all kinds, and carefully dry and preserve them in envelopes.

1. Examine closely a branch, and find out how and where a leaf breaks away from the twig. Does the petiole or leaf-stalk break? What kind of a mark or scar remains?

2. Are there any buds newly formed? What is the relation of these, in position, to the leaf?

3. Are there more buds than one to the leaf?

4. Can you find, on the older twigs, buds of previous years which did not open?

5. What influences cause the leaves to change color and drop off?

6. Does the bark peel readily from the twig? Is it merely *drying* fast to the wood?

7. How much new wood has been formed this year?

8. Where has it grown, in the center or at the circumference of the branch?

9. Nuts, and the seeds of most weeds, are classed as dried fruits.   Why is it they are uniformly of dull colors ?

10. Can you understand why the edible portion of nuts is protected by a shell, while in berries and such fruits it is not so covered ?

11. What animals devour nuts ?   Do they in any way assist in scattering them ?

12. How else are nuts distributed ?   Will they float in water ?

13. How are they protected while unripe and on the tree ?   How, when they open and fall ?

14. Can you make out the various layers of the ovary in the acorn, hickory nut, walnut, and chestnut ?

15. Is the form of the nut of any advantage to it ?

16. Note the various contrivances by which the seeds of weeds, etc., are scattered.   How do some manage to use the wind ?   What part of the flower in the dandelion and thistle becomes the sail ?

17. What sized plants bear seeds with prickles ?   Do you see the reason why the size varies within narrow limits ?

18. What part of the flower becomes the prickle ?

19. Are the prickles in any case fastened to the seeds themselves ?

20. If the seeds are caught in the fur or hair of animals, does it not defeat the aim of the plant in producing the prickle ?

21. Examine a number of these under a lens, and sketch, showing the structure.

Books for Reference.   Humboldt Library : No. 116, chapter xi.   No. 33, Vignettes from Nature, chapters xi, xvi, xvii, xxi, and xxii.   No. 64, The Distribution of Life.   No. 26, chapter xvii.

Physics.

EVAPORATION.

1. Place small amounts of water in various shaped vessels and allow them to stand exposed to the air for several days.

2. What becomes of the water?

3. Under what circumstances will it evaporate most rapidly?

4. Note varying effects of a wide extent of surface, depth, currents of air passing over the surface, surface protected from currents as in a corked bottle, direct sunlight, darkness, heat, and cold.

5. What causes mud to dry up?

6. What becomes of the dew? Frost?

EBULLITION.

1. As heat is added to a vessel, what effect is there upon the rate of evaporation?

2. Note the changes that occur as the water comes to the boiling point?

3. What becomes of the first bubbles? What do they contain?

4. What causes the peculiar noise when a vessel of water simmers?

5. Note the bubbles when boiling begins. Where do they originate? How do they change in size? Why?

6. What are these bubbles?

83

7. Hold a thermometer in the steam above the water; does the temperature vary after boiling begins?

8. Is the water still receiving heat from the flame?

9. What becomes of this heat? If you hold your hand near the flame, does the heat continue to increase while you hold it there? Why does it not in the same way increase the temperature of the water?

10. Try boiling alcohol. Does the thermometer, used as before, show the same temperature?

CONDENSATION.

1 Where does the water go when the mud dries up? Is it destroyed?

2. How does water change its form when it evaporates? What is its form before it evaporates? (Liquid.) Afterward? (Vapor.)

3. Is it visible as it disappears from the pan by evaporation? Explain this.

4. Can it be rendered visible? What is it then called?

5. What change takes place in the vapor when it becomes visible?

6. Explain why it is sometimes foggy in the mornings?

7. What causes the fog to disappear?

8. Can you account for the formation of clouds?

9. When are they lowest? Why?

10. What is the history of a drop of rain?

DISTILLATION.

Take a quart or more of the "hard cider" produced by the fermentation of yeast. (See Chemistry for September.) Put it into a retort with a long neck, or an ordinary bottle with a bent glass tube fitted tightly through the cork. Suspend this in a vessel of boiling water, and conduct the vapor through the tube into a small bottle partly immersed in a vessel of cold water. Distil until about one-third has passed over into the smaller bottle. Redistil until alcohol is obtained sufficiently pure to show by the flame test.

1. Why is the smaller bottle immersed in cold water?

2. Why suspend the other one in boiling water instead of placing it next the flame directly?

3. Does the liquid in the flask boil?

4. Why not boil the liquid in the flask?

5. How is it that we can gradually separate the alcohol from the remainder of the liquid by this process?

6. In how many ways does the alcohol obtained differ from fresh juice of the fruit from which it was distilled?

7. Try burning it ; taste it ; note the odor ; allow a little to evaporate from the back of the hand.

8. Compare with water.

· Books for Reference. Humboldt Library : No. 2, Forms of Water.

Chemistry.

SOLUTION.

Provide some or all of the following substances : common salt, alum, saltpeter, chalk, washing soda, bichromate of potash, blue vitriol, copperas, and prussiate of potash. Each pupil should have a small bottle, about the size of the one-eighth-ounce morphia bottle, which may be procured at a trifling cost of any druggist. Fill each nearly full of cold water and label. Take the temperature of the water, before beginning, with a thermometer.

1. Drop a small amount of the different substances, finely powdered, into the different bottles. What becomes of it ?

2. Drop a small lump in ; does it disappear ? Why is the disappearance more rapid when the substance is finely powdered? How has the temperature changed?

Continue to add the finely powdered substance with constant stirring, until it no longer disappears, but begins to settle on the bottom. Gradually warm the water by placing the bottle on a sand-bath. If not heated slowly the bottle will crack. Test-tubes or thin glass beakers are much better for this purpose.

3. What effect does the heat have upon the substance at the bottom ?

4. Add more of the substance until the water boils and no more will dissolve, and then set aside to cool.

Those substances which disappeared in the water are

said to be *soluble in water.* Water is a *solvent.* They are said to dissolve, and the mixture of water and the dissolved substance is a solution.

5. Are all the substances named soluble ?

CRYSTALLIZATION.

Pour a little of the above solutions while hot into shal·low dishes, and set aside until the liquid evaporates. Suspend a string in the solution remaining in each of the bottles, and observe for a few hours.

1. How does the form of the solid, which soon appears, differ from what was added to the water ?

2. Do the crystals which form in the solution differ from those which remain after evaporation from the shallow dishes ?

3. Take a small amount of a solution and evaporate it by boiling ; how does the rate of evaporation affect the crystals ?

4. Are the crystals of each substance all alike ?

5. Solids which are deposited from solution, or which solidify from a melted state in such regular forms, are said to be crystalline. Those which solidify without the crystalline form are amorphous.

Meteorology.

1. How does the temperature at evening, night, and morning compare with that at similar times during September? Will the changes noted in any other column of your record suggest the cause for this?

2. How does the average temperature of the day differ from that of September?

3. What is the direction of the prevailing wind? Compare with September.

4. How has the prevailing wind affected the temperature?

5. Has it shown any marked influence upon the barometer?

6. Has it brought cloudy or clear weather, wet or dry?

7. From what direction did the heaviest rain come? From what direction did the greatest number come? Can you assign reasons for this? Consult maps and the globe.

8. What influences, if any, has the nearest mountain range or large body of water had upon the temperature and rainfall? How can you tell what their influence is?

9. What kind of cloud has been most frequently noted? Does the general character of the clouds differ from that of last month?

10. Does any particular kind of cloud usually immediately precede a heavy rain?

11. Have you noticed any fogs? When are they most dense? At what time do they disappear?

12. In what regions are they most dense ?

13. What was the character of the day and night preceding the fog ?

14. Does it always follow rain ?

15. What becomes of it when it is dissipated ?

STUDY OF THE WEATHER BUREAU MAPS.

16. Compare the temperature of the " Low " with that of the " High " area. Can you account for the exceptions to the rule ?

17. Does the heaviest rainfall, as given on the margin of the map, accompany the " Low " area ?

18. Do the isotherms show as marked a deviation from the general direction as they did in September ? Do the deviations occur in the same regions ?

19. What is the direction of the wind with respect to the " High " area ?

20. Where was the storm center during the heaviest storm in this region for the month ?

Astronomy.

1. What change noticed in the length of day and night?

2. Compare with the change during September.

3. Compare with the change in position of the noon shadow.

4. Are the spaces between two successive marks of the same length as they were in September for the same period of time? Can you show why there is variation?

5. Using the globe and sun, explain the differences discovered.

6. What time elapses between two successive full moons?

7. By means of a globe and sun, and another object to represent the moon, show what the relative position of the three bodies is when the moon is full.

The constellations to be observed are all of those given in preceding month, and in addition : Perseus, Andromeda, Serpentarius. Note the change in position, since last month, of the different constellations.

How can we account for it?

Geography.

GENERAL CONDITIONS.

1. What becomes of the water that falls as rain upon the land ? Mention three ways by which it is removed from the surface. (See Physics and Geology for October.)

2. What determines the direction of the flow of waters from the land?

3. What conditions determine its velocity ?

4. What conditions affect the size of a river, (*a*) its length, (*b*) its volume of water?

NORTH AMERICA.

1. Which ocean, with its arms, receives the larger amount of water from the continent of North America?

2. What does this indicate as to the number of the great slopes of the continent ?

3. Where do they show the line of the great continental water-parting to be ?

4. By modeling, represent the continental outline with this great water-parting and the two slopes.

5. Do the rivers in the eastern slope indicate the position of a secondary water-parting ? What is its direction and position ? Represent the two slopes from this water-parting.

6. Judging from the direction of the rivers in the northern slope, where are the great depressions?

7. Are there any minor divisions in the slope, as indicated by rivers?

8. In the southern slope of the continent, do the rivers indicate any other water-parting?

9. Where is this, and what is its direction? Indicate it in the model.

10. What directions do the rivers flow from this water-parting?

11. Where is the lowest line between the great continental water-parting and the last one found?

12. Study the course of the rivers in the southern continental slope between these two water-partings; what must be the general form and character of the surface of this region?

13. What things contribute to form the great rivers of this region? (See Studies of Signal Service Maps.)

14. In the eastern half of the Mississippi basin, is there any well-marked transverse water-parting?

15. Compare the two halves of the basin in this respect.

16. Since no great river systems are found on the coast slopes, what must be the character of those slopes? What is their direction from the water-partings?

17. Make a complete model of the continent, showing the water-partings and slopes, the lines of lowest depression, the chief rivers and lakes.

18. In what way did the continental slopes affect the settlement of the country?

19. Why were the earliest settlements in the interior made along the northern border of the United States?

20. What advantages did the early French routes into

the interior possess over those of the English and Spanish ?

21. In what way have the different slopes affected the occupations of the people ?

22. Why has the Atlantic coast slope always been a manufacturing region ?

23. Why does New York excel Philadelphia in trade with the interior ?

24. What has determined the location of the great cities of the Mississippi basin ?

25. What natural features have fixed the chief routes of commerce ? (The line where the slopes meet at their lower edges or borders.)

26. How do the continental slopes affect the commerce between the North and South ?

27. How do the slopes affect the commerce between the East and West ?

28. How have the great slopes affected the development of the Pacific coast region ?

29. How have the continental slopes affected the commerce between the Atlantic and Pacific coasts ?

BOOKS FOR REFERENCE. How to Study Geography, Francis W. Parker ; Earth and Man, Guyot.

Geology.

EROSION AND SEDIMENTATION.

Select some small stream that may be studied for some distance along its course. The small gullies formed by a heavy shower will answer very well. Certain river valleys in northern Italy that were once partially filled with glacial drift now abound in stone-capped clay pillars many feet in height. These have been formed by the rain wearing away the earth around the stones while that immediately under them was protected from its action. Similar pillars in miniature may be seen after a hard rain on any exposed clayey surface where there are small bits of stone. The height of the pillars indicates roughly the amount of soil torn away by the rain. The sun then dries them out, and, crumbling down, they are soon again at a common level with the surface. Trifling as this process may seem, the amount of soil thus beaten up and removed by the rain, in the course of a year, must be enormous.

1. How does a heavy rain affect the surface of the ground? How do you account for any minute elevations that remain standing after a hard rain?

2. What causes a stream to be crooked? Does it ever tend to straighten its channel? How?

3. In what part does it cut the deepest channel?

4. In what part the widest?

5. Upon what does the swiftness depend?

6. When two branches unite, is the single channel thus formed as large as that of both branches put together?

7. Can you notice any difference in the character of the sediment in different parts of the course? Dip up a little of the water in different places and allow it to settle.

8. In what part of the course of the stream do you find the largest pebbles?

9. Where are they most rounded and worn?

10. What determines where in the course of a stream they shall be deposited? Study the order of deposition in a pool or lakelet. As a further illustration, shake up different kinds of material in a glass jar, and allow them to settle.

11. In what part of the stream's course is the finest mud dropped?

12. Does the stream build new material along its banks? Under what conditions?

13. Cut down through some of the material thus deposited, and note the arrangement; is there any regularity?

14. Examine the material deposited at the mouth of the stream; how is it arranged?

15. Under what conditions will it not be deposited?

16. What are some of the things which assist the stream in widening its channel? What influence does drift have upon it?

17. What causes the formation of waterfalls?

18. What determines whether the descent from a higher to a lower level shall be by a cascade or by rapids?

19. Study the face of some cliff, a railroad cut, the sides

of a trench, or newly made excavation ; is there evidence of deposition from water ?

20. Can you tell whether it was deposited by running or still water ?

21. Can you see any reason why certain rocks are to be found in strata ?

22. Can you tell if the rocks that dip were deposited in that position ? Compare with the depositions in the glass jar. (See 10.)

23. If not deposited thus, what evidence is there that they were uplifted ?

24. Did the upheaving force act slowly for a great length of time, or rapidly for a shorter period ?

Mineralogy.

Gather a handful of coarse sand. Put it into a jar and thoroughly wash by shaking it up with water repeatedly, until freed from silt.

1. Examine some of the grains under a lens ; can you find any crystals ?

2. Are they entire or fragmentary ?

3. How many different kinds can you find ?

4. Can you tell where the sand came from ?

5. Examine particles of the soil and compare with a bit of the powdered rock which underlies it ; are they the same ?

6. Has the soil been formed by the weathering or rotting of the underlying rock ?

7. What other agent has aided in the soil formation ?

8. Examine the rough surface of a piece of marble ; can you see any crystals ?

9. In the same way examine a piece of granite ; how many different minerals does it contain ?

10. Coarsely powder a small piece ; are the fragments crystalline ? Which is the softest ? Which the hardest ? Granite is made up of quartz, feldspar, and mica ; the feldspar decomposes and becomes clay. What becomes of the quartz ?

Zoology.

There is hardly a more useful auxiliary to the science work which relates to animal life than an aquarium. If it be possible to have a strong metal-framed one connected with a steady water supply, it will save much trouble, but one may be managed very well without such conveniences. If no connection with pipes can be made, it it better to have several of medium size than to have one large one. Fish globes, eight or ten inches in diameter, are inexpensive and will be found very useful.

A small aquarium may be made thus : use an inch board one foot wide and one foot long for the bottom, and two boards of the same thickness and width, ten inches high, for the ends. Three-eighths of an inch from the edge on either side, with a saw, make a groove one-quarter of an inch deep, and wide enough to receive loosely double strength glass. Groove the end boards and fasten them to the bottom with screws so that the grooves will exactly match. Partially fill the grooves with soft putty, or better, aquarium cement, and press into each side a pane of glass. By making the bottom board eleven and one-half inches long, an ordinary ten by twelve window pane will be the proper size. When the glass is pressed to the bottom of the groove, draw the two ends in at the top until the glass is held firmly and then fasten them in place by narrow strips of wood, one on each side of the tank, placed on top of the glass and screwed to the end pieces. These strips also pro-

tect the hands from injury while working with the specimens in the aquarium. Before filling with water, the
inner surface of the bottom and ends should be well
rubbed with oil or paraffine and the grooves inside the
glass well packed with putty. The bottom should be
covered with an inch or two of sand and coarse
gravel.

Two or three of this size will enable one to preserve
safely a large variety of specimens, and sufficient in
amount to keep up an interesting study of animal life
throughout the winter. Indeed, if the supply falls short,
they may be restocked at any time of the year. By drag-
ging the bottom or edges of a pond or ditch, which is
covered with leaves and grass, with a hand rake, using a
net, one may usually in the midst of winter gather an
abundance of minnows, tadpoles, snails, crawfish, frogs
water-beetles, etc.

GENERAL OBSERVATIONS.

1. Are any birds to be found at this time ? Are the
birds that have migrated superior to those that remain in
intelligence ?

2. Are they winter residents ?

3. Have they been here all the year or have they come
from some other locality ?

4. What is their food ? How do they find protection
from storms ?

5. Where do they stay at night ?

6. Is their winter garb different from that of summer ?

7. Are they mated, in flocks, or solitary ?

8. Look for insects under stones, boards, leaves, etc.
Have they lined their nests in any way as a protection
against the cold ?

9. If they are not active keep them for a short time in a warm room.

10. Do they show signs of life?

11. In the same way, search for earthworms.

12. What substitute have these animals for migration?

13. What do they do for food?

14. Animals lying through the winter in a dormant state are said to hibernate.

15. Put a common mud-turtle in a box of wet sand and cover loosely with a lid. Keep the sand wet.

16. Note the time when he disappears; he will probably not be seen again for months.

17. How do you think the chances for life of a hibernating animal compare with one that is migratory.

18. Why does the animal hibernate when kept in a warm room in winter time? Does the animal display intelligence in hibernating?

ANIMAL COVERINGS AND WARMTH.

1. What changes do we make in our clothing as winter approaches? In material? Color? Thickness? Texture?

2. How do the brute animals make similar preparation?

3. Is the winter plumage of birds the same as that of summer?

4. How do birds preen their feathers? Why?

5. How are the coverings of water-fowl especially adapted to their mode of life?

6. Study the arrangement of the feathers on a bird; a pigeon or sparrow may be readily obtained for the purpose. Are the feathers distributed evenly over the body?

7. Is there any obvious advantage in the manner in which the feathers are distributed?

8. Mention the uses you can see for feathers?

9. What animal can you name that is covered with fur? Name one covered with hair? What difference is there between fur and hair? Examine a dog and a cat.

10. Can you suggest any reason why one animal is provided with fur and another with hair?

11. Which is the better protection against injury? Which is the warmer covering?   .

12. Where are fur-bearing animals found? Where are those with a hairy covering found? Compare wool with both hair and fur?

13. Read something of the history and habits of the fur and wool bearing animals.

14. Study the scales of a fish and snake; what is their chief use in each case?

15. Do the coverings of fishes and snakes change in any way with the seasons?

16. If possible, secure a snake skin that has been shed and examine it closely; how does the snake get out of it? Are the scales shed?

17. Is the right side out? Note the transparent covering that was over the eye.   .

18. How does the covering of the turtle differ from that of both the snake and the fish?

19. Do insects have skins? How does the outside of an insect's body differ from most other animals studied?

20. What peculiarity in the covering of a crawfish? What is its most important use?

21. Can you see how it is possible for the animals which have such hard coverings to grow?

22. How do the different modes of life of the various animals observed correspond to their coverings ?

THE SKIN OF THE HUMAN BODY.

1. Compare the skin on the back of the hand with that on the palm in color, thickness, sensitiveness, and markings.

2. Why is the greater thickness on the palm ?

3. On what other parts of the body is the skin similar to this ?   Why ?

4. What is the effect of manual labor on the skin in the palm ?

5. Is there any difference in the causes which operate on the palm and on the sole of the foot ?

6. What causes the creases in the palm ?

7. Note the short hairs covering the back of the hand ; examine with small magnifying glass.   At the root of each hair is a small oil gland which pours out upon the surface a minute quantity of oil.   Notice the softness and flexibility of the skin.

8. When is it that the skin on the hands becomes harsh and chapped ?

9. How is oil affected by cold weather ?   How must it affect the flow from the glands in the hands ?

10. How do the hands feel after having had them in soap-suds ?   What must be the effect of the soap on the oil ?

11. Why should the skin be wiped dry after washing ?

12. What is the best way to prevent the hands from becoming chapped ?

13. What would you suggest as the natural remedy ?

The outer layer of the skin which sometimes may be rubbed up as white scales, and which forms the clear skin in a blister, is the cuticle or scarf skin. As it dies and is worn off it is replaced by the true skin underneath. When dry, it cracks and exposes the sensitive layer lying under it.

A small cake of pure mutton tallow rubbed over the hands at night is a simple and effective remedy. It should not be smeared on in great quantity. Nature never oils the skin in that way, and we should imitate her in this respect.

14. What is perspiration ? Is it pure water ?

15. What causes tend to increase perspiration ? To diminish it ?

16. Passing outward through the skin, and opening at its surface, are very many minute tubes that convey the perspiration from the sweat glands ; these are situated in the deeper layers of the skin. The openings of these glands may be seen through a magnifying glass in rows in the palm.

The sweat glands in health are continually throwing off from the body waste matters which are carried to them by the blood.

17. How must the heat of the body be affected by the evaporation of perspiration from its surface?

18. Do you become warmer or cooler when you per-spire freely. Since the skin thus assists in maintaining a proper heat in the body, it is a *heat regulator.*

19. Rub a little oil briskly on the hand ; what becomes of it ? Has it evaporated ?

20. Why is it that liniments may be applied to the skin for ailments that lie deeper, as in case of a sprain ? The skin is an organ of *absorption.*

21. On what part of the body is the skin most useful in giving us the sense of touch ?

22. The sensitiveness of the skin in different parts may be tested by using a pair of dividers with sharp points thus : close the eyes and allow some one to touch the skin in various places, now with the single point, then with the double point. Find where you can distinctly distinguish the two points when they are closest together.

23. Try in this way the palm, back of hand, cheek, tongue, lips, back of neck, arm, ear, etc.

24. How many important uses have we found for the skin ?

25. Examine one of the finger-nails. Note the opaque area near the base called the lunula, and also how the skin is attached around the inner end.

26. Does the skin grow fast to the edge of the nail ?

27. Why does the skin sometimes break and peel backward from the base of the nail ?

28. To prevent this, loosen the skin by running around the edge the dull point of a knife.

29. In what way are the nails most useful ? What happens if they are allowed to grow too long? If trimmed too closely ? How does the care of the nail affect the shape of the finger-tips ?

30. How does biting the finger-nails spoil them ?

31. Why is a knife better than scissors for trimming them ? The nail is made of thin layers, and scissors, especially dull ones, tend to separate them.

32. Of what use to us is the hair on the head?

33. Can you give a good reason for brushing and combing it ?

34. Note the white powdery flakes that may be sometimes brushed from the head. Where do they come from ?

35. Compare these with the cuticle which may be rubbed from the back of the hand.

36. What gives the softness and flexibility to the hair ?

37. What is the effect of using soap and water upon it ? Why is it so ?

38. Why is it necessary to wash the hair ? If the scalp is healthy no oil is needed ; and if it is not, oil will do but little good. Treat the scalp much the same as you do the skin on other parts of the body.

39. How many distinct uses of the skin may be named ?

40. How may it best be cared for as an organ of pro-tection ? Contrast the effects of indoor and outdoor occupations upon it. What are the effects upon the skin of bodily exercise in fresh air ?

41. How may its usefulness as an organ of touch be increased ?

42. In what occupations is a refined sense of touch necessary ? Of what use is it to a physician ? How do the blind utilize it ?

43. Test yourself as to this sense. Can you distinguish by touch a one-cent piece from a dime ? A five-cent piece from a two-cent piece ? Sugar from salt ? Salt from sand ? Can you distinguish flannel from heavy cot-ton cloth ? Printed from unprinted paper ?

44. How is the usefulness of the skin promoted by bathing ?

45. How does the work of the skin necessitate frequent change of clothing ?

BOOKS FOR REFERENCE.   As a text-book, Martin's Human Body. Humboldt's Library, No. 4, Man's Place in Nature. See also the Nos. previously recommended in work for September and October.

Botany.

The activity of plant life outdoors has ceased, and but little can be done with the study this month except to examine the dormant condition of those plants which live through the winter, and to note the provisions made for the succeeding season by those that do not. The nice adaptation of the plants to their changed environments is the chief point to be observed.

1. Have the plants completed their preparation for winter?

2. Can you find any that continue to grow until the leaves fall?

3. Do the first frosts kill any of the newly grown twigs? Examine as many different kinds of trees as possible.

4. What changes have the new twigs undergone since summer?

5. Can you find any plants that have been entirely killed?

6. How will such plants be reproduced next season?

7. How does the number of seeds produced by plants that are killed each year by frosts compare with the number produced by plants that live from year to year? . Which class of plants seems to have the better mode of scattering its seeds? Take plenty of time in working up this topic so that a large number of examples can be cited by the pupils.

8. Are there any seeds to be found? Can you find

any which by some means have been planted? Remove a small pan-full of earth to the warm school-room and see if any self-planted seeds will grow.

9. Can you find any plants which came from the seed last spring that have been entirely killed by the frost? Such plants are called *annuals.*

10. Plants which live over from year to year are called *perennials.*

11. Look through the garden for plants whose roots or underground stems are still alive, but whose tops may be dead. Do you know what the entire life history of such a plant is? Examples, parsnip and turnip. Such plants are called *biennials.*

REFERENCES. See October.

Physics.

HEAT.

In the experiments to be performed, it is the intention to have the pupils prepare the apparatus under the direction of the teacher and do all the work.

The teacher must see that the directions are closely followed that the conditions may be as nearly perfect as possible. Ideal results are not to be expected, but for what is lost in this respect, compensation may often be found in a close study of the disturbing elements which rendered them inaccurate. Interpretation of the results of all the experiments must be insisted upon, and concise statements, together with descriptions of the apparatus, in many cases accompanied with drawings, should be required.

In some instances, teachers fail because they do not allow the pupils sufficient time in which to prepare their apparatus. With the mind fixed upon an expected result, they too often force the experiment regardless of proper precautions which should have been taken. In describing an experiment the pupil should always be required to state what precautions are necessary to be observed. There is as much for the pupil, often, in the careful preparation and manipulation of the apparatus as there is in the outcome of the experiment itself.

In the following work, with a little care on the part of

the teacher, a good deal may be accomplished in the cultivation of a "temperature sense" in the pupil. While it does not rank high among the senses in usefulness, and in most persons it is but poorly developed, it should not by any means be neglected. With but little practice the pupils will be able to judge, with considerable accuracy, of the different degrees of temperature of water between the freezing point and that of 130° or 140° Fahrenheit.

The central thought to be developed in these lessons on heat is, that heat is energy which expresses itself in different ways owing to the manner in which it is directed and to the medium employed. Almost the only expression with which the pupils are familiar is that of temperature, and that heat should be able to perform work without increasing the temperature is something that is hard to get them to realize. The fact, however, that heat continually passing into a vessel of melting snow or ice does not raise the temperature while the ice is melting is enough to start them to thinking in an intelligent way upon the subject. The uniform temperature of water after it has been raised to the boiling point, although heat is constantly added, is illustrative of the same point. To the question as to what this excess of heat which passes into the water, in either case, does, the pupil can hardly find a wrong answer, if cautiously and properly directed.

RADIATION, ABSORPTION, AND REFLECTION.

1. Heat an iron rod or bar in a flame till red hot, remove, and hold the face or hand near it on different sides. What is noticed as to the direction in which heat passes off? Heat thrown from a body thus is said to be *radiated.*

2. What becomes of the heat radiated from a body? Is it destroyed?

3. Does the rod radiate all its heat? When will radiation cease?

4. By what contrivances are rooms heated by radiation?

5. Why does the earth become cooler after sunset?

6. Which becomes cold faster, the land or the water?

7. Why is it that dew forms at nightfall?

8. Why is the formation of dew dependent upon the clearness of the night? Consult your Meteorological Record for the facts upon which to base your answer.

9. Compare and contrast with (8) the conditions under which fog forms.

10. When any body is held near a warmer one, how is the former affected by the latter? Anything so warmed is said to get its heat by *absorption*.

11. Is the absorption of heat affected by the smoothness or roughness of the surface of the body?

12. Does color affect the result? When opportunity offers, spread two small squares of cloth, one white and the other black, upon snow in the sunshine ; after a time notice the rate of melting underneath each one. Try different materials of each color ; is the rate of melting dependent upon the color or material and texture of the cloth?

13. Heat which strikes a body and is again thrown off is said to be *reflected*.

14. Are good radiators also good reflectors?

15. Are good radiators good absorbers?

16. Which of the above qualities should a good stove possess?

17. Should a stove be kept with a brightly polished

surface? Should the surface be smooth or broken by ornamentation?

TEMPERATURE.

1. Provide a small vessel of water and a thermometer. The water should have a temperature of 50° or 60°. Hold the fingers in this till familiar with the sensation. Place the thermometer in the vessel and note the temperature.

2. Apply heat until twenty degrees hotter, and again let the pupils test with the fingers and then measure with the thermometer. In this way, test with the hand and measure with the thermometer until the fingers can be held in it but a few seconds only.

3. Begin again with the temperature first taken and by adding snow or ice reduce to the freezing point, testing with the fingers and reading the thermometer as before.

4. Repeat these experiments, changing the temperature ten degrees each time instead of twenty.

5. After holding the fingers a short time in ice water, dip them in water having the temperature at which you began; does it feel warmer or cooler than before? The pupil should test with his fingers and express his judgment as to the temperature in each case before using the thermometer.

6. Why is testing the temperature in this way with the fingers likely to be untrustworthy?

7. Note the temperature of the school-room; it should be about 68°. Compare with that of a hall-way. Daily practice should be given in judging the temperature of the room.

EXPANSION.

1. Fasten one end of a small iron rod or wire, a foot long, tightly in a small support of some kind. Against

the free end arrange an index finger in such a way that it will move over a dial. The index should be several inches long and the wire should rest against it near the pivot.

2. Apply heat to the rod throughout its length; note the movement of the index. What does its movement indicate?

3. Withdraw the heat; does the rod still rest against the index?

4. Substitute a brass rod for the one of iron and note the movement of the index.

5. Cut or punch a hole in a piece of tin large enough to just allow a rod to pass through it smoothly. Heat the rod and try passing it through the hole. What does this indicate? Cool the rod and try again.

6. Can you see any reason why a blacksmith should heat the tire of a wheel before putting it on?

7. Why is there a space between the ends of the rails in a railroad?

8. Why heat the bolts and rivets used in putting together the parts of iron bridges and boilers?

9. Allow each pupil to fill a small bottle level full of boiling water which has been colored with a little indigo or ink. Pass a glass tube a few inches long and of small bore, say one-eighth of an inch, just through the cork; it should not project below the under surface of the cork. Press the cork tightly into the bottle and the water will rise in the tube; see that no bubble of air rests underneath the cork and that none are clinging to the inside of the bottle. The water should stand in the tube so as to be visible above the cork, and the point to which it rises should be marked. This is easily done by slipping down over the tube a small piece of paper. Set the

bottle aside until the water becomes cold. Does the water stand at the same height in the tube? Why? Why fill with boiling water?

10. Place the bottle when cooled in a shallow pan containing sand, and heat gradually over the alcohol lamp.

11. Can you notice any movement of the water in the tube? Why is the tube used?

12. What is the effect of heat upon the water?

13. Make a drawing of the apparatus used and explain why each successive step is taken in its arrangement.

14. Using the same apparatus, place the bottle in a vessel containing snow or ice mingled with salt. Watch sharply the column of water in the tube.

15. Compare its movements with those when the bottle was heated.

16. In order to test the temperature, one bottle with a wide mouth should be prepared with the tube and also a thermometer through the cork. At what temperature does the water begin to rise in the tube? Does it expand beyond its original volume?

17. From these two experiments can you think of what changes and movements the water in a pond must undergo in being frozen?

18. Why does ice form at the top and not at the bottom of a pond or stream?

19. What would likely be the result if the ice should begin to form at the bottom?

20. Prepare the bottles again as above, but fill them only about half full of water and push the tube through the cork until it reaches nearly to the bottom.

21. Clasp the upper part of the bottle in the hands and watch the tube.

22. Compare carefully the conditions of this experiment with those in the last. What essential difference between them?

23. Heat the bottle, as before, over a lamp ; account for the result observed.   ·

25. If possible, procure a bladder or a small rubber bag partially filled with air ; warm it gently and account for the result.

Books for Reference.—Humboldt Library, No. 120. The Modern Theory of Heat; and The Sun as a Storehouse of Energy.

Chemistry.

In this and other science work it will sometimes be necessary to have a means of getting a strong heat without smoke. If gas is at hand it is best to procure a Bunsen burner and attach it to a jet with a rubber tube. An alcohol lamp, however, will make a good substitute. To make one of these, take a small bottle and perforate the cork, making a round opening three-eighths of an inch in diameter. With a small piece of tin make a tube an inch or two long that will tightly fit the hole through the cork, allowing it to project a short distance above. The seam of the tube need not be soldered. Roll a small flat lamp wick tightly and pass it through the tube. A large-sized thimble may be used as a cap for extinguishing the flame and to prevent waste of alcohol when not lighted. The cork should rest loosely in the bottle when in use. A much better lamp is made by using a metal-capped tooth-powder bottle that may be bought of any druggist for five cents. This equals any alcohol lamp of its size that is made specially for the purpose, and it is much cheaper, and will answer all purposes where heat is required in performing the experiments suggested in this book.

1. Take a small stick of wood and cut it into fine pieces ; set fire to another similar one and let it be consumed. Watch closely the changes taking place.

2. How has the wood been changed in the first instance ? Are there any changes in amount ?

3. Has there been any change whatever in the substance of the wood ?

4. What was the first change noticed in the burning wood ? Note the charring.

5. Does anything remain after burning has ceased ? What is it ?

6. Does it in any way resemble the wood ?

7. Is there in what remains either as great bulk or weight as there was in the wood ?

8. What has become of the part that has disappeared ?

9. Allow the smoke to strike a piece of porcelain or glass ; what collects on the surface ?

10. Does the soot in any way resemble the wood ?

11. Was it a part of the wood ?

12. Hold the flame of an alcohol lamp under and near the soot on the plate ; what becomes of it ? Is it totally consumed ?

13. What is the greatest difference, in result, of the above operation on wood ?

14. In the first instance there was a *physical change ;* in the second a *chemical change.*

15. Try lowering the lighted stick into a wide-mouthed bottle ; try again with a bottle or jar of larger size ; compare the burning under such conditions with those in the first instance.

16. What conditions seem to be necessary for the burning of the wood ?

17. Is the air in the bottle changed when the stick is burned in it ?

18. Pour into a clean bottle half an inch of lime-water and shake it ; does it change ?

19. Now burn a match in the bottle and shake again ; is the lime-water changed ?

20. Does this recall the results of any experiment of a previous month?

21. Drop a piece of marble into a small bottle of strong vinegar or into water mixed with hydrochloric acid; how does the action differ from what takes place when it is put into water? (See Chemistry for October.)

22. Use a piece of limestone in place of the marble; describe closely what occurs.

23. What do the bubbles contain? Lower a lighted match into the bottle.

24. By means of a bent tube through the cork, draw some of the gas formed out into a small amount of lime-water; do the results with the lime-water and match recall any previous experiments? This is a test for carbon dioxide gas.

25. What tests proved it to be different from air? In what respects is it like air?

26. Place in a Florence flask or pint bottle a handful of pieces of marble, cover them with water and add hydrochloric acid till gas comes off freely. Through a bent glass tube in the cork convey the gas to the bottom of another wide-mouthed bottle or a beaker.

27. After a few minutes, with a movement as of pouring, invert the beaker over a burning taper or match? How do you account for the result?

28. Why is it possible to collect this gas in an open beaker as we did? Why is it possible to pour it like water?

29. When the bubbling ceases, pour off the liquid and dry the solid that remains; does it differ from what was used originally?

30. Will acid act upon it again as it did at first?

31. Try the vinegar with chalk or limestone or marble that has been mixed with water.

32. Have the substances in the above experiments undergone physical or chemical change ?

33. Take a small amount of sulphur and mix thoroughly with about the same quantity of iron filings ; can you distinguish the two substances in the mixture ?

34. Can you separate the two substances ?   Blow upon the heap.

35. Pass a magnet back and forth near the mixture ; what is the result ?

36. Make another similar mixture of sulphur and filings in a cup ; warm gradually over the burner.

37. Watch closely and describe the changes that take place ?

38. After the action ceases, examine the substance formed and compare with the original materials.

39. Can you distinguish the sulphur ?   How does it differ from the filings ?   The new substance thus formed is called iron sulphide.   Instead of writing the word iron in full, the symbol Fe is generally used, and instead of the word sulphur the symbol S is written.   Iron sulphide has for its symbol, Fe S.   In the first instance the iron and sulphur formed merely a mixture ; in the second a combination.   What is the difference ?

40. Which experiment with the filings and sulphur more closely resembles that with the acid and marble ?

41. In what important particular are they different ?

42. In how many of the experiments performed could you distinguish new substances that were formed ?

43. What were the tests used which proved their presence ?

44. How does the new substance which was formed in the bubbles of vinegar differ from the Fe S in the last experiment ?

BOOKS FOR REFERENCE.   Remsen's Introduction to the Study of Chemistry.

Meteorology.

1. How does the mean temperature for the first week compare with that of the first week in October ? What causes the difference ?

2. Is the direction of the prevailing wind the same as it was for October ? Is it a cold or a warm wind ?

3. How can you account for its direction ?

4. What wind is accompanied by a clear sky ? How does this wind affect the temperature ?

5. What wind has accompanied the rains ? Are the rains more or less frequent than they were in the preceding months ?

6. How does the amount of rainfall compare with that of the preceding months ?

7. What is the most common form of cloud observed ?

8. How have they changed in character ? Are they higher or lower than they were in September ?

9. Which is the more common this month, frost or dew ?

10. What is the character of a night preceding a frost ?

11. Does the frost form upon all objects outdoors ?

12. How does a windy night affect the formation of frost ? A cloudy night ?

13. Examine some frost crystals under a lens.

14. Are they uniform in shape and size ? Are frost crystals frozen drops of dew ?

15. What difference is there between the conditions for forming dew and those for forming frost ? In what respects are they the same ?

16. Has the barometer in any way indicated the change noted in the weather ?

17. What was the mean height of the barometer on the clear days ?

18. What was its mean height on the rainy or stormy days ?

19. In what month has the barometer shown the greatest range of movement ?   In which the least ?

20. In what month has there been the greatest fluctuation in the weather ?   In what month the least ?

21. Is there any uniformity in the temperature which accompanies a falling barometer ?   Is it the same or different with a rising barometer ?

STUDY OF THE WEATHER BUREAU MAPS.

22. Do the isotherms vary more or less this month from their general direction than they did last month ?

23. Where is the variation greatest ?   What cause can you assign ?

24. In what part of the country has there been the heaviest rainfall ?

25. Where has there been the most snow ?

26. Where is the region of lowest temperature ?

27. Have the mountains the same effect upon the isotherms that they had in September ?

28. Do the coast lines exert the same influence upon the isotherms as last month ?

29. What was the lowest isotherm that passed through this locality during the month ?

30. What was the lowest latitude of that isotherm in September ?   In October ?

31. What inference may be derived from its varying position ?

Astronomy.

The facts that have been noted from time to time as to the variation in the length of day and night, the change of season, the changing shadow, the different position of the rising and setting sun on the horizon, should all be used in giving the pupils a clearer idea of the earth and the sun in their relative positions, and also broader conceptions of these bodies themselves. To accomplish the latter end, the pupils should be trained to think of the earth and the sun without the use of the globe for illustration. Make the same use of the symbol in this case as in all others ; use it only as an aid to the conception of the object, but do not let it entirely take the place of the object, inasmuch as then the pupil's conception must be of the symbol only.

1. Compare the length of day and night with that of preceding months.

2. Is the rate of variation each day the same during the month ? How does it differ from that of October and September ?

3. In what direction is the noon-mark changing? Why ?

4. Is it changing more or less rapidly than it did in the preceding months?

5. Are the facts observed thus far sufficient to prove the revolution of the earth around the sun ?

6. What other supposition can you make that would account for the phenomena observed ?

7. Use a globe, if necessary, to illustrate your meaning.

8. Has the diminishing day had anything to do with the changing season ?

9. Show to what other cause the change in season is due.

10. What time elapses between two new moons ?

11. Show what the position of the moon must be with respect to the earth and sun when it is new. Why is it crescent shaped ?

12. In what direction do the horns point ? Why do they point in this direction ? Does the direction vary ? Why ?

13. Does the moon always follow the same path across the sky ?

14. Where does the new moon always appear first ? Why ?

15. Where is it when between old and new ?

16. The constellations to be observed are the same as those for October.

BOOKS FOR REFERENCE.   Astronomy Science Primer, by Lockyer. Newcomb's Astronomy, Briefer Course.   See previous months.

Geography.

CLIMATE OF NORTH AMERICA.

By a judicious reference to the Signal Service Maps, and to maps of the continent, upon which are marked the isotherms, a detailed study of the climate of North America may proceed from month to month. It must not be expected that the pupils will generalize sufficiently to be able to see all the laws underlying the distribution of heat and moisture ; yet such use of the maps will assist them to collect in a practical way a large number of the facts upon which the laws are based, and which open the way for a clear understanding of the laws further along. The data gathered from the study of physical maps should be used to supplement and extend the knowledge and experience they have gained from their own observations recorded in the Meteorological Record.

1. What regions of the United States show the greatest contrasts as to rainfall during the month ?

2. Note the latitude of the two regions ; also the elevation, the winds which traverse them, and their nearness to the sea.

3. Can you tell what conditions have most affected the rainfall ?

4. Which condition has the most to do with the temperature of the two regions ?

5. What difference is noted in the temperature of the two places?

6. Contrast the character of the prevailing winds upon the Pacific slope with those upon the Atlantic. How do the two regions differ in temperature in the same latitude?

7. Is the difference in temperature dependent upon the winds? Note the direction from which they come in each case.

8. Compare the rainfall of the interior between the two great mountain systems with that on the coasts. What is the direction of the prevailing wind in the interior?

9. Compare the rainfall in the northern and southern regions of the interior. Upon what does the difference depend?

10. How can you account for the difference in temperature of the northern and southern divisions of the interior?

11. What contrasts in temperature and rainfall are noted between the mountainous parts and the lowlands?

12. What contrasts, that you know of, between the people of different regions are due to difference in climate?

13. Are any differences that may exist between the people on the Pacific coast and the Atlantic coast due to difference in climate? Are the differences as well marked as they are between the North and the South? Why?

14. Contrast the people of the far north with those of the extreme south, as to character, habits, occupation, etc. How does the climate affect them?

15. How does difference of climate affect the productions in our latitude?

16. Where are there the greatest contrasts in the pro-

ductions in the same latitude ?   Are these due to climatic differences ?

17. Compare the rainfall for the month of the region just east of the Rocky Mountains with the region just west of the Appalachian Mountains ; how do you account for the difference ?

18. Where do the winds that sweep the two regions come from ?

DRAINAGE OF SOUTH AMERICA.

1. Note, by the examination of a good map of South America, the ocean which receives the greatest part of the drainage waters ; compare in this respect with North America.

2. From the flow of the rivers, how can you tell the location of the continental slopes ?   Bound the slopes.

3. Where is the great continental water-parting ?

4. How does it compare in relative position with the great continental water-parting of North America ?   How does it compare in direction ?

5 What resemblance in the two continents as to their great slopes ?   Compare the two Pacific slopes.   The Atlantic slopes.

6. Do the rivers in the north of each continent indicate any similarity in the slopes in these regions ?

7. What minor water-partings are indicated by the rivers of the eastern slopes ?

8. How does the position of the minor water-partings differ from those of North America ?   How do they compare in direction ?

9. Compare the slopes of the interior with those of North America.

10. In what directions does the interior slope ?

11. What resemblance and difference can be discovered in the great river systems of the two continents?

12. What differences as to their minor river systems?

13. What part of the continent must receive the greatest rainfall?

14. Compare the northern and the southern parts as to rainfall, basing the comparison upon the size of the rivers.

15. Compare the regions as to rainfall with corresponding parts of North America; what difference noted? Why?

16. What inference, based upon the great rivers, can you make respecting the fertility of different regions of the eastern slope? What inference in this respect about the western slope?

17. Where is the greatest river basin? What are its boundaries? The second, and third in size?

18. How does the general slope of these basins as wholes differ?

19. Compare the Brazilian Highland with the Appalachian.

20. In what latitude are the greatest rivers? In what latitude are the smallest rivers? Compare with North America.

Geology.

PEBBLES.

Have each pupil take the entire collection of pebbles gathered during the preceding months and assort them with respect to their different characteristics, such as shape, color, material, etc., and by a careful consideration learn something of their history. This work should be preceded by as much actual field work as possible. No teacher ought to hesitate to begin such field work, simply because of a lack of experience. It is the want of actual contact with things that renders so much teaching unsatisfactory to the teacher and obscure to the pupils. Visit some stream and spend a few hours studying the pebbles that line its banks. No matter how insignificant the brook may be, it will hardly fail to afford abundant illustration of the force of water in pebble-making. Fortunate indeed is the teacher who can also visit, with his classes, the shore of a lake or the sea, and there study the same force at work under different conditions. The wind here plays a part equally important with the water, and the two together, through the ceaseless rolling waves, are as destructive as the swiftest current. The mobile water curling in graceful breakers and spreading itself out in thin layers on the beach, seems to possess but little of the force necessary to accomplish the results wrought out along every shore. But a cupful of water taken from one of these waves will show that it carries a multitude of sand grains that rasp each other and the shore continually. In the larger waves, great quantities of pebbles are constantly rolled in and out with the advancing and retreating waters, and the grinding, grating sound accompanying the alternate movements tell something of the great work that is going on. In times of tempest, the force is increased a thousand fold. With a thundering roar, the water, laden with great bowlders, hurls itself in some places against the shore with a force sufficient to demolish the most substantial works of man ; elsewhere, it rolls up immense heaps of sand, gravel, and stones, and leaves them perhaps hundreds of miles from the starting point of their journey. If in addition to these illustrations it is possible to study and compare with them the action of the glaciers, the interest will be greatly increased.

The different forms of the glacial pebbles, the different manner in which they are deposited, the means by which they were carried, will all furnish rich material for careful thought and study. It is an excellent exercise for the reasoning powers to trace the history of a pebble from its present condition and surroundings, back through its various stages to its origin in some distant cliff in a remote age. How much of this history can be written, will depend upon the age and experience of the pupils ; some will perhaps read its history only to water which rolled it and made it round ; others will follow it to a particular lake or stream, and still others may see its footsteps leading to some cliff. It little matters how far they go, or how far short of the end they may have to stop, if in accounting for them they learn to properly use and interpret the conditions under which the pebbles are found. It is not enough for a full conception that they follow merely the footsteps of the pebbles through space; the element of time is one of greatest importance, but it is a factor that can never be anything but vague in the minds of the most highly trained, and too much must not therefore be expected of young pupils. No effort should be spared, however, to broaden their ideas in this direction, inasmuch as a lack of this conception stands in the way of many people who cannot receive the modern theory of the earth's development.

Whether all or but one of the above illustrations of the results of water action are at the command of the teacher, let it once more be urged that the means at hand be used. It is the universal experience that not only do the facts so learned remain longer in the mind, but that such lessons often prove to be initiative of a line of observation and thought that lasts through life.

1. Where were the pebbles in your collection found?

2. Can you distinguish those that were found on the banks of a stream from those found on the shore of a lake?

3. What have you observed in the arrangement of pebbles on the river bank or lake shore? Is it exactly the same in both cases?

4. Have you found pebbles in any considerable quantity at a distance from water? Does the water reach the place in times of floods?

5. How can you account for this remoteness of pebbles from water? Are they like the rocks found in the quarries in the vicinity?

6. Can you tell whether they were deposited by running or still water?

7. Can you tell whether the water was shallow or deep?

8. Were they deposited on a shore or in the middle of a lake or stream?

9. Are there any other evidences of water action near by ?

10. Can you form any estimate as to the length of time since they were deposited ?

11. What things on the surface will assist in giving some idea of the time?

12. Are there any large trees in the vicinity ? What is the depth of the vegetable mold? Is the sod well formed ?

13. Which gives the best evidence of the length of time since the pebbles were deposited, the trees, the vegetable mold, or the sod ?

14. What is the nature of the ground with which they are mingled, sandy, clayey, or loamy ?

15. How does the surface of a pebble differ from that of a freshly broken stone ?

16. How does it differ from one that has been exposed to the air for a long time ?

17. What makes this difference in surface ?

18. Assort the pebbles with respect to shape ; what is the most common form ?

19. Why should they be rounded ? Upon what does the shape appear to depend ?

20. Is it the hardness of the material in the pebbles or its arrangement that does the more to determine their shape ?

21. Assort and rearrange the pebbles again with respect to the material composing them ; compare as to color, hardness, etc.

22. Can you tell how it is that many different kinds are found together?

23. Does any one kind of material prevail to any great extent more than the others?

24. Is any of the rock composing the pebbles to be found in neighboring quarries?

25. Can you recall whether or not the ledges that may usually be seen projecting from a cliff or hillside are of the same kind of rock?

26. What evidence have you seen that such cliffs are wearing away?

27. A great variety of rock may be picked up by a stream traversing many miles of country, but how is this variety possible with a lake?

28. How does the force which rounds off the pebbles in a stream differ from that in a lake or on the seashore?

29. What part does the water really play in both cases?

30. Can you think of any conditions which affect the rate at which pebbles will be transported? Is this course a direct one to the mouth of the stream?

31. Under what conditions will they be deposited along the banks?

32. Under what circumstaces will they be dropped in mid-stream? When will such be moved again?

33. Upon what conditions will those along the bank be allowed to remain?

34. Is it likely that pebbles left in sand on the building bank of a river will be again disturbed?

BOOKS FOR REFERENCE. See September. Also Humboldt Library, No. 38. Chapter i.

Mineralogy.

An interesting variation in the study of this subject this month will be found in a consideration of common mineral fuel.

The pupils should supply themselves, as far as possible, with specimens of bituminous, anthracite, cannel, and splint or block coals ; also, with examples of peat and coke. A good specimen of lignite is likewise needed to complete the list.

Compare the different specimens as to weight. Which is the heaviest ? The lightest ?

1. The weight of a solid or liquid compared with an equal bulk of water is called its specific gravity. To find the specific gravity of a solid, weigh it first carefully on an ordinary balance ; then suspend it from one of the scale pans by means of a fine thread, and immerse it entirely in a small vessel of water, and obtain its weight submerged. The weight in air divided by the loss of weight in water is the specific gravity.

2. Which specimen has the greatest specific gravity ? which the least ? Do you notice any correspondence between the specific gravity and the hardness ?

3. What difference in luster do you notice ? Are they sufficiently well marked to enable one to distinguish the different kinds of coal ? Some kinds show a play of different colors, and are known as peacock coal.

4. How do they differ in hardness ? If you have

different varieties of the same kind, *i. e.*, specimens from different mines, can you notice differences in them?

5. Try with a lighted match to set fire to the different specimens, selecting sharp edges or corners for the purpose. Which one burns easiest? Which with most difficulty?

6. Note the odor of the burning substance in each case ; how does the peat differ from the rest?

7. What difference in the ways of burning in grates and stoves?

8. Compare the coke with the different coals. It is the carbon left after burning the coal to rid it of other substances in its composition. It is used in smelting iron. (See Mineralogy for December.)

9. All the coals, and peat included, originate in the same way, but each different kind represents a different stage in formation. It is the result of immense beds of vegetable material becoming deeply covered in succeeding ages by the rock and earth now found above the coal seams. Peat is coal in its earliest stage of formation, and anthracite is coal in its latest and completed stage. It has been changed from the bituminous variety, to that of its present character, by means of heat and pressure.

10. Examine a piece of the "lead" of a pencil ; this substance is called graphite and is pure carbon. It is also known as plumbago.

11. If possible, get a piece of native graphite ; note its luster and peculiar feel.

12. What other use has this mineral besides that in the manufacture of lead-pencils?

REFERENCE. Read Applied Geology, by S. G. Williams.

Zoology.

GENERAL OBSERVATIONS.

1. Can any of the summer birds be found? If so, where do they stay?

2. Have you found any newcomers? Have they come from the north or south? What is their food? Do they sing? Are they building nests?

3. Is there any insect life abroad? Watch sharply on warm days and in sheltered places.

4. Hunt for earthworms. How deep do they burrow in winter?

5. In what condition do the fish spend the winter? The craw-fish? Frogs?

6. Look for these under leaves and in mud along the sides and in the bottom of ponds.

7. Do tadpoles live over winter?

ANIMAL MOVEMENTS.

The following studies should be based upon what the pupils have been able to observe about their own movements, as well as those of the common domesticated animals. Ample opportunity should be given beforehand for the observations to be made, and the discussion should not be carried beyond the limits set by those observations. By this, it is not intended to circumscribe too closely any legitimate reasoning that the pupils may attempt, but merely to guard against the really vicious habit that some pupils have, in the beginning, of setting up some theory independent of any actual observation, and trying to defend it by vague speculations. That rapid progress may be made, pupils should be encouraged to be candid and to be ready to give up promptly any theory or supposition as soon as it can be shown to be inconsistent with the facts of observation.

1. Why is it necessary for most animals to move from place to place? Such animals are said to have the power of locomotion.

2. Do you know of any animals that cannot move about? How do they get their food? How are they protected from their enemies?

If possible, secure specimens of coral, sponges, and oysters in the shell. The points of attachment may easily be discovered and something of their modes of life may be learned.

3. How does the power of flight affect the life and habits of birds? Consider the advantages in food-getting, and in means of escape and attack, that are due to flight.

4. How has it affected their distribution? What barriers are difficult for birds to overcome?

5. Make a study of the way different animals walk; first examine those that walk on four legs, as the cat, dog, horse, cow, rabbit, squirrel, and any others that can be seen.

6. Contrast the cat and dog; what is the order in which they place their feet in taking a step?

7. Note the motions of the trunk of each as they step; what difference do you notice?

8. What gives the cat its stealthy tread? Its velvety

paws contribute partly to it, but they are not the only cause. Notice as the cat steps how the body sinks slightly at the joints where the fore-limbs are hinged to the body at the elbow, and that the same is noticeable in the hind limbs at the heel joint, though somewhat less in amount. These movements, due to the great flexibility of the joints in the foot, and to the fact that when the fore-paw is put to the ground the leg is not vertically under the body but obliquely forward, give a spring to the step that is wanting in all other classes of quadrupeds.

9. Compare the movements of the cat with those of the dog ; what reason can you think of for the difference in their gait ?

10. What habit or need of these animals has done most to fix their gait ?

11. Compare the movement of the horse and the cow ; in what order do they place their feet in walking ?

12. In what order are the horse's feet placed in trotting ? What is the order in pacing or the rack ? In galloping ?

13. Does a cow trot ? How does the movement of the hind legs differ from that of the horse ?

14. Can you see wherein lies the greater capacity of the horse for speed ?

15. How does the locomotion of the rabbit differ from that of the cat and dog ? What is the order in which the rabbit moves his legs ?

16. How do the rabbit and the cat differ in making a spring ?

17. What is there in the life of the rabbit that makes him draw his hind legs under him in a crouching attitude ?

18. In which are the hind quarters, compared with the

fore quarters, the more developed, the rabbit or the cat ? Compare both of them with the dog.

19. How do the movements of the squirrel's legs differ from those of the rabbit's ?

20. Which of the animals studied does the squirrel resemble most in locomotion ?

21. Compare the development of its different parts with that of the rabbit, dog, and cat ; which does it most closely resemble ?

22. In what kinds of places do these animals live in their wild state ? How are their movements fitted for such places ?   .

23. In animals that walk on two legs, to what uses are the other pair of limbs devoted ?

24. How does the movement upon two limbs affect the position of the body ? Why is the position of the bird less upright than that of man ?

25. What are the advantages of the upright position for man ?

26. Is there any advantage in turning the toes out in walking ? What joint permits of this turning of the toes outward ?

27. Which is the easier mode of walking, with the feet parallel, or diverging outward at the toes ? Which is the natural and which the acquired way ? Observe children learning to walk.

28. What difference in the bearing or carriage of persons is caused by the direction given the foot in walking ? Take a few steps very slowly, and study the position of the body at each step.

29. In walking with the feet parallel, compare the transverse space between the tracks with the space when the toes diverge.

30. Which mode of walking contributes more to erect-ness of attitude ? Why ? Test by walking slowly. It will be noticed that in walking with the feet parallel, there is a slight rolling motion at the hips, and that the body sways somewhat from side to side. The swaying is increased since the feet are usually placed a little wider apart transversely, in order to broaden the base. The body is bent slightly forward when taking steps thus.

When the toes are turned outward, the distance trans-versely between the feet is less, and the swaying motion at the hips is partially lost.

The body is more easily held erect in walking with the diverging steps.

The Indian in his long journeys seemed to prefer carrying his feet parallel, while the white man turns his toes outward, as a rule. If one practices until he can walk well either way, an alternation of the two methods will be found to be restful when taking long walks.

31. By what means is the body protected from jars in walking ? Which of the above-described modes of walk-ing gives the more elastic step ?

32. With the shoe removed, notice how the foot spreads gradually as the weight of the body is thrown forward upon it ; what part of the foot should touch the ground first in order to reduce the jar most ?

33. Why do tight shoes make the step inelastic ?

34. Why do high-heeled shoes render it difficult to walk with the natural step ?

35. What is the chief use of the arms in man ? To what is their difference in function, from that of the fore limbs in most animals, due ?

36. Compare their movements with the wings of a bird ? the fore legs of the horse, dog, cat, and squirrel.

37. What general modification in form and attitude of the trunk accompanies the increasing freedom of movement in the fore limbs ?

38. In what movements is the hand superior to the corresponding part in other animals ?   Note the position of the thumb and fingers.

39. What change in the position and attachment of the arms is associated with their great mobility ?

40. What substitutes for legs do such animals as worms and snakes have ?

41. Study the movements of a fish in the aquarium ; what is the chief organ of locomotion ?

42. What seems to have determined the shape of the body ?

43. How does it turn itself ?   How does it rise and sink ?

44. Does it require any effort on the part of the fish to remain in the usual position ?   Observe the position in which a dead fish floats.

45. By what means is it kept in an upright position ?

46. Since the flight of a bird through the air and the swimming of a fish in the water are somewhat analogous, why is it that the modes of propulsion in the two cases are so very different ?

NOTE. Additional topics will be given under this head in the spring.

THE SKELETON.

It is desirable in this study to have some prepared skeletons ready for class use.   A human skeleton should be procured if possible, both on account of its size and of the practical interest it possesses for pupils.   Skeletons may be prepared quite easily from any small animal.

After killing the animal, such as a frog, mouse, or bird, with chloroform or ether, cut all the meat away that comes off without danger of breaking a bone or separating a joint, and remove the contents of the body cavities. Then make a caustic potash solution, one ounce to a pint of water, and soak the carcass in this, at short intervals, removing the flesh as fast as it softens. To remove the brain separate the skull from the spinal column, and use a crooked wire. With care in preparing the solution so that it will not be too strong, the flesh may be cleaned off before the ligaments soften enough to allow the bones to separate at the joints, and one may in this way secure an articulated skeleton. If the bones become separated, however, they may be mounted diagrammatically by sewing them to stiff cardboard.

1. Name several animals that you are sure have bony skeletons.

2. Name some that do not have skeletons.

3. Name some that have the skeletons on the outside of the body.

4. Of what use is our skeleton to us?

5. Of what use are the bones of our limbs? Of what additional use are the bones of the skull?

6. What uses can you discover for the ribs? Notice carefully the act of breathing.

7. Note in the prepared skeletons the two parts : the trunk, including head and neck, and the limbs, upper and lower.

8. Can you find such divisions in the skeleton of a frog? In the bird? The mouse? The squirrel?

9. Which, on the whole, most closely resembles our own?

10. In what respects are they all alike?

11. Which is most unlike our own? Which animal most closely resembles us in action?

12. Examine the skull of each. Wherein do they differ most?

13. Which contains relatively the largest cavity?

14. Which animal shows the greatest amount of intelligence?

15. Which the least?

16. Note the bones composing the skull. Look for the notched lines where they are joined. These are called sutures.

17. Do the bones move one upon the other?

18. Do they form a complete box? Are any of the skulls incomplete in this respect?

The large opening at the base of the human skull, the *foramen magnum*, is the passage for the spinal cord; the smaller openings, front and back, are for the passage of nerves and blood-vessels.

19. How can you account for the difference in the shape of the heads of these animals?

20. What gives this difference of aspect chiefly, the bones of the face, or those of the skull?

21. In what respects are the trunks all alike? Which are most alike? Between which are the greatest differences?

22. Which of the animals are most alike in their resting attitude?

23. Which are most alike when in action?

24. Can you tell whether it is the movements that determine the general form of an animal, or the shape that determines the general movements?

25. Can you see how the movements of the animals have determined any of the features noticed in the trunk?

26. Which has done more to give shape to the trunk as a whole, the position of the body while in motion or while at rest ? Are all the animals alike in this respect ?

27. In which animal is the trunk the most flexible ?

28. How is the trunk rendered flexible ? In what part is it most rigid ? Why ?

29. What are the advantages we derive from the flexibility of the trunk ? Between the vertebræ are elastic pads of cartilage. Each pad is fastened to the vertebra above and the one immediately below it. The elasticity of the pads and their attachments permit of flexibility without the gliding of one bone over another, as in most joints, which in this case would endanger the delicate spinal cord within. These pads, with the curves of the spinal column, are usually thought to be largely instrumental in protecting the brain from jars and shocks incident to walking, jumping, and similar movements. That this is not so to any great extent is evident to every one who has unexpectedly stepped into a hole a few inches deep. When knowingly taking such a step, the leg is so held as to remove the jar by bending slightly at the joints ; otherwise the position does not admit of this bending, and the shock is conveyed to the base of the spinal column and thence to the brain, and, even in a trivial misstep, it is one that is very generally dreaded.

30. In which animal are the fore and hind limbs most alike ? In which most different ?

31. Which animal uses its fore limbs most nearly as we do ?

32. In which animal is there the greatest difference between the fore and hind limbs ? In which is there the greatest similarity ?

33. In which animal is there the greatest difference in

the use of the fore and hind limbs? Note the relative length of the fore and hind limbs.

34. Count the bones in the fore limb or arm of a man, and compare with the other skeletons.

35. In which skeleton do the bones admit of the most varied movement? Which the least?

36. What is the chief use of the fore limb that has the greatest range of movement?

37. Note the relative length of the bones in the upper and lower arm in each animal.

38. In which animal are they relatively strongest? Note the relative length in each case.

39. Can you find bones in the fore limbs of the other animals to correspond with all those in the arm of man?

40. Which is most like man's arm in use?

41. How are the upper limbs fastened to the trunk in each case? Are they all alike in this respect?

42. What cause can you see for the difference, in this particular, between the mouse and bird? Between man and the mouse?

43. In which animal are the hind limbs relatively strongest? How do they compare with the fore limbs as to the number of the bones?

44. Note their attachment to the trunk; how do they differ in this from the fore limbs?

45. How have the bodily movements affected the hind limbs in each case?

46. How do the movements of the bones in the hind limbs differ from those of the corresponding bones in the fore limbs? Note the relative length of the bones of the hind limb, and compare with the fore limb.

47. How has the attitude of the body modified the hind limbs in each case?

48. How are they adapted to the movements of the animal?

49. In which skeleton is the foot most unlike the hand? In which is the greatest resemblance?

50. In which are the movements and uses of the foot and hand most nearly alike? In which most unlike?

51. Locate in four-footed creatures like the horse, dog, cat, etc., these joints found in man; toe joints, heel joints, knee joint, hip joint, wrist joint, finger joints, elbow joint, and shoulder joint.

Botany.

A few observations should be kept up this month on the effects of frost and freezing on plants.

1. Sometime during a hard freeze examine the smaller twigs. Are they frozen through? How protected?

2. Open the buds; are they frozen? What are the ways by which the buds are protected?

3. Are they wet through when it rains?

4. Can you still distinguish the newly formed wood?

5. Is any part of the twig still green?

6. Look for seeds of weeds and other plants that have been scattered about; do they freeze? Can you find any that are sprouting?

7. Can you tell whether or not it kills them?

8. Are those that are buried in a few inches of earth frozen?

9. Look for acorns and other nuts; how does the freezing affect them?

10. Can you find any plants whose stems have been killed, but whose roots are still living?

11. Do the roots of the trees freeze?

12. Can you find any injurious effects of frost and freezing on the trunks of trees?

13. Can you find any growing plants?

Physics.

THE LEVER.

It is the intention that the lessons given upon the lever should supplement those given in Zoölogy this month on the movements of animals. The pupils must provide themselves with small sticks about a foot long, and a block of wood, stone, or iron an inch or two in diameter.

1. Suppose the block were a weight that could not be conveniently lifted by hand, illustrate with the stick the different ways in which a bar might be used in lifting it.

2. The pupil should work with this problem until he finds the three ways of using the stick as a lever. He should see that in each case there is a fixed point about which the lever moves which is called the fulcrum. Also that in each there is a point where the power is applied and another point where the weight is placed. He should note that the form of the lever depends upon the relative position of these three points, which are usually represented by the letters F, W, P. The distance from F to P is the power arm, and from F to W the weight arm of the lever. The three kinds are distinguished as first-class, when F is between P and W; second-class, when W is between F and P, and third-class, when P is between F and W. It will be noticed that one need remember only the point which lies between the ends in

order to tell the class of lever, and in the order of first, second, and third, the letters stand *F W P*, initials which no pupil of Cook County Normal School will find it difficult to remember.

3. How must the lever of the first class be used to lift the greatest weight? What do you notice about the relative length of the two arms *P F* and *W F*?

4. Use it again so that it will be of the least use in lifting a weight; is there *any* advantage in such use? Note again the relative length of the two arms.

5. In the same way, use the second and third class forms of the lever. Note each time the relative length of the two arms, and also as to whether the advantage gained in each case is one of *power* in lifting the weight or of *distance* through which it is moved.

6. Can the lever be so used that there will be no gain of either power or distance?

7. Is it possible to gain power with each form of lever?

8. What do you notice about the relative distance through which the power and weight move in the second class lever? Notice the same in the third class.

9. What determines the distance through which the power or weight shall move?

10. What forms of the lever have you seen workmen use? When do they use the first class? When the second class? When the third class?

11. Study some of the parts of the animal body as levers. What are their uses?

12. In studying the levers of the body, the pupil should first be required to fix the limits or ends of the lever, then the fixed point or fulcrum, then the weight and power. If this order be followed carefully, one step

at a time, it is not difficult to fix the levers of the body and to tell the different orders.

13. In the manner suggested, locate and describe the levers concerned in the following movements : (1) Flexing the forearm ; (2) extending forearm ; (3) lifting the entire arm outward and upward from the body ; (4) opening the mouth ; (5) closing the mouth ; (6) neck rigid, tipping head backward and forward ; (7) throwing the head from one shoulder to the other ; (8) straightening up when the body is bent at the hips ; (9) lifting the body to tip-toe position ; (10) standing on the heels and lifting the toes ; (11) hold the foot clear of the floor and tap it with the toes ; (12) in same position lift the toes ; (13) flexing the lower part of the leg ; (14) in swinging the leg at the hip joint ; (15) in the rib movement in breathing.

14. What class is most commonly found in the animal movements ?

15. What advantages are derived in most cases from the form employed ?

16. What disadvantages in the lever of the forearm ?

17. In what position can you get the most strength or lifting power in the forearm ? Test this by straightening the arm out on a table and then slowly flexing it against the upper arm.

18. Can you find similar levers used in the movements of other animals ?

19. Why is it so difficult to hold an animal by its hind legs ? Note the leverage and the class of lever in the four-footed animals in the leg below the heel.

20. What kind of a lever is there in the wing of a bird ?

21. How do animals move that are not provided with bones for levers ?

22. The pupil should be asked to trace out the levers that may be found in the wheel work of different machines.

EQUILIBRIUM OF BODIES.

In this subject many interesting experiments may be devised and many illustrations may be drawn from the experience of the pupil which will acquaint him somewhat with the force of gravitation and its action upon bodies of different size, shape, and mass.

1. When a ruler or any body is held at rest in the hand is there any evidence that there is a force acting upon it? How is that force measured? What is the measurement of it called?

2. When the hand is removed, what happens to the object? What kind of a line does it follow in its movement? What is this particular line called?

3. Can you balance every body upon a point of support that is smaller than the base of the object? Can you balance any of the bodies in more than one position? Try such bodies as blocks of wood, balls, sticks, etc.

4. The point in a body upon which the body will balance in any position is called the center of gravity. Where is such a point in a ball of wood or iron? Where is it in a cube of wood?

5. In order to find the center of gravity in any body, suspend it from some point and note the direction of the vertical line from the point of suspension through or across the body ; now suspend it from another point and note when the vertical line from the second point of suspension intersects the first. The point of intersection is the center of gravity. Does the center of gravity lie within the body or on its surface?

6. Is it always within the body ?   Where is it in a ring or hoop ?   In a hollow sphere ?

7. The vertical line from the center of gravity is called the *line of direction.*   In considering the stability of bodies it is of the highest importance to keep the *center of gravity* and the *line of direction constantly before the mind.*

8. When a cube rests on a table on one side, can you see where the line of direction must be?

9. When you roll the cube from one side so that it will rest upon another, what kind of a line does the center of gravity describe ?

10. Compare the rolling of a ball with the turning of the cube ; which is easier?   How does the line described by the center of gravity in the ball differ from that described by the cube ?

11 Place a cone on its apex and try to balance it ; as it falls over, what kind of a line is described by the center of gravity ?

12. A body is said to have stable equilibrium when any movement which disturbs its equilibrium *raises the center of gravity ;* when any such movement lowers the center of gravity it is in unstable equilibrium.   When the center of gravity moves in a line parallel with the floor or other support the body is in indifferent or neutral equilibrium.   Test various bodies that you have handled, such as the cube, cone, pyramid, ball, prism, etc.   These may be modeled in clay.

13. Can you place a cone in stable equilibrium ?   In unstable equilibrium?   In indifferent equilibrium ?

14. In tipping any body over notice the path of the line of direction at the point where the body refuses to come back to its original position.   Under what condi-

tions will the body always resume its first position when
, its equilibrium is disturbed ?

15. Under what conditions do you find a body most
stable ?   Least stable ?

16. Where is the center of gravity of your own body ?

17. Why is it more difficult to push one over forward
than backward ?   Why may one be easily pushed over
sidewise ?

18. Why is a wagon with a high load of hay more
easily upset than one with the same weight, but less
bulk ?

19. Can you understand why tight rope walkers
always carry a heavy balancing pole?   Why does a
porter with a pack on his back lean forward, while if
the same weight were in a pail and carried in his hand
he would walk upright ?

20. Why is it difficult to walk on stilts at first ?   Why
is it impossible to stand steadily upon them ?

21. Why does a ball roll down hill?   Why does a bi-
cycle rider fall over sidewise when he stops ?   A somewhat more difficult thing to explain is why he and his
wheel can remain upright while in motion ; can you see
the reason ?

22. Thrust a pin half-way to the head in a medium
sized cork.   Stick two penknives into the cork one opposite the other and so that the handles will slant downward below the end of the pin.   Why will the cork
remain upright balanced upon the pinhead ?

HEAT.

A study of the following topics in this subject should
be applied in the explanation of whatever natural phenomena the pupils may have observed, which rests upon

the principles here illustrated as a cause. Among the points which may be mentioned, are the cooling of surfaces upon which dew is formed, the origin and direction of air currents, modes of ventilation, effects of different kinds and colors of clothing upon the heat of the body, and so on. Careful consideration of the differences in bodies as to their capacity for heat will assist to a clearer comprehension of the relation of land and water masses to climate.

Liquefaction.

1. Take two wide-mouthed bottles as nearly alike as possible and fill one with ice and the other with the same weight of water ; place both in a pan of boiling water over a lamp or gas jet.

2. Note the temperature of each at intervals until the ice is all melted.

3. Have the two vessels received the same amount of heat ? Note the conditions carefully under which each is placed.

4. What difference in temperature when the ice is melted ?

5. Had the temperature of the bottle with the ice in it risen at all at the moment it was melted ? What change did the heat bring about in the bottle ?

6. After the ice has melted, does the thermometer indicate any change ?

7. Remove to a sand bath and raise the temperature of the water until it boils. A thin glass beaker or vessel of tin should be used for the purpose.

8. What is the temperature at which it boils ? Hold the thermometer in the steam over the liquid.

9. Increase the heat by means of more burners ; does the temperature rise ?

10. What has been accomplished by the heat in these experiments with the water and ice?

11. When heat is applied to a body or fluid does it always show itself as temperature? When not shown as temperature how is it expressed?

Conduction of Heat.

1. In heating the metallic rods (1) at one point, what did you notice as to the effect upon the entire rod?

2. Did the parts farthest from the flame become heated by radiation?

3. What parts became heated first? What parts last?

4. How does the heat get from one end of the rod to the other?

5. Procure pieces of different kinds of wire or rods, such as copper, iron, and brass, one foot long. Twist them together in pairs for two inches at one end and from the point where they are twisted spread them apart in something of a U shape. At some distance from the twist, and at equal distances from each other, fasten by means of shoemaker's wax small bullets or shot to each wire. Support horizontally so that the twisted ends may rest in the flame of the lamp. Protect the balls from the *radiant* heat from the lamp with a screen.

6. From which wire do the balls drop first? What does that indicate?

7. Which is the last in losing the balls?

8. Bodies which become heated from particle to particle as in the case of the wires are called *conductors.*

9. What difference between heating by radiation and conduction?

10. Which is the better conductor, iron or copper? Brass or copper? Iron or brass?

11. Why does a piece of iron become heated when held in the hand ? Why does it at first feel cold ?

12. Why does wood feel less cold than iron to the touch ? Why are iron handles sometimes tipped with wood ?

13. Is the iron really colder than the wood ?

14. Why does our bed feel cold at first ? How does it become warmed ?

15. Why does a blanket seem warmer than a sheet ?

16. Why is linen clothing worn in summer and woolens in winter ?

17. Why is it regarded safer for one's health to wear light woolens next the body, even in summer ?

Convection.

1. Fill a good-sized test-tube, or, better still, a glass beaker, nearly full of water. Sprinkle into it a little powdered chalk and heat gradually.

2. Look closely for any currents that may be started as indicated by the particles of chalk.

3. Make a drawing of the beaker, and mark with arrows the direction of the currents.

4. Where does the water become heated first ? How do the other portions become heated ?

5. Using light pieces of paper, look for currents of air in the room. Try the space over the stove or register ; also the cracks above the doors and at the bottom. Open the window at top and bottom half an inch. Use a lighted candle or taper in looking for a draught.

6. What is the cause of the air movements in the room ?

7. Can you account for their direction ? Using a

thermometer, find out where the lowest temperature is in the room, and whether it is at the top or bottom.

8. Recall the experiment illustrating expansion of air, which was performed in November.

9. How are those parts of the room distant from the stove or register heated?

10. Compare the heating of the air in the room with the heating of the water in the beaker.

11. The manner in which the water in the beaker and the air in the room are heated is known as *convection*.

12. How does convection differ from conduction?

13. Fill a test-tube nearly full of water, and *very cautiously* heat it near the top in the flame of the lamp ; test at intervals with a thermometer the top and bottom portions. A small piece of ice held at the bottom of the water by a fragment of lead or a pebble will make the contrast stronger. Great care must be exercised in heating the test-tube in the last experiment, or it will crack ; why is this?

14. Does the water become heated throughout more or less quickly than before?

15. What makes the difference? By what process is it heated in the latter case?

16. Why is it not heated by convection?

17. Study the mechanism of the kitchen range, and explain how the water in the boiler is heated.

18. When the fire is starting, which part of the boiler gets warm first? Place the hands at different points on the outside.

19. How does the water in the lake become heated? Explain why it is always cold a little distance below the surface. How does the ocean become heated, by conduction or convection?

20. How does the sun warm the earth ?

21. Is the air warmed directly by the sun ?

22. Can you see any reason why it is colder on a mountain peak than it is on a low plain ?

23. Hold a piece of plain glass between the hand and the sun ; can you notice any change in the amount of heat that reaches the hand ?

24. Instead of the plain glass, use a common magnifying glass or lens ; hold it so that the sunlight passing through it is reduced to a small point. Allow this to fall upon the hand or upon paper. How can you account for the great heat at that point ? Is it hot outside the area of this spot ? Try to make a drawing showing by lines the way the heat must come to the lens and the way it must leave it on the opposite side. Heat bent out of a straight course by some substance which it passes through is said to be *refracted.* Compare reflection with refraction.

Capacity for Heat.

1. In two vessels of the same kind, place equal amounts of water ; raise the water in one of the vessels to the boiling point and take the temperature. Find the temperature of the water in the other vessel, and then add it to the boiling water.

2. What is the temperature of the mixture ? How much was the cool water warmed ? How much was the warm water cooled ? Is the number of degrees the same in both cases ? Is the result what you would expect from the experiment ?

3. Take a piece of lead weighing three or four ounces. If not already in a sheet, pound it out thin and roll loosely. Suspend in a vessel of boiling water, and allow it to remain until it has the same temperature as the

water. Into another vessel put a weight of water equal to that of the lead, and take its temperature. As quickly as possible drop the lead into this vessel of water and take the temperature. How much does the temperature of the water rise ? How much does that of the lead fall ? What are the sources of error in these experiments? In what way will the errors change the results ?

4. In the same way use different substances, as zinc, sheet iron, tin, brass, and copper.

5. Notice how much the water gains in each case and how much the metal loses.

6. How much heat must have been in the metal when taken from the boiling water ? What became of this when it was dropped into the cooler water ?

7. Does the thermometer always tell us when heat is added to a substance ? Recall the experiment of the melting ice in the November work.

Sources of Heat.

1. How do we warm our houses ? What are necessary in order that we may have a fire ?

2. When the wood or coal burns what kind of a change takes place ? (See Chemistry for November.)

3. Have you ever known heat to be produced without the use of fire ?

4. Try rubbing a nail with a file. Rub two sticks together. Rub the edge of a penny over the sleeve. What results in each case ?

5. Pound a nail on a stone or iron block with a hammer ; what is the result ?

6. What is the real difference between the two ways of getting heat, that of burning the wood, and that of making it warm by rubbing it ?

Chemistry.

PREPARATION OF OXYGEN.

Materials Needed.

1. Test tubes, one for each pupil if possible, about six inches long and three-quarters of an inch in diameter.

2. A six-ounce Florence flask.

3. Corks to fit the above.

4. Glass tubing having a bore of about three-sixteenths of an inch. A piece about eight inches long for each pupil. Bend the tubes at a right angle two inches from one end, and put the short end through a hole in the cork.

5. Glass bottles with wide mouths, at least one for each pupil, and a few empty glass fruit jars. Morphia bottles are very useful.

6. A pneumatic trough. Any vessel holding five or six inches of water will answer. A small bench with a hole in the center must be used for supporting inverted vessels in the water with their mouths below the surface. To make this take a strip of tin about eight inches long, four inches wide, and bend up two inches at each end. This will be strong enough to support small jars and bottles.

7. Alcohol lamps or bunsen burners.

8. About an ounce of potassium chlorate and an equal amount of black oxide of manganese for each pupil. Test these materials by powdering a little of the potassium chlorate and mixing with the same amount of the

black oxide and heating in an open tube ; if the mixture melts quietly they are safe ; if slight explosions occur, throw the materials away, as they are not pure and are dangerous.

Experiments.

1. Mix the powdered crystals of the chlorate with an equal amount of the black oxide ; put about one inch depth of this into a test tube and fix with a cork having a tube through it as described above. Fill one or more small bottles with water and invert in the pneumatic trough, which should have four or five inches of water in it. Place one of these upon the bench with the mouth over the hole. Support the test tube over the flame so that the end of the glass tube will be under the surface of the water in trough, but *not under the bottle on the bench*. After the bubbles have escaped for a few moments, arrange the end of the tube under the hole in the bench so that they will rise into the bottle:

2. Why not put the end of the tube under the bottles at once ?

3. Why fill the bottle first with water ?

4. Can you see anything passing out through the tube ?

5. What change do you notice in the materials in the test tube ?

6. What is the nature of the substance rising into the bottle of water ?

7. When the water has left the bottle, remove it from the hole, but keep the mouth below the surface. If gas still comes off, collect it in another bottle.

8. Slip a piece of glass as a cover under the bottle filled with gas, and holding it tightly in place, remove the bottle and turn it quickly right side up.

9. Provide a number of fine splinters. Light one of them, and, when fairly blazing, blow it out and quickly thrust the glowing end into a jar or bottle that contains air; note carefully all that happens.

10. Light again, and in the same manner thrust it into the jar filled with gas from the test tube ; what difference do you notice?

11. What evidence that there is something in the jar different from air?

12. With a fresh supply of gas, repeat the experiment suggested above in (9), using a short piece of a candle. Fasten a light piece of wire around the candle by which it may be lowered into the jar.

13. After the pupils have made oxygen for themselves, it may be desirable to have a larger quantity and have it collected in the fruit jars. To do this take about an ounce of the potassium chlorate and mix with the manganese as before, and use the Florence flask. Heat gradually, and when enough has been collected remove the end of the tube from the water before removing the flame. If this precaution is not observed, the water will run back into the flask and break it.

14. Put a small amount of sulphur into a thimble and ignite it; by means of a wire wrapped around it for a handle, lower it into a jar of the gas.

15. Ignite a piece of well-charred charcoal and lower into a fresh jar of gas.

16. Fasten a small splinter to an iron wire, and after lighting lower it into a jar of the gas.

17. Get a worn-out watch spring from a jeweler and draw the temper by heating, and then straighten it; fasten to a stick as in (16) and, after igniting, lower it into a jar of the gas.

18. In the same way try a narrow ribbon of zinc.

19. In the foregoing experiments, does the gas in the jars burn?

20. In what respects is it like air?

21. What happens after burning a substance, as wood, in the jar for some time? Compare this result with what was observed when burning a taper in a bottle of air.

22. The gas collected in the jars used in these experiments is called *Oxygen.* It is the element in the air which enables us to have fires in our stoves and grates.

23. It is also the life-giving element of the air for animals. How does it enter our bodies?

24. Why should chimneys have a good draught to make good fires?

25. Why do we fan or blow a fire to start it?

26. Why do we need ventilation in a room?

27. In what respects does oxygen differ from the carbon dioxide gas? (See Chemistry for November.)

28. Write a list of the experiments performed and state the results obtained.

Meteorology.

1. Has the prevailing wind changed direction within the last three months? What may be given as causes?

2. Has the cloudiness increased or diminished?

3. How does the character of the rains differ from those in September? What causes the difference?

4. From what direction do the heaviest rains come?

5. In what month has the greatest number of fogs been noted?

6. What conditions are most favorable for the production of fogs?

7. Is the wind more or less variable than it has been in the preceding months?

8. What wind precedes the heaviest rains?

9. What wind accompanies clearing weather?

10. Is the temperature increasing or diminishing this month? What cause can be given? (See Astronomy for December.)

11. Is the rate of change in temperature more or less rapid than it was in the preceding three months?

12. When have most of the rains occurred, in the daytime or during the night?

13. Of those rains which occurred in the daytime, did the greater number fall in the forenoon or afternoon?

14. Have the frosty mornings been followed by fair or foul weather?

15. On what date did the first snow fall?

16. From what direction do the snows come?

17. Do all the rains come from the same direction?

18. Examine some single snowflakes closely ; are they all alike?

19. Are they all of regular form? Why are some flakes larger than others?

20. How do snow clouds differ in appearance from rain clouds?

21. How does the history of a snowflake resemble that of a raindrop? In what respect is it different?

22. Does the barometer in any way herald the approach of a snowstorm?

23. At what temperature did the heaviest snow fall? Did the temperature rise or fall after the snowing ceased?

STUDY OF THE WEATHER BUREAU MAPS.

24. Draw a line across the map connecting the points farthest south where snow has fallen during the last month. This may be called the snow line for the month.

25. Where does the snow line extend farthest south?

26. Where is its most northern point?

27. How many degrees of latitude are they apart? How many miles are they apart north and south?

28. How do the coast lines affect the snow line?

29. On which coast is it farthest north? Why is it so?

30. Which mountains have the most marked effect upon it, the Rocky Mountains or Appalachian system?

31. How does the course of the storms for this month compare with that for the preceding months?

32. Have the courses of the great rivers affected, apparently, the direction of the storms?

33. Have the mountains determined the course of the storms?

34. Have there been any great storms with rain in one part of its area and snow in another part?

35. Contrast the Pacific slope with the Atlantic as to rainfall and temperature this month.

Astronomy.

1. Compare the relative length of day and night in December with that of preceding months.

2. What has been the average rate of change in the length of day during the month? Compare with the former months.

3. Note the position of the noon shadow about the 21st of the month. Has it changed its position more or less rapidly this month than it did in September?

4. Stretch a string from the top of the upright piece at the end to the point touched by the noon shadow in September when the day and night were equal, and another string to the point touched by the shadow in December when the day is shortest. Note the size of the angle between the two lines. If possible, measure it. If these two lines were continued into space, what two points in the celestial sphere would be found?

5. Note as directed in September the points on the horizon where the sun rises and sets. Why is it that when the shortest day is reached in this month the shadow does not at once begin a retrograde movement on the shadow stick. The time of the shortest day of the year is called the winter solstice. This means the sun stands still. Can you see a reason for the use of the word solstice?

6. How have these positions changed since September?

7. What suppositions can you make regarding the earth and sun which will account for the changes?

8. Suppose you were to draw lines across the sky marking the apparent path of the sun every day since September, what would be the relation of these lines to each other ?

9. How much of the quarter circle on the horizon has the sun traversed since the day and night were equal?

10. Compare the number of degrees estimated in (9) with the size of the angle measured in (4).

11. Can you show, by means of the globe, on the supposition of revolution, what part of the earth's orbit has been traversed since the autumnal equinox ?

12. How many days have elapsed since then ?

13. Does the fraction of a year which has passed since the equinox correspond to the part of the orbit over which the earth has passed since then ?

14. What supposition can you make that will explain the lack of correspondence ?

15. Explain, by means of a globe, if necessary, why the sun has seemed to change its position since September.

16. Write a brief description of the condition of animal and plant life. Compare with September. To what cause or causes are the differences due ?

17. Do you always see the same side of the moon ? By means of a globe, sun, and moon, explain.

18. Can you see any reason for believing that the moon revolves round the earth ?

19. If the moon revolves round the earth as the earth moves through its orbit round the sun, can you tell what kind of a line the moon must describe ?

20. Have any of the constellations which were seen last month disappeared ?

In addition to those of last month that are still visible are Auriga, Orion, and Gemini.

Geography.

NORTH AMERICA.
Soil and Productions.

1. What things can you name that affect the fertility and productiveness of soils ?

2. Make use of a good physical relief map and study the conditions which affect the productiveness of the different regions. From what you know of plant life, what are the primary conditions necessary for it.

3. Contrast the growth and general appearance of a plant during a wet season with its condition during a dry one ?

4. What is the effect of heat and moisture upon the plants that you have noticed ?

5. Use a map which shows the character of the vegetation in different regions ; what climate have those parts where vegetation is most luxuriant ?

6. What contrasts in the products of the Atlantic and the Pacific coast regions ?

7. Compare the northern half with the southern on each coast ; on which coast is the contrast greater ?

8. In the great central plain, contrast the eastern and the western halves ; in which half within the United States are the productions more uniform ?

9. In which half do the agricultural productions extend farther north ?

10. Where are the great wheat-growing regions? How can you account for the wheat-growing region of Texas, since a similar one is not to be found in Mississippi?

11. Where is the rice production greatest? Contrast the conditions that it requires with those necessary for wheat.

12. Note the cotton-growing region; does the belt reach the Rocky Mountains? Can you see a reason for this?

13. Contrast the corn-producing regions with those mostly devoted to wheat.

14. What is the relation of the tobacco and hemp regions to those of cotton and corn?

15. What grains flourish in a cooler climate than that best adapted for wheat?

16. Make a study of the different fruit regions; what part of the continent includes the greater part of the fruit-growing regions?

17. Compare and contrast the Atlantic and the Pacific coasts. What are the staples of each?

18. Where is the southern boundary of the apple region? Where is the chief apple-growing district?

19. What effect, if any, do the Great Lakes have upon the surrounding country in the production of fruit?

20. What climate seems best suited to peach raising?

21. What is best adapted for oranges?

22. What fruits are produced south of the United States? What ones are produced north of the United States?

23. Where do the fruits grow farthest north, along the coasts or in the interior?

Minerals.

24. From what parts of the continent are the minerals chiefly obtained ?

25. Contrast the eastern and western highlands as to the variety and kinds of minerals produced.

26. Locate the iron mines that are now being worked most extensively.   Where are the copper mines ?

27. Where are the bituminous coal regions?   The anthracite coal fields ?

28. Where are the gold and silver mines ?   The mines of quicksilver?   Of lead ?

29. Where are the petroleum deposits ?

30. What cities are the chief agricultural depots in the north ?   In the south ?

31. What are the chief mining cities?   What is the chief coke manufacturing city in the country ?

SOUTH AMERICA. CLIMATE.

1. Use a good physical map, upon which the ocean currents and winds are clearly marked.   Model the map to get an idea of the climatic effect of the highlands, river basins, and coast lines.

2. How does the latitude of South America affect its climate ?   Contrast it in this respect with North America.

3. Contrast the area of South America that lies within the tropics with that of North America in the corresponding latitude ; what climatic differences must be due to these contrasts ?

4. In the same way compare the temperate regions of the two continents.

5. What climatic difference must be due to the difference in the character of the coast lines of the two continents ?

6. What modification of the climate in the tropical regions must be due to the difference in relief?

7. How does the position of the great Andean highland affect the climate within the tropics?

8. What is the direction of the prevailing wind within the tropics? What must be its character as to moisture?

9. What agencies for condensing the moisture in the northern half of the continent?

10. Contrast the western slope of the Andes within the tropics with the eastern; to what are the differences due?

11. What do the rivers indicate as to the amount of moisture east of the Andes?

12. What ocean current sweeps the eastern shores in the temperate regions? Does it set toward or away from the coast? What is the direction of the wind?

13. What ocean current skirts the western coast? What wind west of the mountains?

14. Contrast the southern half of the Pacific coast with the northern; what causes the differences?

15. Contrast and account for the differences noted between the eastern and the western coasts of the southern half of the continent.

16. Latitude 50° north or south is noted as embracing regions where fogs are prevalent; can you account for this?

Geology.

During the winter season, opportunity should be taken to study atmospheric and aqueous agencies that are constantly but slowly changing the face of the earth by means of frost and ice. The action of these may be seen and studied on a large scale, if one has a chance to visit a cliff, a river shore, a pond or lake beach, and quarries. One or more of these can hardly fail to be convenient in almost every neighborhood, and, of course, whatever is present should receive the larger share of attention. In lieu of a cliff, however, a stone wall will sometimes make a good substitute ; or, what is generally better, the bank of some ditch will show how the water, soaking down and then freezing, loosens masses of earth which fall off and form a *talus* at the bottom. A small stream, a roadside brook it may be, will often show exactly how a river's banks are clutched by the icy fingers which sooner or later carry away masses of earth, rock, and drift, and deposit it elsewhere. The ice which forms under a cliff, as will be illustrated by that formed along any steep bank, receives considerable material dropped from above, which it bears away when thawed loose from the shore. Sometimes in beds of finest clay, large bowlders are to be found that cannot well be accounted for, except on the supposition that they were dropped by floating ice, which doubtless bore them to the spot from some distant place. When the ice breaks up after a rain, its work in gouging and cutting the banks as it is carried along by the current may be observed. The formation of ice dams or gorges, and their subsequent bursting with the effects of the flood which follows, may also be noticed in any stream, at almost any sharp curve, or where some obstruction chokes the channel.

The freezing and thawing of the ground is also an interesting subject for observation and study. The freezing of the soil uplifts and loosens it, so that erosion takes place more easily. By the uplifting and consequent settling movements, the roots of grasses and other plants are sometimes left exposed, and are then killed. On hillsides, the effects are still more marked. Water falling in hollows above stumps, trees, and rocks, by its alternate freezing and thawing tends to push such objects a little farther down the slope. This will be noticed in the spring after a thaw, when trees will frequently be found uprooted, and rocks will be moved a little from their winter bed.

In quarries, or where rocks have been long exposed to the weather, by means of cracks or seams of softer material which has been washed out, water finds access to a greater or less depth below the surface. When frozen it operates with great force in splitting the rocks apart.

1. Examine the ground in various places and find out something as to the depth it is frozen. Study the influences which cause variation in the depth.

2. Compare places near a building, and on the different sides ; on which side is it frozen deepest ?

3. Find a place where the ground is composed of clay ; compare the depth to which it freezes with a place composed of sand. Compare both with vegetable mold and loam. What precautions must you observe in the selection of places of observation, that your results may be trustworthy ?

4. How can you account for the different depths frozen in the various places ?

5. Compare a piece of ground covered with heavy sod with one without vegetation ; which is frozen deeper ?

6. What difference in the freezing of the ground under a large flat stone and that around it uncovered ? In the same way examine the earth under a board, and compare with that under a thin stone.

7. Compare wet with dry places ; which freeze deeper and the sooner ?

8. What effect does a forest have upon the freezing of the ground ?

9. Compare places covered with snow with others where the snow is blown away ; how do you account for the different depths to which the ground is frozen ?

10. Does vegetation increase or diminish the possibilities of the soil for taking up water ?

11. Does the depth to which ground freezes seem to depend upon the water it soaks up ?

12. If there is opportunity, examine a freshly plowed field and compare it with one that has settled compactly.

13. Can you see any signs of weathering away of the stones in the walls in different buildings ?

14. Secure specimens of the different kinds of stone, and study the closeness of the grain in each.

15. Can you see a cause for their wearing away ? Are there any cracks or seams ?

16. Does a stone freeze through like a lump of earth ?

17. When broken, can you find any frost crystals below the surface ?

18. Do stones take up water like the soil ? To test this, dry specimens of these, taken from walls and elsewhere,

and weigh them ; then soak in water for awhile, dry with
a cloth as much as possible, and weigh again.

19. Which ones gained most weight? How do they
rank as to durability in walls, etc.?

20. Test in the same way pieces of mortar or cement
from walls or pavements, and also pieces of brick.

21. Compare in this manner different kinds of stone,
such as limestone, marble, flint, granite, sandstone, and
slate ; does their durability correspond in any way to
their absorptive powers ?

Mineralogy.

If the pupils, during the preceding months, have been reasonably industrious in making their collections, they will, no doubt, have found, among the rest, one or more varieties of iron ore. Good examples of this valuable ore may usually be picked up along railroads where it has been dropped from passing trains laden with it. If there are smelting furnaces near, it may be easily obtained in quantity, and, usually, in great variety. If possible, also, secure good specimens of pig iron, slag, rolled bar, cast iron, and steel. With younger pupils a collection of tools, utensils, instruments, etc., would be valuable in illustrating the properties of each. Sample sets of these may often be procured from manufacturers, who are almost always willing to furnish them to any school that will give suitable space for the exhibit. Much of the wall space, between the blackboard and ceiling, too often bare and unsightly, may well be given up to this purpose. Such displays, by no means necessarily confined to this one subject, will often be used directly, as means of illustration in teaching; and indirectly, by their constant presence, they will, in many pupils, stimulate thought and impress the mind with some notion of the useful industries.

The richest ores from which iron is obtained are magnetite, hematite, and limonite, classed as oxides; and siderite and clay iron-stone, among the carbonates. For specific descriptions of these, the teacher is referred

to " Crosby's Tables for the Determination of Minerals,"
a copy of which every teacher should have, and to Dana's
Manual of Mineralogy. The latter contains a brief description of the different kinds.

Pupils are generally anxious to know the names of the
different minerals that they find, and it is proper that the
teacher should give the names when convinced that the
questions are based upon something higher than idle
curiosity. As a rule, the teacher should give no help
until sure that the pupil himself has invested some
thought in the subject. To insure this, a blank form for
the description should be given the pupil, to be filled
out from his own study of the mineral. (See Mineralogy for September.) When this has been done, the
teacher may then give the name, and feel fairly assured that he is helping one who really wishes to
know. Of course, these blanks cannot be completely
filled until the preceding lessons, upon the physical
characteristics of minerals, have been given and understood. But they may be used to advantage from the beginning, the pupil filling them out as the work proceeds.
Simple methods of making the tests with acids and
the flame are described in this book under the head of
Mineralogy in the work outlined for January and April.
The teacher is referred, also, to Crosby's Tables, or any
manual of determinative mineralogy. The acid test
is easily made, and will add interest from the start. The
flame tests should not be attempted until the pupils are
familiar with the more obvious characteristics.

1. What strongly marked characteristic is common to
all iron ores ?

2. Find the specific gravity of the different varieties ;
what one is heaviest ?

3. Powder a small piece of each kind and test with the magnet ; which is most strongly magnetic ?   Are any not attracted at all ?

4. What is the hardness of each ?

5. What is the difference noticed in the streak.

6. Compare as to color ; what color distinguishes the magnetite ?

7. What difference in shade between limonite and hematite ?   If a specimen of specular iron ore, the purest variety of hematite, can be found, it will be recognized by its shining mica-like blades with a metallic luster.

8. Siderite, iron carbonate, is another variety less rich in iron and varying much in its appearance.

9. Examine specimens of pig iron, cast iron, wrought iron, and steel.   How do they differ in appearance?   Can you find any evidence of crystals in any of the specimens ?

10. What different properties do they possess?

11. Pig iron is obtained directly from the ore by smelting it in a large furnace with an intense heat.   The ore is mingled with broken limestone and coal.   By means of a hot blast the iron is melted out and settles to the bottom, and the lighter impurities remain on the top. At intervals the melted iron is drawn off into a number of molds formed in sand, called pigs.   This process gives the crude iron.   The succeeding processes, puddling, hammering, and rolling, are designed to rid it of its impurities and give it fiber and toughness.

Cast iron articles are made by pouring the melted metal into molds of the desired form.

12. How many uses can you name for cast iron ?

13. What would seem to be its most useful property ?

14. Compare it in appearance with cast steel ?

15. What useful articles are made from steel ? What are its valuable properties ? A most useful characteristic of steel is that it may be so treated as to have different degrees of hardness and elasticity. Take a fine steel knitting-needle and bend it. On being released it regains its former shape by its elasticity. Heat to redness and plunge into cold water, and it will become hard and brittle and break easily. Heat again and allow it to cool slowly, and it becomes softer. The process of reheating and cooling of steel is called tempering, and by it many different degrees of hardness and elasticity are obtained.

16. What are the chief uses of rolled iron ? How does a freshly broken surface differ in appearance from that of cast iron or steel.

17. What are its most useful properties.

Zoology.

GENERAL OBSERVATIONS.

1. What animals are you sure must remain over winter with us that are not to be found abroad ?

2. Why do not all animals migrate ? Is it due to superior or to less intelligence, or to neither ?

3. What animals that you are sure must remain here during the winter provide themselves beforehand with a supply of food ? Will such animals lay up a store of food when kept as pets ? How do you explain this ?

4. What is the character of the food with which they supply themselves ?

5. Where do such animals usually stay ?

6. Are there any that do not lay up a store of food which live through the winter ?

7. Where do such animals live ?

8. Can you see any reason why all animals do not store food for winter use ?

9. Does the activity of animals vary with the season ? Is it economical for them to remain in a state of rest at certain times ?

10. What animals that remain here during the winter are active ? What is their food ?

11. Do you see any relation between the activity of an animal and its food supply ?

12. Do animals which remain quiet during the winter take precautions against the cold ?

FOODS. DIFFERENT KINDS.

1. Do you notice any difference between your summer and winter diet?

2. Compare closely the character of the food which makes up a meal in January with that of a meal in July. What articles especially relished in July that are omitted now?

3. Does the character of the food vary with the occupation? Contrast the diet of a man who does physical labor with that of a book-keeper. Does your own desire for particular foods vary with the kind of work you do?

4. What influences affect the amount of food you take?

5. Can you notice any change in your weight at different times? How can you account for your losing in weight at times and for your gaining at others?

6. From your own observations, what different uses can you see for food?

7. What means have you of knowing whether an article is fit for food or not? How does the nose assist in making selection?

8. Is the taste assisted by the sense of smell? Close the eyes and hold the nostrils, and try distinguishing different articles of food by tasting them.

9. What parts of the mouth are concerned in tasting? Try touching different substances to the tip and back part of the tongue, to the inside of the cheek, to the gums, to the under side of the tongue. Where is the sense of taste most acute?

10. Is the same part equally sensitive to different substances? Try sour, sweet, and bitter articles to different points of the tongue.

11. By means of a mirror and a good light observe carefully the surface of the tongue ; note the roughness and the small individual elevations which cause it. Compare with the tongues of the dog and the cat.

12. These elevations are called papillæ. The smallest in size are the filiform papillæ, and the less numerous but larger rounded dots are the fungiform papillæ. Draw the tongue well forward and press it down with a spoon handle and notice a V-shaped row on the back part ; these are the circumvallate papillæ. The papillæ aid in giving us the taste of food.

13. Do all articles give us the sense of taste ? Mention those easily tasted. Mention some that have little or no taste. Can you taste a stone ? Salt ? What causes the difference ?

14. Can the acuteness of taste be cultivated ? With whom is *tasting* a business ?

15. What influences our likes and dislikes of certain tastes ? Do young children sharply discriminate by taste ?

16. What distinction is there between gratifying taste and satisfying the appetite ? Is the taste as acute at the end of a meal as it was at the beginning of it ?

17. Are foods that are the most pleasant to the taste, the staple articles of diet ?

18. What seems to be the use of the sense of taste ?

19. Do all the animals that you know of have the sense of taste ? Of what use would it be to grain-eating birds ? Do the dry seeds differ in taste ? How do birds find out what kind of seeds they want ?

20. Do the brute animals determine whether or not an article is fit for food by tasting ?

COOKING.

1. Can you see any good reason for cooking food ? In what way does it change meat ?

2. Does the taste we get from a piece of meat depend upon the way in which it was cooked ?

3. The art of cooking is based upon a few simple principles, which are determined by certain characteristic properties of the different food-stuffs, and which are exhibited when brought into contact with heat. The principles are easily understood, and the facts may soon be learned, but to become an expert in this most useful art nothing will take the place of long and patient practice.

4. Put a small amount of the white of an egg in a test tube, and subject it to a sudden and strong heat ; what change does it undergo ?

5. Try again, but let the heat be very moderate, not enough to cook it ; does it undergo change ?

6. Put a little more of the white of an egg into a tube or bottle, and pour boiling water upon it; note the change. Try again, and use slightly warm water ; what difference in the results?

7. The principal substance of lean meat is similar in its properties to the white of an egg. Now suppose you wished to roast meat ; is it desirable to keep the juices within the meat, or should they be allowed to escape into the pan ?

8. Which would you advise at first, a quick or slow heat ? Why?

9. In boiling meat, would you put it into hot or cold water at the start ? Why ? How would it be if you wished to make soup ?

10. In frying meat, should the pan be hot or cold when the meat is put into it? Why?

11. Why is broiled meat usually juicy?

12. Many vegetables, such as beans, peas, and potatoes, are rich in starch, which when cooked swells up and becomes dry and mealy. In this condition it is more easily digested than it is when in a compact mass.

13. Obtain a little wheat and dry it; when well dried pound or grind it up very fine in a mortar. Add a little water and stir well.

14. Note the tenacity of the dough thus formed. It is due to a substance called gluten, which is the most nutritious part of the grain. Starch is also present. The bran is rich in mineral constituents.

15. Take a lesson at home in bread making, and write a description of the process.

16. At what point is the yeast added? Why knead the dough?

17. What is the use of the yeast? Recall the lessons on fermentation. Why does bread sometimes sour before it is baked? Why must it be kept warm while rising?

18. Why bake the bread? Why is baked bread full of little cavities? Why is fresh bread less healthful than dry bread?

HUNGER AND APPETITE.

1. How does the character of one's occupation affect his appetite?

2. What seems to be essential for a regular appetite?

3. What seems to be the function or use of the feeling of hunger?

4. Does the character of the occupation, mental or physical, affect the location of the feeling? The demand for more work material in the brain worker as well as in the muscle worker is made through the appropriate organ in the feeling of hunger. We never are hungry in either our heads or our hands ; both of these parts refer their wants to certain parts of the alimentary canal, the organ that shall speak for them.

5. Is the feeling of hunger, if not satisfied, a persistent one?

6. If the hunger of a brain worker is not satisfied when it occurs, what feelings are likely to follow? What feelings in the case of the muscle worker?

7. What do these feelings which succeed hunger indicate as to the effect of labor upon the body?

8. At what time is the appetite sharpest? When is it least?

9. If you retire at night hungry, are you hungry when you awake? Why is this?

10. Are there any emotions or external conditions which tend to abate the feelings of hunger?

11. Are there any external conditions which tend to increase the feelings?

12. How is one to know when he has taken enough food? If the meal be an agreeable and an uninterrupted one, the loss of the hungry feeling may, perhaps, be taken as a guide to the amount of food that should be eaten. But it is possible for the pangs of hunger to be satisfied by a greatly insufficient amount of food, as any one can testify who has been called away from a meal before he has eaten the usual amount. On returning the feeling of hunger is generally entirely gone ; but that there was an insufficient amount of food is shown by

the subsequent feelings which come when work is resumed.   It would seem that the feelings of hunger cannot accompany the work of digestion ; if any food is
taken into the stomach, no matter how small in amount,
and there is a pause in the meal, digestion begins and
hunger is no longer felt.

13. What have you noticed about the habits of different animals after they have taken food ?   Notice the dog,
cat, horses, and cattle.   Are they active or do they rest?
How is it with a baby ?

14. How do your own inclinations and feelings change
after a full meal ?   Can you account for this ?

15. Do domesticated and wild animals seem to observe
any regularity in their times of taking food ?   Observe
the dog and the cat.   When cattle are left quietly to
themselves, with good pasturage, they feed with tolerable
regularity about four times a day.   They begin very
early in the morning, and feed for an hour or two ; and
then, if the day be warm, they seek the shade or a stream.
Before noon they sally forth again to graze and then they
spend the heated noontide in the shade.   Another meal
in the afternoon is followed by a drowsy rest in the
shade ; then a full supper as the sun goes down brings
their day to a close.

16. Can you see anything in the habits of animals or
in the nature of their food which affects the periods of
their eating?   Does the age of the animal have any
effect ?

17. How do you account for the fact that many people eat but twice a day ?   In considering this question
account should be taken of the habits and occupations
of the individuals.

18. Under what conditions is it better to have a light-

lunch at midday and a full meal in the evening ?   When the reverse ?

19. Do you know by experience of any ill effects from taking a full meal of good food just before retiring at night ?

20. What reasons can you suggest for the regular recurrence of the times at which food is taken by animals ?

BOOK FOR REFERENCE.   Humboldt Library, No. 48, Life in Nature.   Chapters on Nutrition.

Botany.

During the winter occasional observations should be made upon plants, and the effects of frost and freezing may be noted. The phenomena of growth are perhaps entirely absent, though in particularly mild winters it is not unusual to find dandelions in full bloom at this time. A very few days of mild weather in midwinter will be sufficient to coax the chickweed, in sheltered places, to spread out its delicate petals. But for most part, plants seem to understand the treachery of these exceptional warm periods, and refuse to pay them any heed.

1. Can you find any buds that have been killed by the frost? Collect a large number and get the percentage killed.

2. Where are the living parts of the buds?

3. Do the central parts of the buds freeze?

4. What can you find about the buds that acts as a protection against frost?

5. Do any birds or other animals use the buds for food?

6. In what condition are the acorns and other nuts that may be found at this time?

7. Can you find any seeds that have sprouted and afterward have been killed?

8. Have the nuts and seeds that are covered with fallen leaves been frozen?

9. Is there any sap between the bark and the wood?

10. Is there any moisture in the wood? Does the water in the twig freeze?

AIR.

There are few experiments requiring simpler apparatus than those which will well illustrate many facts and phenomena relating to air ; and it may be added, there are few possessing greater attraction, or that are more useful in explaining many interesting phenomena daily observed. From the simplicity of the apparatus, however, and the common occurrence of the phenomena due to air pressure, etc., it must not be imagined that the conception of the real character of air is one easily gained. The fact that the air is invisible renders its study difficult and stands in the pupil's way of getting a definite idea of what it really is. Some things indeed seem to lead straight to a misconception ; for example, since it floats above the surface of the earth, the ordinary experience of the child leads him to believe that it is without weight. It will be found that very few pupils in grammar schools associate the rising of water in a tube " by suction " with air pressure outside, which is its true cause. They almost invariably have the notion that there is some mysterious kind of pulling power inside the tube. The experiments, therefore, which will assist in giving the correct idea, should be repeated and extended until the pupils have the conception that the rising of a liquid in the tube, and in all similar instances, is due to an unbalanced pressure. The explanation of why water will rise in a pump stock is really as simple as the one necessary to show why one end of a see-saw goes up if only one person is on the board. The only reason why the former is not understood as well as the latter is because of the difficulty in conceiving that the air has weight.

Elasticity of Air.

1. Fill a small bottle half full of water. Through the cork pass a small, tightly fitting glass tube, which should reach to the bottom of the water. If the cork is not air-tight, cover with wax. (See Chemistry for January.) If the tube is drawn to a fine point at the upper end, the experiment will be more interesting.

2. Blow strongly through the tube into the bottle and quickly remove the end of the tube from the mouth; explain what you observe.

3. What occupies the space in the bottle above the water before blowing into it? Why is it possible to blow air into the bottle?

4. Does the air which was blown into the bottle escape again?

5. Is the water all driven from the bottle? Upon what does the amount which escapes depend?

6. Can you explain why the water is not driven out of the bottle by the air already there before blowing into it?

7. Can you think of any solid body which the action of the air in the space above the water resembles?

8. Remove the cork and invert the bottle in a small basin or cup of water; does the water enter the bottle? Why?

9. Push the bottle, mouth downward, into the vessel of water; does the water fill the bottle? Why?

10. Pass a small funnel through the cork and connect it tightly with wax ; press tightly into the bottle and fill the funnel with water. Can you fill the bottle with water in this way ? Why ? Try filling the bottle when the funnel fits loosely in the mouth of the bottle.

Pressure of Air.

1. Warm gradually a test tube or bottle in the flame of the alcohol lamp, invert it, and press it closely upon the back of the hand ; as it becomes cool, what do you observe ?

2. Was the bottle or test tube entirely empty before it was heated ? What was accomplished by warming it ? Recall an experiment performed in Physics in the November work to explain this.

3. What must have taken place when the bottle cooled ?

4. Hold the arm in different positions ; does the bottle still cling to it ?

5. Remove the bottle (noting any sound made as it is pulled away) and heat it again ; invert it over a saucer of water with the mouth below the surface.

6. As it cools, what takes place ? How does it differ from what happens when a cool bottle is so inverted in water ?

7. Boil an egg until hard and remove the shell ; heat as above, or by dropping a lighted taper into it, a bottle with a mouth somewhat too small to allow the egg to pass through readily. Moisten the edge of the opening, and when quite hot, quickly place the egg in it, the small end down.

8. Consider what takes place as the bottle cools. If the opening is of the proper size the egg will pass into

the bottle. By recalling previous experiments (see Physics for November), devise an easy means of getting the egg out of the bottle without injury to either.

9. Bend a glass tube, the size of a lead pencil, into something like a U-shape so that each arm shall be three or four inches long. Immerse completely in water until filled. Fit a piston, made by wrapping a greased string or strip of cloth around a stick or wire, into one end of the tube, and push it half-way down the arm and then partially withdraw it. Watch the water in the tube.

10. Repeat the experiment, holding the tube in different positions—upside down, horizontal, etc.

11. Hold the tube upright, and push the piston down half-way; see that the other arm of the tube stands level full of water. Place a finger tightly over this end and slowly withdraw the piston. Does the water follow the piston? Remove the finger and note the result. In this exercise note whether or not the piston is air-tight; how can you find this out?

12. Repeat the experiment suggested in (11), and withdraw the piston entirely from the tube; can you account for what takes place?

13. Place a small tube of any kind between the lips, and, with the finger over the other end, suck the air from it and apply the tongue to the end; what takes place? Remove the finger and note the difference.

14. Close the lips and try drawing or sucking the cheeks in between the teeth; when well drawn in, what is the effect of slightly opening the lips?

15. Using the tube mentioned in (9), immerse it partly in an upright position in water; does the water rise in it? Lift it out of the water slowly, and watch the water inside the tube.

16. Immerse it again in the same way, close the upper end tightly with the finger, and remove from the water ; what difference do you see ? Remove the finger and notice what takes place.

17. Fill a large bottle with a small opening level full and invert it; does the water run out ? If a small-necked bottle cannot be obtained, get one with a good cork, through which a small hole may be drilled.

18. Sink a bottle or a tube below the surface in a vessel of water, and let it lie on its side until it is completely filled ; turn it up mouth downward, and raise it so that the mouth is just below the surface. Is there any water still in the bottle ?

19. Can you give any reasons for what has taken place in the foregoing experiments ? In the first one did the bottle make any mark upon the hand ? ' How could you make such a mark with the bottle without first heating it ? Try pressing the bottle firmly against the hand for some time.

20. Why does heating the bottle first enable the water to rise in it, as in (6), when it does not do so as in (8) under elasticity ?

21. Is the water drawn up into the bottle, or is it pushed into it ? Is there anything inside to draw it? Is there anything outside to push it ?

22. Is the egg in (7) drawn into the bottle or pushed into it ? What is there to draw or push ?

23. Can you make the air in the bottle push the egg out again ?

24. When the piston is pushed down in (9), is the water pushed or drawn out of the opposite end ?

25. While the piston is being withdrawn, is the water when following it being pushed or drawn ?

26. Does the water refuse to follow the piston in (11) while the finger remains on the opening in the tube? Has the piston any means of drawing it? If the piston is not air-tight, how will it affect the results?

27. If possible, procure a thick glass tube thirty inches long having a bore of about one-fourth of an inch, and also a small bottle of mercury. Stop one end of the tube and by means of a small funnel fill it with mercury. Place the thumb over the upper end, and then invert in a small cup of mercury. Does the mercury run out? Measure the height of the column. If a barometer be at hand compare the height of the mercury in the tube with it.

28. Repeat the experiment, using water instead of mercury. What difference between the water and the mercury? Mercury is thirteen and a half times as heavy as water : how high a column of water would be sustained by a pressure equal to that in (26)?

29. What force holds these fluids up in the tube? Explain how the same force has acted in previous exercises.

30. What use can you see for the barometer? Why does the mercury sometimes stand higher than at others in the barometer?

31. Why must the barometer tube be closed at the upper end? Is there air in the space above the mercury? Why?

32. Why is it that the mercury of the barometer enables us to measure the pressure of the air and that in a thermometer measures temperature?

33. From the foregoing experiments can you tell in what directions air presses?

34. The actual pressure of the atmosphere is about

fifteen pounds to each square inch of surface ; calculate the pressure on top of a desk ; of a table ; on the floor of a room. Why does not this great weight crush every. thing beneath it ?

35. Why are our bodies not crushed by this weight, which on an average-sized man equals twenty tons ? How does it affect people who ascend to great heights in balloons ?. Can you account for this ?

THE PENDULUM.

To follow the work on the equilibrium of bodies planned for the previous month, an interesting series of observations and experiments may be made with the pendulum. They will afford fine opportunity for the pupils to develop skill in making and delicacy in manip- ulation.

1. Suspend from any convenient support a large bullet by means of a small thread, two feet long ; when the bullet is drawn a little to one side of its position of rest, can you see why it swings?

2. What kind of a path does the ball describe in swinging? It is called an arc. When the ball is at one extremity of the arc, what two forces are acting upon it? Note carefully the line of direction of each force. Com- pare with these two lines the direction through which the ball really moves at each point in the arc. Why does the pendulum begin to swing in the opposite direc- tion ?

3. *An oscillation* or *vibration* is the motion from one extremity of the arc to the other. The angle measured by the arc is the *amplitude of vibration.* The time it takes the ball to move through this arc is the *time of vibration,*

4. Swing the pendulum through a short arc and note the number of vibrations to a minute. Vary the experiment, making the arc longer and shorter, and count the vibrations per minute; what fact do you learn?

5. Make another pendulum of same length, but use a cork ball of same size as the bullet. Compare the oscillations of the two pendulums.

6. Suspend another bullet by a shorter thread; how do its oscillations compare with the first one made?

7. How long must it be so that it will vibrate just twice as fast? Compare the length of the two.

8. What do you notice about the *times of vibration* and the *number of vibrations* in a given time of the two pendulums? Try those of other lengths.

9. Can you make one which will vibrate seconds? How long is it? What does the pendulum of your clock at home vibrate?

10. What advantage in using the pendulum in measuring time? What is the use of the spring or weights and the other parts of a clock?

11. What means were used for measuring time before clocks were invented?

12. Suppose a clock runs too fast, how can you properly regulate it? Why? Why do the extremes of winter and summer affect the running of a clock?

13. Suspend bars of wood having same length, but of different shapes, such as conical, one suspended by the base and the other by the apex, prismatic, spindle-shaped, etc., and observe the oscillations of each; can you account for the variations?

14. Which is really the longest pendulum mentioned in (13)? Which the shortest? How can you decide?

Chemistry.

In making hydrogen, and performing experiments with it, the pupils should follow with great care all the directions given. It is easier and much better to prevent an accident in laboratory work than it is to repair the mischief done by one. The pupils should be trained to make themselves certain of each step in any process before taking it. *When hydrogen is mingled with air or with oxygen, the mixture is explosive.* Upon this fact are based all the precautions necessary to be observed in the making of hydrogen, and in its management in the following exercises. With this single point in mind, it is easy and practicable for pupils to perform a number of interesting and profitable experiments. It is doubtful, however, if it be advisable for the teacher to undertake such a course of experiments when the pupils cannot do all or the essential part of the work for themselves. It should be planned to have the pupils *do*. It is not denied that they may be instructed by what they see and hear the teacher do ; but there is so much that the pupils can do for themselves, and the power they gain by doing, by working out patiently all the details for themselves, is so much greater, that it is nothing less than depriving them of their rights to fail in meeting their capabilities for work. Teachers are as far astray when they *do* what the pupils should do, as they are when they assume to *think* for them.

Materials Needed.

1. Procure a wide-mouthed bottle, holding two to four ounces, for each pupil. Fit a piece of glass tubing, three or four inches long, through the cork ; the upper end of the tube should be drawn to a point. To do this, heat the tube an inch from the end in the flame until soft, and then pull it out to a fine thread and break it. The hole in the upper end of the tube should not be larger than a small pinhole. The cork, unless it be a good one, should be well coated with wax. An excellent wax for the purpose may be made and applied as follows : Hard paraffine, two parts ; soft paraffine, one part ; melt together, and, while hot, pour a few drops into a vessel of cold water ; remove these quickly while still warm, and apply to the cork. A coating of tallow on the cork will answer the purpose.

2. The bent tube used in making oxygen in previous lessons ; a short piece of rubber tubing ; a clay pipe.

3. A piece of glass tubing, about half an inch in diameter and two feet long.

4. A handful of scraps of zinc.

5. Hydrochloric acid.

6. Test-tubes, or small two-dram bottles.

Experiments.

1. Clip the zinc scraps into small pieces, and put enough into the wide-mouthed bottle to, at least, cover the bottom. Cover with water and add the acid until a brisk bubbling takes place. Allow this to continue three or four minutes till the air in the bottle has been driven out.

2. Press tightly into the bottle the cork with the tube in it. What evidence is there of a change taking place in the bottle. Wrap a towel or cloth around the bottle as a precaution against a possible explosion. This will prevent injury from flying pieces of glass.

3. Apply a lighted match to the tip of the glass tube. This is called the philosopher's candle. What evidence have you of the character of the work being done by the acid and zinc ?

4. Are the bubbles formed inside the bottle filled with air ?

5. Feel the sides of the bottle ; is the gas coming out at the top of the tube steam? How can you decide this question ?

6. Is the gas oxygen ? Is it carbon dioxide gas ?

7. How does the flame differ from that of ordinary gas or a lamp ?

8. Hold a small piece of iron wire in the flame for a short time, and then, when cool, hold it for the same length of time in the flame of a candle ; what difference in the result ?

9. How does the light-giving power of the flame differ from that of a candle ?

10. Take the large glass tube and lower it gently over the flame ; with the flame at different heights inside the tube, can you detect any sound ?

11. While the sound is being produced, watch the flame closely ; what changes, if any, does it undergo?

12. Can you account for the sound ? The full consideration of this question had probably better be referred to some future time when the subject of sound is being studied. If possible, try tubes having different diameters and of different lengths.

13. What forms in the upper part of the tube when it is held over the flame ? Can you account for it ?

14. Extinguish the flame ; hold a test tube inverted over the tube through which the gas is escaping. After two or three minutes, remove the test tube, and, still keeping it inverted, apply a lighted match to its mouth. Compare the result with a similar experiment performed with oxygen.

15. In the same manner fill a test tube and remove it and turn the mouth upward ; after a minute apply a lighted match to the mouth. Is there any evidence of gas in the tube ?

16. Fill the test tube again, remove, and keep it inverted. Bring the mouth of the tube close to the mouth of a second tube, also inverted, and incline it until the mouth of the first is turned upward under the second. Apply a lighted match to the mouth of the second while it is still inverted. These operations should be performed as quickly as possible.

17. Connect the glass tube by means of the short rubber tube with the stem of a clay pipe. With some strong soapsuds blow some bubbles. When they break loose from the pipe touch them with a lighted taper. Do not apply the flame to the pipe bowl, nor to the bubbles until they are entirely free from it.

18. What do the experiments, 14 to 17 inclusive, show you as to the character of this gas? The gas formed is called *Hydrogen.* Its symbol is H.

19. In what respects is hydrogen like air ? How does it differ from air ?

20. Compare it with the CO_2 (read carbon dioxide) that was studied in November.

21. How do the pouring processes by which the

gases were transferred from one vessel to another differ?

22. Compare the effects of CO_2, O, and H, and air, upon the lighted match.

23. Compare the methods by which CO_2, O, and H are obtained; in what respect is the process the same in all the cases?

24. Examine the contents of the bottle after the bubbling has ceased; is the zinc changed? What kind of a change has taken place?

25. Try some of the fluid which remains upon fresh zinc; is it like the acid you started with?

26. Will fresh acid continue to act upon the solids left in the bottle?

BOOK FOR REFERENCE. Humboldt Library, No. 99, Nature Studies, chap. i.

Meteorology.

1. In which month during the period included in your record has the temperature been most diminished? Can you see a reason for this?

2. In which month, in the same period, has there been the least variation in temperature?

3. Does the rate of variation in temperature correspond in any way to the variation in length of the noon shadow?

4. Judging from the slant of the sun's rays, are we receiving more or less heat from the sun than we received in December? What does the thermometer tell us?

5. What has been the prevailing wind for the month? Compare with previous months.

6. Is the wind more or less variable than it was during the autumn months?

7. How has the prevailing wind affected the temperature?

8. What wind has accompanied the lowest temperature? The highest?

9. What was the greatest range of temperature noted in any week? What was the range during the month?

10. How does the number of rainy or snowy days compare with that of December?

11. How does the *amount* of rainfall compare with previous months?

12. From what direction do the rains come? The snows?

13. Do you notice any uniform variation in temperature before, during, and after a storm?

14. At what temperature has the most snow fallen? The heaviest rains?

15. Does the size of the snowflakes vary with the temperature?

16. Does the barometer in any way indicate uniformly the approach of a storm?

17. Do rain and snow storms affect it in the same way?

18. When does it show uniformly the greater height, on warm or cold days? What has been its greatest range in each week and during the month?

19. How do the clouds during this month compare in kind and elevation with those of the previous months?

20. What differences, if any, do you notice between a rain cloud and a snow cloud?

STUDY OF THE WEATHER BUREAU MAPS.

21. What quarter of the United States has had the Low Area most frequently during the month? The High Area?

22. What region has been visited by the severest storms? Compare with December in this respect.

23. What has been the most southern point reached by the zero isotherm during the month? What range of latitude was crossed by this isotherm?

24. What was the most southern point reached by the isotherm 32°? What range of latitude did it cover?

25. Can you determine the direction of the great storms during the month? In what regions have they originated?

26. What places stand on the snow line during this month ? Compare with December.

27. Where does the snow line bend farthest south ? Farthest north ? What is the range of latitude covered by the snow line ? Can you see any reason for this variation ?

28. What influence have the Great Lakes had upon the snow line ? The mountain systems ? The river valleys ?

29. How does the climate west of the Rocky Mountains differ from that on the east ?

30. Contrast the Atlantic coast with the Mississippi valley.

BOOK FOR REFERENCE. Humboldt Library, No. 99, Nature Studies. Chapter on Snow. .

Astronomy.

The problems in this subject which offer themselves for study in the changing seasons and recurring day and night, and through the observation of the stars and the planets, have been of deep interest to mankind since the earliest times. They present every degree of difficulty ; the simplest lie within the grasp of the primary pupil, while the solution of those most abstruse has engaged the highest intellectual power of the human mind.

It is not necessary to take up all the problems that may suggest themselves during any month ; but enough should be considered to give a meaning to the daily meteorological record that has been kept, so that keeping it may not sink to the level of lifeless routine work. If the records have been faithfully made, by this season abundant data will be at hand, which will form a good basis for most interesting work.

1. How is the length of day and night changing this month ? Is the change the same that occurred last month ?

2. Compare the rate of change during the first week with that during the last one. Can you account for the difference ?

3. Compare the rate of change during January with the corresponding weeks in December. Can you explain why the rate is much the same ?

4. Is the period of daylight this month being length ened by additions at both morning and evening ?

5. At which time is the greatest addition made? Why should the additions not be the same at both ends of the lighted period?

6. Refer to the record for previous months; is there a corresponding difference while the day is growing shorter? Make use of a globe in trying to find out why the lighted period is not either increased or diminished by *equal* times, morning and evening.

7. When is the increase or decrease in day's length nearly equally divided between morning and evening? When is it most unequally so divided?

8. Examine the noon marks made this month. (See description of apparatus in September work.) How do the spaces between the marks compare with those of previous months?

9. What does the variation in the length of the space indicate? Try to illustrate by use of a globe.

10. Is the limit of the shadow moving in the same direction as it did last month? What is the meaning of this? Is it moving at the same rate? Show why, using a globe, this is so?

11. Can you tell from a study of the noon marks whether we are receiving more or less heat from the sun than we received last month? Consult your meteorological record and note the variation in the temperature this month.

12. What is the smallest angle that the sun's rays at noon have made with the horizon? Use the instrument described in the September work for making the measurement.

13. Try to show why this angle is smallest during this part of the year.

14. What effects depend upon the size of this angle as

a cause ?   Is the angle increasing or diminishing at present ?

15. What effects are noticeable at present that are due to its changing size ?   Is it affecting temperature ? Why ?

16. In which of the previous months was the angle about the size that it is the last of January ?   How does that month compare with January as to temperature, length of day and night, etc. ?   Try to explain why they are alike in some respects and different in others.

17. How are the points at which the sun rises and sets moving on the horizon at present?   Can you show why this is so, using a globe ?

18. What is the greatest variation in the time of the rising or setting of the moon on two successive days ?

19. Can you think of the conditions necessary that would cause it to rise at the same time every evening ?

20. Under what conditions would the moon rise in the west and set in the east ?   Would its appearance change during the night ?   (This is true of one of the moons of the planet Mars.)

21. The planet Venus (see Astronomy for September) moves around the sun in two hundred and twenty-five days.   Can you explain why this planet has changed from an evening to a morning star ?   Try to see the planet moving in its orbit and in its proper relation to the earth and sun.   Use symbols sparingly and only to illustrate, not to take the place of the real objects.

22. How long does it shine as morning star and as evening star respectively ?

23. Suppose the earth and Venus are on the same side of the sun and in a line with it, what will be the position of the three bodies at the end of one year ?

24. Can Venus ever appear to us except as a morning or an evening star ?

25. Will she exhibit phases corresponding to those of our moon ?

26. In what position will we see the largest part of the disk ? In what position will we see the smallest part of it ?

27. Constellations the same as last month ; how have they changed their positions ?

BOOKS FOR REFERENCE. Humboldt Library : No. 14, Wonders of the Heavens. No. 20, The Romance of Astronomy. No. 1, Light Science for Leisure Hours, Chapter on Venus.

Geography.

SOUTH AMERICA. PRODUCTIONS.

The pupils should model a relief map, and with this before them endeavor to work out the reason for the character of the various productions, as far as they are results of the climatic conditions of latitude, elevation, winds, rainfall, coast line, and ocean currents.

1. Judging from the range of latitude covered by the continent, what contrasts must be expected in animal and vegetable productions?

2. Compare South America with North America in this respect. What different conditions will tend to produce contrasts in the two continents in corresponding latitudes?

3. What contrasts in productions would you expect to find in South America in the equatorial regions?

4. Is it possible that the productions belonging usually to the temperate regions may be found within the tropics?

5. What contrasts would you expect to find on the opposite sides of the Andes Mountains within the tropics?

6. How must the productions of the Atlantic and the Pacific coast lines differ within the tropics?

7. Would you expect much contrast between the Atlantic coast line and the interior in the equatorial region?

8. Would you expect a similarity or contrast between

the Pacific coast of South America and that of North America?

9. What are the most active influences which determine the productions on these coasts in the two continents?

10. What must be the character of the Pacific coast productions of South America in the temperate zone?

11. Do you see any reason for their being different on the eastern side of the mountains?

12. Contrast this region with the corresponding latitude of North America.

13. Where are the fertile river valleys in South America?

14. Locate on molded map the great forest area of the continent. What are the conditions favorable for it? What valuable woods are obtained from this great forest region? Read a description of the Amazon river basin.

15. How do the climatic conditions favor the great grass plains of the Orinoco basin, the Llanos? Are the same conditions favorable to forests?

16. Where else are there grass regions in South America?

17. To what regions of North America do they correspond?

18. Locate on the map the region from which spices, gums, and medicinal plants are obtained.

19. Locate in the same way the coffee-growing region.

20. What do the exports from Buenos Ayres tell as to the productions of the surrounding country? Compare with the exports of Rio Janeiro.

21. Locate the regions of greatest mineral wealth.

What minerals are found in the Andes Mountains? In the Brazilian highland?

22. What are the chief cities of the mining regions? Read the Story of the Incas and the history of the conquest of Peru.

BOOKS FOR REFERENCE. Guyot's Physical Geography. Humboldt Library, Nos. 11 and 12. The Naturalist on the River Amazon.

Geology.

The observations of the effects of frost and freezing as agencies that are at work during the winter season in changing the face of nature should be continued this month along the lines commenced in December. The experiment suggested under Physics for November, showing the expansive force of freezing water, may with profit be recalled or repeated and applied in this connection. Examination should be made of the soil in different places to determine the depth to which the ground is frozen under various conditions. It will be a matter of interest and profit at this time, while outdoor work is impracticable, on account of the inclemency of the season, to consider the nature of fossils, and to try to read some of the earth's history recorded by them. The early ideas as to the origin and meaning of fossils were as monstrous as they now seem curious and amusing. Of all the observed acts in nature which man has, from time to time, endeavored to reconcile to his preconceived notions of the origin and history of this world, nothing has proved more refractory than these foot-prints of a long bygone age. Although it required some hundreds of years for early scientists to get the first glimpse of the truth concerning fossils, yet so obvious are the general facts of their history, it was only necessary for the mind to approach the subject unbiased by preconceived notions and beliefs to have their true character recognized. The course of early inquiries into the nature of fossils affords one of the strongest illustrations given on the page of history of how one's prejudice or belief may become an insurmountable barrier between him and the simple truth. Even children of primary grades will, without prompting, reason correctly about the origin of fossils, though of course they lack almost totally the idea of the time involved.

The fossil in itself is a matter of comparatively little interest, but when it is used as a key to unlock the secrets of the past; when through it the child calls up a great picture of the world and nature as they must have been when it was a living thing; when, with it in hand, he sees the succeeding ages roll by, each with a character of its own, then it becomes one of the most powerful means at the teacher's command for broadening and strengthening his pupil's conception of the universe. The teacher must carefully avoid the mistake of being in too much haste. The idea to be attained is vast, and is destined to forever grow. Let the pupil have ample time to fill in his picture of those distant ages with land, water, sunlight, darkness, plants, animals, air, blue sky, lowering clouds, lightning, thunder, rain, snow, ice, and everything that the existence of that one living thing, which we now know as a fossil, implied. Without due deliberation and thought, something will be omitted which will mar the symmetry of the creation and spoil the beauty of the scene.

For an excellent resumé of the early theories regarding fossils, the teacher is referred to Lyell's Principles of Geology, vol. i, page 33, *et seq.*

1. Examine the ground in the locations observed last month; has it been frozen to greater depth?

2. If opportunity offers, notice a trench dug through

the street ; is the ground frozen deeper under the cobble stones than it is under the sod ? Can you account for the difference ?

3. Can you find any stones that are being crumbled by frost ?   .

4. Where is the ground frozen to a greater depth, under the trees or in an open space ? Where there is sod or where the ground is bare ?

5. Can you notice any differences in freezing that you know are due to differences in soils ?

6. Among the fossil plants that are perhaps most easily obtained by pupils are some of those, ferns it may be, of the Carboniferous or Coal Period. The following questions and suggestions refer specially to such a fossil, though they may readily be adapted to any fossil plant. These, or at least the impressions of them, are frequently found in the lumps of coal in the bin, and pupils should watch for them.

7. Is there any doubt as to what has left its imprint upon the stone or coal ? What are the marks that make you certain of the correctness of your answer ?

8. Does it in any respect resemble any plants of the present time ? Can you tell what part of the plant it is ?

9. Is the fossil under examination the original plant, or a cast of it ? By *cast* this is meant : that the space that was once occupied by the plant has been filled with a stony substance that bears the shape and marks of the once living thing. If neither a cast nor the original substance, can you make out whether it is more than merely the *imprint* of some plant ?

10. Can you discover any evidence that the leaves were veined like those of the present day ?

11. Can you form any idea as to the size the plant must have been ?

12. From what you know of ferns which you have seen, within what range of heat and cold is it likely that this plant lived ?

13. Was the cold as severe as that of Greenland at present ? Is it possible that snow may have fallen where it grew ? Did it rain there ? Do you suppose the sun shone upon it ? How much warmer may the sun have shone upon it than it shines upon us in summer?

14. Do you know where it was found ? Do ferns now grow in that region? How *may* that region have differed from its present condition when the fossil grew there ?

15. Is it likely that it grew on a high mountain ? Did it grow in a desert ? Could it have grown in a marsh ?

16. Is there evidence as to whether it grew in a forest or in open fields ? What would you suppose concerning the fertility of the soil that produced it ? .

17. Can you tell whether or not it belonged to a plant that shed its leaves? Was this fossil decayed before it fell to the ground ?

18. Do you think this fossil plant bore as many leaves as our plants do at present ? Were plants growing as thickly on the ground as they do now ?

19. How does it happen that fossil leaves are not more abundant? Are the leaves that you noticed fall last autumn likely to become fossilized ?

20. Did this fossil leaf decay after falling to the ground as soon as most leaves do that you have noticed ?

21. What must have happened soon after it fell, which started it on the way to become a fossil ?

22. Which is the more likely, that it fell in a wet place

or in a dry one? In which place would it probably be more quickly covered?

23. In which kind of covering, wet or dry, would the more perfect imprint be made? In which kind would the leaf be the longest preserved? In which would the imprint be the better preserved before the rock hardened?

24. Was it covered with fine or coarse material?

25. If you think it was buried in a dry place, what agency, probably, did the work? Can you by digging down into the soil find leaves that are as perfect as this one?

26. On the supposition that it fell into a swamp, or into water, by what means do you think it could have been buried?

27. If you think it fell into water, can you find any evidence as to whether it was running or standing water?

28. If the fossil you have is a cast of the plant form, how was that cast made? Would it be more easily formed in dry or in wet ground?

29. In case you have but the imprint, can you tell what has become of the plant? Why was the imprint not destroyed?

30. If your fossil came from a coal mine, or near it, do you know what thickness of earth there was above it? How deep are some of the coal mines that you have seen or read about?

31. Are there layers of solid rock above the coal seams?

32. In what way, most likely, was this great covering deposited?

33. If this mass of earth and rock was deposited by

water, what change must have come over the region where the fern grew ? What can you infer about the depth of the water ?

34. Can you find any evidence that will show whether the change was gradual or sudden ?

35. What is the most reasonable supposition that you can make which will account for the region where the fossil grew becoming covered with water.

36. What other change in the region must have occurred after the mass of earth was deposited ?

37. What supposition can you make which will explain how the water was removed ?

38. Is there any evidence of more than one sinking, and one elevation of the land ?

39. After the water finally disappeared, by what means do you think the fossil became exposed, if it was found on or near the surface ? What agencies that you know of are now at work that would tend to gnaw away its covering ?

40. In looking back over the possible history of the fossil, can you form any estimate of the length of time included in it ?

41. In any region that you may be familiar with during the past few years, has there been any perceptible depth of material deposited ? What has placed it there ?

42. Has there been any perceptible deposition in any lake, large or small, that you have had opportunity to observe ?

43. Is there any way of telling how long it took the water to gather to this region or recede from it ?

44. It has been estimated that the Mississippi River carries down enough sediment each year to cover a square mile two hundred and sixty-eight feet deep. At

that rate, how long would it take that river to remove a layer one foot thick from its basin ?

45. At the same rate, how long would it take to expose the fossil after the water had receded, supposing it to have been buried five hundred feet deep? If each of the other periods in the history of the fossil were as long, what would be its age ?

BOOKS FOR REFERENCE. Humboldt Library: No. 6, Town Geology. No. 38, Geological Sketches, chap. vii.

Mineralogy.

If the pupils have been industrious in collecting specimens of the various kinds of rocks and minerals of the
neighborhood, it will be interesting to examine them with
a view to learning something of their chemical properties. A few cents' worth of hydrochloric and sulphuric
acids in separate bottles will be all that is necessary. If
these cannot be obtained, use strong vinegar.

1. Powder a small amount of limestone and put it into
a small bottle or test tube, add a little hydrochloric acid,
and note the result. Gently warm the test tube over the
lamp; what difference is noted?

2. In the same way try the limestone with dilute sulphuric acid; compare with the changes that occurred
with hydrochloric acid. Dilute the sulphuric acid with
five or six times its bulk of water, and allow it to cool
before using; add the acid to the water, allowing it to
run slowly down the sides of the tube.

3. In a similar manner treat a piece of marble and
compare with the limestone.

4. Take some small pieces of shells, those of oyster or
clam, and treat with acid; how are they like the stones?
If it can be obtained, try in the same way a piece of *chalk*
—not crayon. What is the result?

5. The bubbling noticed when the stones were placed
in acid is called effervescence. Stones which dissolve in
acids with effervescence, a gas being formed, are said to

be calcareous.   They are composed of the elements calcium, carbon, and oxygen.

6. Treat a small piece of gypsum with acid, compare it with the action of the acid on marble and limestone.

7. Break off a small piece of quartz from one of the pebbles found on the lake shore or the banks of a stream, and drop it into the acid; is there a change?

8. In the same way try a piece of flint or any other flinty hard stone in your collection; does the acid affect them?   Test also a piece of slate.

9. Treat a small piece of clay with acid; does it dissolve?

10. In the same way try a piece of sandstone; does it differ in any particular from any of the above?

11. These hard stones, insoluble in acid, are called silicious stones.   They are composed of the elements oxygen and silicon.   The clay is silicious, but contains some impurities.

BOOK FOR REFERENCE.   Humboldt Library: No 6, Town Geology.

Zoology.

GENERAL OBSERVATIONS.

1. Keep a sharp lookout during the month for returning birds. It is too early to expect the return of any great numbers, yet some may occasionally be seen.

2. Have the winter visitors returned northward yet?

3. Are there any signs of returning spring through the awakening of animal life?

PREHENSION OF FOOD.

The various ways in which different animals seize their food and convey it to their mouths form interesting subjects for study. The wonderful precision of the human arm and hand in these movements is worthy of more than passing attention. When baby begins to help itself at the table, the movements are neither graceful nor accurate. In attempting to seize the morsel, the unruly shoulder-muscles, which at an early age are the ones chiefly used in guiding the hand, bring the hand down wide of the mark. After repeated efforts, almost by accident the hand comes within grasping distance, and the fingers, without the slightest effort at individual arrangement, close like the claws of a bird. The return movement is equally awkward ; the shoulder-joint is stubborn, the elbow refuses to bend, the wrist fails in its duty, and the chubby fist is sent on an excursion from ear to ear before the morsel is finally lodged within the anxiously waiting mouth. But, see the result of persistent training. After a little time the shoulder makes just the right swing, the elbow makes exactly the right angle, the wrist gives the hand the proper droop, and by an accurate and definite turn of the hand and arm the fingers are marshalled into their appointed positions and the food is carried to the mouth with grace and ease. Absolute freedom and precision of movement are acquired, and the difficulties are mastered so early that, from our own experience, we could not even know that they ever existed. If teachers and parents were to give as much care to muscular training for other movements, such as writing, walking, lifting, etc., as they do to those concerned in getting food to the mouth, it is hardly too much to say, that, in the child's life, years of time and tons of effort would be saved.

1. What animals, besides man, make use of their fore limbs in managing their food? What animals, that you know of, make no such use of these limbs?

2. Is there an essential difference in the character of the food of these two classes of animals?

3. What movements of the squirrel's foreleg are like the arm and hand? In what respect are the paws unlike the hand?

4. What is the foot-like character retained by the fore-paws? Why is this?

5. If possible to do so, examine the hand of a monkey; in what respect is it more hand-like than the fore-paw of a squirrel?

6. What differences between the cat and the dog in the use of their forepaws in food getting?

7. Are the cat's forepaws more or less hand-like than

those of the squirrel? In what respects? The limbs used in grasping are said to be *prehensile.*

8. How do animals without prehensile limbs seize their food?

9. Does there seem to be any correspondence between the shape of the head and the mode of food prehension? Notice the contour of the heads of the different animals that make no use of their fore limbs in the prehension of food ; compare them with the heads of those that use their limbs for prehension.

10. Does the attitude of the body vary with the prehensile character of the limbs?

11. What parts of the face are concerned in the prehension of food? What parts are most used in taking liquids? In taking solids?

12. Study and explain the process by which we take a drink? (See Physics for January.)

13. What organs are concerned in this operation?

14. Do the dog and the cat drink in exactly the same way?

15. How do birds drink? Why do they throw their heads backward?

16. How do the horse, the cow, and the sheep seize their food?

17. Why is the tongue of a cat rough? Is the dog's tongue similar? Can you see a reason for what you observe? Keep in mind the wild state of these animals.

18. A cow's food differs very much from that of a cat ; yet her tongue is rough and rasp-like ; what reason can you see for this similarity in the two animals?

19. Can you account for any differences observed between the cow's tongue and that of a horse?

20. What use does the snake make of its tongue?

21. In what way do we use our lips in taking food?

22. What animals have you observed that make greater use of their lips for this purpose?

23. Can you trace any correspondence between the character of the food and the kinds of lips of different animals?

24. Are the teeth employed in the prehension of food? Compare different animals in this respect, such as the horse, the cow, the sheep, the squirrel, the rabbit, the snake, the dog, and the cat, with yourself.

25. Notice the movements and the work done by the different parts of the mouth in chewing or masticating food.

26. What appears to be the function of the tongue? Of what tissue is it composed? In how many ways can you change its form? How many different movements does it have?

27. With the finger-tip examine the surface of the teeth. How many teeth have you?

28. How many different kinds of teeth can you find in your mouth?

29. Compare your teeth as far as possible with the animals mentioned in (24). What variations?

MASTICATION OF FOOD.

1. Notice the movements made by the jaws of different animals in masticating their food. What are the movements of your own jaw? Is the movement always in the same direction?

2. Is the movement dependent upon the kind of food?

3. Do the teeth correspond in either arrangement or form with the movement of the jaws?

4. What organs keep the food between the teeth during the process of mastication?

5. What appears to be the particular function of the
tongue? How many movements has it?

6. What part do the front teeth play in mastication?
How are they adapted to their work? How many are
there that are alike? They are called *incisors*.

7. What appears to be the use of the teeth next to the
incisors on either side? In what animals are they prominent? Do you make any such use of yours? These are
canine teeth.

8. What use is made of the teeth behind the canine
teeth? How are they adapted to their work?

9. In comparing yourself with other animals that differ
from you in their food and mode of mastication, do you
find corresponding differences in the teeth?

10. The two teeth immediately behind the canine teeth
are called *bicuspids*, and the remaining ones are the
molars. How many teeth have you in all? The last
molar, or wisdom tooth, is not cut until much later than
the rest, usually between the ages of seventeen and
twenty-five years.

11. The parts of a tooth are the crown, which is that
portion exposed above the gums ; the root or fang, which
is embedded in the jaw ; and the neck, that part beneath
the gum, but not in the bony socket.

12. What teeth are most prominent in the dog and in
the cat ? In the squirrel ? Why the difference ?

13. What is the movement of the jaws when the incisors are employed ? The molars ?

14. Do the cat and the dog have the grinding
motion when using their back teeth ? What adaptation do you see between the movements of their jaws,

the character of their teeth, and the kind of food they eat?

15. Some of the lower animals show a curious and automatic regularity in the movements of the jaw in mastication. The cow in chewing her cud will move her jaw with great regularity from twenty-eight to thirty times before swallowing the mass thus ground up.

16. What reasons can you see for brushing the teeth? Should a toothpick be used? Never use a pin or metallic toothpick of any kind, as it is likely to injure the thin but very hard and brittle layer of enamel which covers the outside of the tooth. Children should be taught to cleanse their teeth regularly after meals as soon as they are able to manage a brush. People usually begin to pay serious attention to their teeth only after irreparable mischief has been wrought by neglect.

INSALIVATION AND SWALLOWING.

1. What further preparation for swallowing, beside being masticated, does the food undergo? Where does the moisture in the mouth come from?

2. By closing the teeth and drawing the tip of the tongue backward and forward, the fluid called saliva may be noticed collecting under the end of the tongue. This arises from two organs called salivary glands which lie under the tongue, and whose office it is to provide part of the fluid necessary to soften and partially dissolve and digest a portion of the food while it remains in the mouth. The fluid is conveyed from the glands by two tubes called ducts, one of which opens in each half of the under part of the tongue. These openings may be seen by looking into one's mouth, by means of a good

light and a mirror, by turning the tip of the tongue upward. They appear about the size of pin-holes. Near these two, other ducts open which come from similar glands located farther back under the tongue. By drawing the cheeks in between the teeth with a kind of a sucking motion, note the moisture which seems to come from the cheeks. Opposite the second molar teeth a duct opens in each cheek which leads from a gland located about midway betweed the ear and the angle of the lower jaw. These are called the parotid glands; those farthest back under the tongue are the submaxillary, and those in front, the sublingual glands.

3. How does the saliva differ from pure water? What use has it besides that of softening and dissolving the food?

4. When the food has been fully prepared for swallowing, to what point is it gathered? It is then called a *bolus*.

5. How is the bolus forced back out of the mouth? Note the position of the jaws during this act.

6. What part of the swallowing is beyond the control of the will?

7. What prevents the food from being crowded upward into the nasal passages behind the mouth? Notice the muscular curtain with the elongated uvula hanging down in the back part of the mouth. How does it help in swallowing?

8. On the side of the mouth in this region look for almond-shaped bodies called the *tonsils*. They secrete a slippery substance called mucus. Note also the red *pillars of the fauces* on the sides of the mouth at the entrance to the throat; these close in above the food and keep it going downward.

Botany.

This is the last of the winter months, according to the calendar, at least, and it should not be allowed to pass without giving the pupils opportunity to become familiar with the winter condition of plants. Twigs from different kinds of trees and of the same tree in different localities should be examined, with a view to ascertaining what per cent. of buds is killed. It should also be noticed whether the twigs themselves all survive alike. Unfortunately, in this latitude, a few mild days sometimes come in this month which coax the buds into unseasonable activity. These are then caught by later frosts, and the plant must fall back upon its reserve store. It should be noticed which trees and plants are thus most sensitive to the spring-like weather, and what ones are least, or not all affected by it.

1. Can you find out whether the buds are frozen through and through during the winter?

2. What is the location of those buds that have been killed, on the ends of the branches or near the trunk? A bud that has been killed may be easily recognized by its being brown or black in the center, while living buds are green.

3. Have you been able to find any twigs that are killed?

4. Can you tell whether the roots have been frozen or not?

5. Are the grass-blades killed in the winter? Are the

roots killed ?   Dig up some of the roots and find out the kind which some of the different grasses have.

6. Can you find any mosses that seem to be alive at this season ?

7. Look on the different sides of the trunks of trees for the green moss-like covering that sometimes may be seen there.

8. Examine some pine trees of different kinds ; did they shed any of their leaves in the fall ?

9. Are the leaves that remain on the trees living ? Can you see any regularity in their arrangement ?

10. Are the leaves grouped the same way in different kinds of pines ?

11. Notice the pitchy substance under the bark ; what is made from it ?

12. Find out how pitch, turpentine, rosin, and tar are produced.

Physics.

AIR.

A common and interesting application of the facts observed under this head last month may be found in the so-called suction pump. If a short piece of tubing from about a half to three-quarters of an inch bore can be obtained, a model can easily be constructed. The straight-sided Argand lamp chimney makes an excellent tube for this purpose. In this sized tube, the working of the valves may be seen. For these, two corks will be needed ; one tightly fitting the lower end and one passing smoothly into the tube. The latter may be made to fit as desired, by wrapping it with a string. Bore a small hole through the corks, and to the upper surface of each fasten by one edge a thin piece of leather large enough to cover the hole. This may be done by drawing a pin down through it and clinching it on the under side. The piston rod may be made by twisting together two wires, leaving them spread at one end, so that they may be passed through the cork, one on either side of the hole.

The Pump.

1. Why are the valves needed in a pump?

2. Will the pump work if the lower valve is placed some distance up the stock ? How high above the lower end may this valve be located ? Recall the experiment with the mercury last month to explain this.

3. What is the use of the piston ?

4. By what means does the water reach the spout of the pump after it passes through the piston valve? What kind of a lever is the pump handle ? In the force pump there is no valve in the piston, and the water is forced out by a downward movement of the piston through an opening between it and the lower valve. In the fire engine the water is thus forced into an air chamber by two such pumps, and to this the hose is attached. By what means is the water forced through the hose?

5. Can you see any advantages in forcing the water out in this way instead of lifting it as in the suction pump ?

6. What is the advantage of the air chamber? Recall the various properties of air studied in January.

7. Where should valves be placed in the force pump of the fire engine ?

8. Is the flow of water into the air chamber steady or intermittent ? Compare this with the flow from the nozzle of the hose ; can you account for the difference ?

The Siphon.

1. Bend a small glass tube similar to the one used in the January work in Physics (the same one will do) so that the two arms are of unequal length. Place the end of the shorter arm in a bottle of water ; apply the lips to the other end, and by suction start the flow of water through the tube.

2. Can you give a reason for the continuance of the flow ?

3. Reverse the ends and start the flow again ; does it continue?

4. Hold the tube in such a way that the ends shall be

at the same level and start the flow ; what is the result ?

5. What is the force that causes the water to begin flowing through the tube ?

6. Where is the force applied ?

7. Try tubes that have arms of different lengths ; with those having the same bore, what determines the rate of flow ?

8. What is the force applied which causes the flow to stop when the arms are of the same length ?

9. Where is this force applied ?   What is there to overcome this force when one arm of the tube is longer ?

10. The siphon in a modified form is much used in pumping water out of leaky boats.   A jet of steam is admitted at the elbow and forced out through one of the arms ; by doing this, water may be made to flow out through the short arm.   Can you explain why this is so ? Why not use the ordinary form of the siphon in pumping boats?

11. What will determine the greatest length that the short arm may be in the ordinary siphon ?

CAPILLARITY.

1. Examine closely the surface of water in a partly filled glass ; is it exactly level ?

2. Dip a small piece of glass into a vessel of water ; note the water in contact with the glass.   Color the water with a little red ink.

3. Hold two small plates of glass together along two of the edges so that the faces of the glass will be but slightly separated ; notice the water between the pieces of glass.

4. Cover the surfaces of a piece of glass with grease,

and hold upright in water ; is the water the same as before at the line of contact ?

5. Hold a glass tube o^f small bore, open at the end, upright in a vessel of water ; note the water inside the tube. Try tubes of very large and very small bore ; what difference between them ?

6. If mercury can be obtained, repeat the above experiments, using it in place of the water. What difference noted ?

7. When the glass surface is clean in the above experiments, does it become wet when immersed ?

8. Does it become wet when smeared with grease ? What difference noted at the line of contact in the two cases ?

9. Does the mercury wet the glass? Does it rise or fall at the point of contact ?

10. The water is said to rise in the small tubes in the above experiments by capillary attraction. Capillary is from the word *capillus*, meaning a hair. It is so named because water rises best in the slender hair-like tubes.

11. How do the conditions for capillary attraction differ from those which caused water to rise in tubes in previous experiments ?

12. Place one end of a string or strip of cloth in a goblet partly full of water, and allow the other end to hang over on the outside. Can you explain what takes place ? Is the rising of the water due to capillarity? Study carefully the conditions.

13. Place the end of a stick in a vessel of water. Can you explain why it becomes soaked ? Why does water in a cask prevent the hoops from becoming loose ?

14. How does the oil or alcohol in a lamp reach the upper end of the wick.

BUOYANCY OF LIQUIDS.

1. Tie a string to a small stone weighing about half a pound and note carefully the weight as it is suspended from the finger. Lower it into a vessel of water, and note the difference in weight. What reason can you assign for the difference?

2. Place an egg in a tumbler or bucket of water; does it swim or sink? Does it seem to have lost any weight?

3. Fill another tumbler with strong salt water, and pour it slowly into the one containing the egg. Can you account for the change in the position of the egg?

4. Half fill a tumbler with water, and then, by means of a tube reaching to the bottom, add brine until the tumbler is full. Drop the egg in cautiously; does it go to the bottom?

5. In what part of the tumbler is the brine? Why add it by means of a funnel or tube?

6. Suspend a small stone beneath one of the scale pans of a balance and by weights in the other pan balance it. Now hold it so that the stone is completely immersed in a vessel of water.

7. What is the force which causes the opposite scale pan to descend? How is the force applied?

8. How much weight must you add to the scale pan above the stone to make the two sides balance?

Each pupil may make a balance which will answer the purpose very well. Use a small stick about eight inches long for the beam. By means of three threads suspend from each end the scale pans. These may be made from a piece of tin two inches square by cutting it in one quarter of an inch at each corner, so that the edges may be turned up. The tin caps of small baking soda cans may be substituted. Drive pins down through the ends of the beam, and turn them up for hooks from which the pans may be suspended. Drive a pin upward through the middle of the beam by which the balance may be supported. Pass another pin through the bottom of one of the scale pans, and turn it up to form a hook from which the stone may be suspended. Balance the two pans by using fine sand. Small shot may be used for weights. Any druggist will determine the number of these to an ounce for you.

9. Fill a tumbler brimful of water and arrange it so that the overflow may be caught in another vessel. Suspend a small stone under the scale pan and balance it. Immerse it in the tumbler of water and balance it again. Weigh the overflow of water when the stone is completely immersed. How does the weight of the over-flow correspond with that necessary to balance the scales after the stone is immersed? Why is the weight obtained for the overflow likely to be somewhat inexact? Can you see from the experiment what the lifting power of water is?

10. The weight of any solid or liquid compared with the same bulk of water is its specific gravity.

Weigh a stone or other heavy body in the air, and then weigh it in water; the weight of what volume of water does its loss in the latter case represent? Recall the experiment performed in (9).

11. Compare the weight of the body in air with the weight of the volume of water found in (10). This will give its specific gravity.

12. Since tin is heavy enough to sink in water, why is it that a tin cup will float?

13. Will an iron pot float? If broken into fragments, will the pieces float?

14. How is it possible to build iron vessels that will bear heavy cargoes?

15. If a cup of mercury can be obtained, try to sink different bodies into it, such as stone, iron, etc. Can you explain why they float?

16. Weigh a small block of wood; drop it into a vessel brimful of water, so placed that the overflow may be caught and weighed as in (9). By means of a pin stuck into the block, push it down just beneath the surface.

17. Weigh the overflow and compare with the weight of the block; by comparing this with the result obtained in (9), can you explain why wood will float and iron or stone will sink?

PRESSURE OF LIQUIDS.

1. Take a tin fruit can, or one similar to it, and in one side make a vertical row of smooth holes an inch apart, each large enough to admit a large-sized knitting needle. Fit them with smooth pine plugs.

2. Fill the can with water and remove the upper plug; note the force of the jet and the distance the water is thrown out.

3. Fill again and remove the second plug. Repeat until the flow has been observed from each opening separately and from all at once.

4. From which opening is the water thrown farthest? Upon what does the distance that it is thrown depend?

5. Try the experiment again, using cans some of which have larger and others smaller diameter, but of the same height. The holes should be as nearly uniform in every respect as possible.

6. Repeat the experiment, using cans of different heights ; upon what does the force of the jet depend ?

7. Is the force of the jet affected by the volume of water in the can ?

8. What is the force which causes the water to issue in the jet ? In what directions is this force exerted ?

9. Cut a circular piece of cardboard an inch and a half in diameter ; drop it cautiously on the surface of a goblet of water. Press down upon this the end of a lamp chimney (a small one used for a night lamp will answer) and push the cardboard below the surface.

10. What holds the cardboard against the bottom of the chimney ? What must be the direction of the pressure ?

11. Pour water cautiously into the top of the chimney; when does the cardboard fall away from the chimney? How high is the column of water the pressure of which holds the cardboard in place in the first instance ?

12. Make a drawing of the vessel with the lamp-chimney and card pushed into it, and show by arrows the direction the lines of pressure must take to support the cardboard against the bottom.

13. Hold a cork so that it is half-way to the bottom of a goblet of water ; what is the height of the column of water that is pressing it downward ? What is the height of the column pressing it upward ? Why does it rise when you let go of it ? (Recall 17 under Buoyancy of Liquids.)

14. In the same way show why a stone, a piece of lead or iron, must sink ?

15. Under what conditions would a body remain suspended in the midst of a vessel of water ?

16. When you place your hand at the bottom of a

bucket of water, do you notice the weight of the water on top? Would you feel the weight if the bucket of water were set upon the top of your hand? How do the conditions in the last two experiments differ?

17. Why is it that fishes can live and can swim with ease in the water at great depths? Why do they become distended when brought to the surface?

Chemistry.

CARBON.

1. Hold a piece of glass or a plate over the flame of a burning candle close to the wick. What collects on the under side ?

2. Gather a little of the substance formed in (1) and shake well in a bottle or test tube of water; is it soluble ?

3. Take a small amount of sugar, half a teaspoonful, and heat it in a shallow dish or spoon. Examine closely the charred mass; is it sugar ? While the sugar is heating, without burning with a flame, hold a cold glass or porcelain plate over it; what gathers on the surface?

4. What kind of change has taken place ? Is the charred substance soluble ?

5. Instead of the sugar, use a small piece of meat; what result is obtained?

6. Set fire to a piece of wood ; when well ablaze extinguish, and notice the blackened end.

7. Take a small wad of paper, and heat it for some time in a test tube without allowing it to blaze; what kind of substance remains ?

8. Coarsely powder a small lump of soft coal and half fill a common clay pipe. Cover the mouth of the bowl with soft clay (plaster of paris is better) and place it in the flame of the lamp upon some support, with the stem projecting upward.

9. Watch the end of the stem and from time to time apply a lighted taper.

10. Can you tell what is produced from the coal within the pipe bowl ? Note the odor at the end of the stem.

11. What does the flame remind you of ?

12. When the flame dies out, remove the lamp and allow the bowl to cool. Then remove the clay and examine the contents.

13. Has there been a change in the coal? Compare what you find within the pipe with the coal with which you began.

14. Has it burned to ashes? Does it remind you of anything that you have examined in a previous month ? (See Mineralogy for November.) It is in a manner similar to this that coke is manufactured on a large scale. Very large ovens are constructed and are lined with fire-brick. There is one opening in the top through which the oven is charged, and another at the side through which the coke is withdrawn. After the coal has burned for several hours, both openings are closed and the burning is completed without contact with air. The coke is then withdrawn through the opening in the side, and the oven is recharged. The heat of the oven is now sufficient to start the burning without resorting to any other means. The country blacksmith makes his own coke usually on the open forge, but it is neither so easily nor so well made as it is in the closed oven.

15. Where is the great coke-producing region of the United States ? What is coke used for?

16. As directed above, heat a pipe half filled with small bits of oak wood ; can you get a flame at the end of the pipe stem ?

17. How does what remains in the pipe differ from the original wood ?

Wood charcoal is made on a large scale by placing sticks of wood in a compact pile which is covered first with a layer of straw and then with earth and turf. Small holes are left at the bottom and also one at the top. Through the latter the pile is ignited, and when the burning is well started the opening at the top is closed, and the pile is allowed to smolder for several days or weeks, according to its size. Finally the holes at the bottom are closed ; after the fire goes out the pile is uncovered, and the wood is found in much the same condition that you found it in the pipe.

18. Wet a small wad of paper with ammonia and drop it into a clean bottle ; when the odor of ammonia is strong in the bottle, remove the paper and drop in some powdered charcoal. Cork and shake for a few minutes and note the odor. Can you account for the disappearance of the ammonia gas after the bottle has stood for some time ? The charcoal should either be fresh or else heated red-hot and cooled under a glass just before placing in the bottle of ammonia gas.

19. Fold a small-sized circle of filter paper and place it in a funnel. Fill it two-thirds full of powdered charcoal. Pour upon this a dilute solution of indigo ; how has it been changed by passing through the charcoal ? Try some vinegar instead of the indigo solution. Small filters ready cut are very cheap, and may be obtained from any druggist. Fold it first in halves, then in quarters, then in eighths. Press the creases with the thumb nail, but avoid touching the filter between them. Open it up and drop the pointed end into the funnel. Pour a gentle stream of water into the filter, and see that it adheres closely to

the inner surface of the funnel. It is then ready for use.

20. Can you see any reason why charcoal is used in filters and as a disinfectant?

21. The charcoal obtained in the foregoing experiments, is, as was learned in Mineralogy for November, carbon. It is not, however, very pure. It is known as one of the chemical elements ; that is, thus far, no one has been able to separate it into simpler parts. Other forms of carbon are the diamond (which is crystallized carbon), soot, lamp-black, coke, animal charcoal, graphite, and mineral coal. The formation of all of these except the diamond, graphite, and coal, is somewhat familiar to us. It will be remembered that in January we worked out the history of a fossil fern-leaf which was found imbedded in coal. Further search will show that the coal contains traces not only of many ferns, but the remains of large trees and stumps also. In fact the whole coal seam has been shown to be the remains of a vast bed of vegetation that was buried as the fossil fern was, and with it, long ages ago. Underneath is the layer of clay from which the great forest of plants grew. Beneath the sediment that settled upon it, the vegetable mass was gradually transformed into coal. Where the covering was porous and the gases that were formed escaped, the anthracite was formed ; where the gases were retained bituminous coal was the result. It is interesting to consider to what extent carbon enters into all living things. The story of how it does so, though, must be reserved for a future lesson.

22. Recall experiment (15) under Chemistry for December ; what was the substance in the jar after the charcoal or carbon was burned in it? You will remember that a lighted taper would not then burn in it, although it did

burn very freely in the gas O, which is another chemical element.

23. What became of the O when the charcoal was burned in it ? What became of the charcoal or carbon?

24. Where did the new substance come from ? Was it a solid or a gas? How did it differ from O ? How did it differ from C (carbon)? The new substance thus formed by the burning (which was nothing but the two substances forming a union) is carbon dioxide gas (CO_2). Recall the experiments in Chemistry for November by which this substance was obtained. The explanation of its formation then will be given at another time.

Meteorology.

1. Has the temperature increased or diminished since December ? Compare February with January.

2. Is the temperature increasing or diminishing at present ?

3. How does the temperature now compare with that of a previous month in which the days were about the same length as those in February ?

4. Compare the rate of variation in temperature this month with that of December and January ?

5. What is the direction of the prevailing wind ? Has it been a cold or a warm one ?

6. What wind has preceded rain or snow storms ?

7. Is there any uniformity in the veering of the wind during a storm ? Can you see a reason for this ? Consult a signal service map ?

8. How does the character of a rain in this month differ from one in the summer time ?

9. How does the amount of fogginess compare with that of previous months ? When do they appear, if at all ?

10. At what temperature has most of the snow fallen ?

11. Has rain or snow been most frequent this month ?

12. What winds have been accompanied by a thaw ?

STUDY OF THE WEATHER BUREAU MAPS.

13. Can you see any relation in position or as cause and effect between the Low Areas and the place of heaviest rainfall ?

14. Do the Low Areas lie chiefly in the same region which they occupied in previous months?

15. In what quarter of the country have most of the great storms originated this month? Compare with last month.

16. Which way do the storms travel? Have there been rain and snow at the same time in different parts of any one storm?

17. Is there any uniformity in the direction of the wind in these great storms?

18. What is the direction of the winds with respect to the High Area?

19. Trace a line through the most southern points touched by the zero isotherm. How does its position compare with that of last month?

20. In the same way trace the snow line, and compare with January.

Astronomy.

From the almanac it will be learned that Mercury wil¹ appear as morning star February 6.* This planet is distant from the sun about thirty-five millions of miles (see September), and has a diameter one-third that of the earth. Its time of revolution is about eighty-eight days.

With objects to represent the sun, Mercury, and the earth, it will be interesting to study the relative position of the three bodies at different times during the year. A diagram on the blackboard should also be used, and the position of the planets Mercury, Venus, and the earth, as seen at this season, should be marked as accurately as possible. New figures should be added each month which will show how their positions are changing.

1. Why is it that Mercury changes from morning to evening star more frequently than Venus?

2. Why is it seen as either morning or evening star only for a comparatively short period?

3. With Mercury, Venus, and the earth on the same side of the sun, and in a straight line with it, what will be their positions at the end of one month? At the end of Mercury's year?

4. Will Mercury ever be visible at midnight?

5. Show what the relative position of the earth, sun, and Mercury is when the latter is evening star. When it is morning star.

6. Can you find out by studying the rate of motion of

---

* True of the year 1891.

each planet how often it will be either a morning or an evening star during a year ?

7. In which of the preceding months did the day's length correspond to that of this month ?

8. The length of the noon shadow on the measure at the present time corresponds with what previous month?

9. During which of the preceding months did the sun rise and set at about the same points on the horizon that it does now ?

10. Can you explain why at two different seasons there should be the correspondence noticed in the observations suggested by the last three questions ? Try to show this by using the globe or by blackboard diagrams.

11. Is the rate of variation in the day's length increasing or diminishing this month?

12. Compare the day's length at Boston or New York with that at New Orleans ; why should there be the difference noted ? Most almanacs give the length of day at all of these places.

13. Is it the latitude or longitude that affects the day's length ?

14. Is the day increasing in length at both places at the same rate ? Why does the rate differ?

15. Is the difference in the rate of variation uniform throughout the month ?

16. Can you by any observation of the heavenly bodies tell in what direction the earth moves in its orbit ?

17. Note the position of some conspicuous constellation, as Orion, at a certain hour, say eight o'clock in the evening. Observe its position during the month, *at the same hour ;* is it always the same ? Explain.

18. Constellations.—In addition to those mentioned last month, Leo, Cancer, Canis Minor, and Canis Major may be given. See Clarke's How to Find the Stars.

Geography.

EURO-ASIA. RELIEF AND DRAINAGE.

The structure of this great land mass does not present the same simplicity that is noticeable in the double continent of the New World. By beginning with a consideration of the rivers, their size, and their direction of flow, a fair conception of the principal features of relief may be obtained. The many strong contrasts between the Old World and the New World which are due to the difference in direction and position of the great highlands should be carefully considered. The pupils should in every case work out the problems presented by means of map modeling and by use of the best physical maps that can be procured for reference. The study should be accompanied by stories and narratives that will keep the conception of the pupil from being narrowed down to the area of sand in the modeling pan before him. This will not be the case if sufficient time be taken to work in such pictures of the countries as may be obtained from the many good books of travel of the present time, and from the many excellent magazine articles of a similar kind. Too much haste on the part of the teacher is a common fault with many, and it is a most serious one. The conception of a continent is too vast in its scope to be obtained without long and careful study.

1. After modeling the outline of the land mass of Euro-Asia, notice the direction of the chief highland region. What contrast does it present with the corresponding great highlands of America ?

2. Note its position in the land mass ; in this respect does it present similarity or contrast with the New World highlands ?

3. What is the direction of the great slope of the continent ? Note the direction of the longest rivers.

4. What ocean receives the drainage of the greater part of the continent ? Compare this with the New World.

5. Can you understand why the drainage waters are not gathered into a very few great river systems, as in North and South America ?

6. On which side of the great highlands are the greater river systems? Why is it so ?

7. North of the great highlands, do the rivers indicate any secondary water-partings ?

8. Contrast the formation of river systems on the opposite sides of the great highlands. To what is the difference due ?

9. Note the direction of the rivers west of the Ural Mountains ; what does it indicate as to the surface of northeastern Europe ? From what other region do European rivers flow ?

10. What do the rivers on either side of the Ural Mountains indicate as to the character of this ridge? ·

11. From the general direction of the rivers, can you locate the highest region of the great highlands ?

12. Where are the greatest depressions within the continental outlines ?

13. Are there any rivers in Asia that do not reach the sea ? Why is this ?

14. In how many directions do the largest Asiatic rivers flow ? How many large rivers in each group ? Note those on the north, the Obi, the Yenisei and the Lena ; on the east the Amoor, the Hoang-ho and the Yang-tse-kiang ; the Mekong and the Irawaddy on the southeast ; the Brahmapootra, the Ganges and the Indus on the south, and the Amoo Daria and Sir Daria flowing into the Aral sea on the west.

15. Contrast this grouping of the rivers with those of the New World ; what is the cause of the difference ?

16. What effect does the *position* of the highlands have upon the development of Asia ? Why is the effect less marked in Europe ?

17. What effect does the *direction* of the highlands have upon the development of the continent ? Contrast it in this respect with the American continents.

18. How does the direction in which the great rivers flow affect their value to man ?

19. Compare the great plateaus of Euro-Asia with those of the New World, as to their relation to the great mountain system.

20. Compare the position of the highest mountain peaks of Euro-Asia in the great highlands with these in the great highlands of the Americas.

BOOKS FOR REFERENCE. Guyot's Physical Geography. Ritter's Comparative Geography.

Geology.

Last month an attempt was made to trace the history of a fossil plant. In many places the fossil remains of animals are more abundant, and they are certainly of equal interest. There are few schools in which at least some of the pupils have not found fossil animals, or parts of them, and they may be made available for the whole school. ˙The history of such fossils must be worked out along much the same line as that followed with the plant, but the different environment requires a little modification of treatment.

The way in which animal and plant remains become buried beneath the cloud of sediment that is being continually thrown down on the floor of seas and lakes may be illustrated by stirring into a jar of water a quantity of fine mud or sand and then dropping into it bones, shells, water-soaked sticks, leaves, etc. When the silt has settled, pour off the water and allow the sediment to become a dry cake. Then, by cutting or breaking it, the bones, etc., will be found to be in a tightly-fitting mold. Most pupils have noticed how sticks, etc., are buried by every little stream in its sand bars and in the mud along its banks.

1. Continue the observations made last month as to the depth to which the ground is frozen. Is it frozen to a greater depth than it was then?

2. If it is possible to visit a quarry or an exposed ledge

of rock, notice whether the frost is causing it to crumble. Can you find any rocks that have been split by freezing?

3. Notice the exposed sides of ditches or hillsides; can you see any effects of freezing? Does vegetation increase or diminish the effects of frost in such places?

4. Have you ever found, while in the woods or elsewhere, the remains of animals that have died? What do you think must become of these after a time?

5. What animals have you found thus in a state of decay? What parts were missing? What parts will last longest? Have you ever found insects in this condition? Have you ever found worms or birds?

6. Before the neighborhood where you live was settled, do you know what wild animals lived there? What became of their bodies after death? Have you ever found their bones?

7. Do you know of animals that bury their dead? Think of some of the accidents that might cause an animal to be covered with earth soon after death. Which would be more favorable, a forest or desert?

8. Compare the chances of a land animal with those of one living in the sea for being accidentally buried soon after death? Which is more likely to be eaten by some other animal?

9. Which kind of animal, land or water, is likely to decay the more rapidly? Which one has in its body the most material that will tend to resist decay? What are such parts?

10. Have you ever found traces of any kind of the remains of an animal?

11. What are direct proofs you have that such traces are the marks of a once living animal?

12. Can you tell whether it was a land or a water ani-

mal ?   Of which class are the remains most abundant ?
Why ?

13. What animal living now does it most resemble ?

14. If it be the remains of a water animal, can you
imagine something as to what its surroundings must have
been ?   Did it live in sea, lake, or river ?   In salt or fresh
water ?

15. Can you tell whether it lived in deep or shallow
water ?   Was it clear or muddy ?   What other evidence
is there that water once covered the region where it was
found ?

16. Can you tell what range of temperature the water
may have had ?

17. Did it eat ?   If so, what must have been its food ?

18. Did the animal walk, swim, crawl, or was it fixed ?

19. Did it have an inside skeleton or an outside shell ?

20. What were the soft parts of the body ?

21. Could it see and hear ?   Do you see anything
which would show whether it had a voice or the power of
making a noise ?

22. Can you tell whether there were many more animals like this one that lived at the same time ?   What
way could you prove this ?

23. Have you any means of knowing how long the animals lived ?   Have you any means of knowing how long
the water may have covered the region where this animal lived before it was born ?   How would you look for
evidence of this kind ?

24. Can you tell whether it lay very long before it became covered ?

25. By what process do you think it was covered ?

26. Was it covered gradually or suddenly ?   By fine
or coarse material ?

27. Do you have in the fossil the real substance of the animal tissues?

28. If the animal tissues are not present, can you find any evidence as to whether their decay was slow or rapid?

29. How must the stony substance which took the place of the tissues have been deposited there? Is it likely it was deposited there before the animal was completely buried?

30. Is there any way of finding out whether the water remained long in the region where it was buried? What would the amount of rock and earth above the stratum in which the fossil was found indicate?

31. Is there any way by which you could determine whether or not the sea revisited the region where the fossil was found after leaving it the first time?

32. Suppose fossil plants were to be found in strata or layers some distance above the stratum where the fossil animal was found; what chapter in the history of the region would that unlock?

33. When the water this last time left the place where the fossil was found, is there any reason to believe that the surface was higher than it is now?

34. Can you find any evidence as to why the water left the locality where the fossil was found? Was the ground uplifted?

35. If the ground was uplifted, was the movement slow and gradual or rapid and violent?

36. What changes did the soft material in which the remains of the animal were embedded undergo in the course of time?

37. Was the substance of the rock melted or affected by great heat after the animal was entombed?

38. Can you think of any conditions which surround animal life at present that must have surrounded this fossil animal while living ?

39. Can you think of any conditions present now which must have been absent at that time ? Which may have been absent ?

40. If the fossil you have is that of a land animal, can you tell anything of its habits ? Did it likely live on animal or vegetable food ? What part of its body that could be preserved, would be the most useful in answering this question ?

41. Was it warmer or cooler than now when it lived ?

42. In what respects must the history of a land fossil differ from that of an animal that lived in the water ?

43. If animals like those whose fossil remains have been examined do not exist now, can you assign any reason for the race dying out ?

44. What natural change in conditions can you imagine that might take place, which would tend to cause certain of our living species of animals to die out *gradually*, not *suddenly* ?

45. What slight change would affect the earthworms ? What would affect birds ? What would affect fishes ?

46. What artificial causes are removing animals from the earth ?

47. What classes of animals now living will probably never become fossilized ? Is it possible that such animals may have existed when the fossil you have examined lived ?

48. Do you think it would be possible for soft animals now living, such as earthworms, to leave any traces of their existence as fossils ?

49. From what you have studied about fossils, do you think fossilization of animals and plants is the rule or exception after death?

BOOK FOR REFERENCE.   Humboldt Library : No. 33, Vignettes from Nature, chap. viii.

Mineralogy.

Last month certain stones were examined, some of whose properties were learned by means of acids. Some additional facts may be learned this month about these same stones by burning or roasting them in the fire.

1. Hold a small piece of limestone or marble in the flame of the lamp till red hot clear through. It may be done by using pincers or by means of a wire wrapped around it. Lay aside till cool and moisten with water; what change takes place after some little time? The rapidity of the change depends upon the variety of limestone used.

2. What is thus formed? What use is made of the substance thus obtained? When sand is added and the mixture is wet, the lime and the silica of the sand unite and form a strong cement.

3. In a similar manner burn a piece of gypsum; when cool add a little water and allow it to stand a few minutes. What is the nature of the substance found? Have you seen it before? For what is it used? Why is it called plaster of Paris?

4. Make a small model of something of the clay used in January and let it dry partially. Then burn it thoroughly in the flame of the lamp; what change is produced?

5. In what does the value of clay for manufacturing purposes consist? What things are made from it? Where is it found? Pure clay is white, but various impurities impart different colors to it when burned. The

257

redness of bricks is due to the presence of iron oxide, a compound of iron and oxygen.

6. Treat in the same way the silicious stones that were used in January ; compare the results with those obtained above.

7. Make a full comparison of the two classes of stones examined during January and February.

Zoology.

This month is, perhaps, the best one of the entire year in which to commence the study of outdoor life. One may now start, as it were, at the very beginning, and for a time, if his wits be sharp, keep pace with the advancing season as it spreads out on every hand. Every bright, warm day, though it be wedged in between wintry ones, is pregnant with hope to all things that live, and the natural interest of the pupils should be properly encouraged. Discouragement, however, is all too easy, and a fruitful source of it is in much of the science reading of the schools. A great deal of this is devoted to the so-called " wonders " of nature, and when the pupil fails to see anything of the kind about him, he is apt to conclude that he is either not a good observer or that he is in a poor locality.

Two things should be kept clearly in mind : first, that what is read in any one book is not the result of *one* man's observations alone, but, usually, that of very many people whose successive lives have covered, perhaps, hundreds of years ; and second, that the truly wonderful things in nature are rarely the violent ones. Not the flood, the tornado, the lightning, but rather the gentle rain, the soft breeze, and the mild but life-giving sunbeam, have made the earth what it is.

No one locality presents *all* of the interesting things that may be studied in nature ; it is equally true that no locality is entirely void of all of them. It may be said that every region has some feature that will make it distinctively an interesting place of study.   To nature's students her treasures are equally divided, and it should be the aim of the teacher to have the pupils become interested in the things at their feet.   If they can find nothing there worthy of their study, they will probably fail in their search wherever they go.

The pupils should be impressed with the necessity of bestowing great care upon the descriptions which they prepare of the things they observe.   To do this requires no little skill on the part of the teacher.   If a minutely detailed description is insisted upon with beginners, the work becomes tiresome, because it is really beyond their powers of observation, and it is therefore non-educative. What is meant is merely this : whatever is really seen, and attempted in the description, should be clearly defined.   For example, if the color of a bird is gray, it should be stated gray, and not black or brown ; or, if it is said that a bird walks on the ground, it should mean " walk," and not hop.   Pupils are usually anxious to know the names of birds and other animals which they have seen.   Even though the teacher may know the name perfectly well from an imperfect description, it should be a rule (to which, of course, there may be judicious exceptions), that the pupil must give a description sufficiently accurate to enable any one to recognize it at sight, if he be familiar with the terms used.   A pupil who does not have sufficient interest and enterprise to do that much work for the sake of the name he desires, would be very little benefited if it were given him outright.   He must feel from the first that he will not be permitted to get something for nothing ; that if he would have a return he must first make an investment.

This month a calendar should be provided in which the
pupils can record their observations as the season advances. It should be large enough to admit of the record
being made without crowding, and the writing should be
in a clear, bold hand. As a convenient form, the following model is suggested. If a frame with glass be provided, with a hinged back, it will be kept cleaner, and
will present a neater appearance. In this may be recorded the times of the return of birds, the first flowers,
etc.

NATURAL HISTORY CALENDAR.
189—.

OBSERVATION.	DATE.	PLACE.	BY WHOM.	REMARKS.

GENERAL OBSERVATIONS.

1. Does animal life, this month, give any indications of
returning spring?

2. Have you noticed any frogs, toads, or other animals
that hibernate during the winter? Do they show any
effects of their long sleep and fast?

3. Have any of the birds which migrated last spring
returned? Have any of the birds which visit us during
the winter disappeared?

4. Do the returning birds come in flocks, in pairs, or
singly? Can you tell whether the first ones that come
are the young or the old birds?

5. Do the males or females come first?   What do
these birds do if overtaken by a cold snap?

6. What is the food of the birds that return earliest?

7. Do they immediately begin nest-building?   Can
you tell whether or not they repair the old nests?

8. What are the most serious dangers that threaten the
birds that first return?

9. Do the returning birds seem to be as numerous as
those that migrated last fall?

10. Have they changed their plumage?   Do the birds
sing?

11. What kinds of insects, if any, are abroad this
month?   Study their habits.   Where do they live?

12. Upon what do they depend for food?   In what
way are they adapted to getting it?

13. Are they the prey of any other animals?   Upon
what do they rely for safety, defense, concealment, or
flight?

14. Examine some of the cocoons that were spun last
fall, and may now be easily seen upon twigs of trees and
bushes; are there any signs of life about them?

15. Observe some of the ant-hills, or other haunts of
ants, that were noticed last fall; are there any signs of
activity?

16. Have you seen any of the work of earthworms
this spring?   Can you find any near the surface?

THE CIRCULATION.

1. Place two fingers of the left hand over the region
of the pulse, in the wrist of the right arm, and count
the pulsations.   Take the average per minute for five
minutes.

2. Place the fingers in the region of the temples, a lit-

tle in front of and above the ear, and count the pulsations felt there. Compare with the number felt in the
wrist.

3. Rise, and count again in a standing position.

4. Take vigorous exercise of some kind for a minute,
and count again. Place the fingers about the middle of
the chest, a little to the left of the breast-bone ; can you
notice pulsations there ?

5. Do you notice any correspondence between the pulsations of the chest and the wrist ? Between those of
the wrist, temples, and chest ?

6. When were the pulsations slowest? When most
rapid ?

7. Does the number of respirations increase with vigorous exercise ?

8. The pulsations felt in the chest are due to the alternate contraction and expansion of the heart. Each
contraction forces a quantity of blood out into a set of
slightly elastic tubes called arteries. These are distended each time they receive the blood, and in consequence a pulsation is felt wherever the artery lies near the
surface.

9. Cross the legs so that one knee rests over the
other ; notice the toe of the foot uppermost ; can you
explain why it cannot be held perfectly still ?

10. From your own observations, can you tell how
exercise affects the blood-flow ?

11. What effect has violent exercise upon the appearance of one's face ? Can you explain this ?

After passing through the arteries, the blood enters a
dense network of very minute tubes called capillaries.
While the blood passes through the capillaries, important
transfers take place. The nutriment, digested in the

alimentary canal, and received into the circulation by
the capillaries and other absorbent vessels which lie in
its walls, now passes out to renew the tissues by soaking
through the walls of these minute vessels. At the same
time, waste materials, dissolved in the fluids which bathe
the tissues, soak through the walls into the blood, and
are carried to the organs of excretion—the lungs, kid-
neys, and skin. How do we know that the blood circu-
lates? This is by no means an easy question, or it
would not have taken so many centuries for wise
men to find out the fact. Two hundred and fifty
years ago it was not only unknown, but the idea was
ridiculed.

12. Note the blue veins lying just under the skin;
have you any proof that blood is flowing through them?
Which direction?

13. Hold the hand loosely downward and shake it
gently; how do the veins change in appearance?

14. Hold the hands above the head, and shake them in
the same way; what difference is noticed?

15. While holding the hands downward as in (12),
press with a finger on a vein, and slip it toward the fingers; note carefully the appearance where the veins fork.
Small pocket-like valves are placed here to prevent a
backward flow of blood. Can you tell in which direction
they prevent the blood flow?

16. From the capillaries (see 10) the blood passes
through the veins to the right half of the heart, and
thence to the lungs, where it enters the capillaries of
these organs. (See Respiration.) From the lungs, the
blood returns to the heart, the left half, and is forced out
into the arteries again, which carry it to the system.

17. Wrap a string tightly around a finger about an

inch from the end ; can you tell why it swells up and changes color?

18. With a pin, or needle, make a slight prick through the skin, and draw a large drop of blood. This operation is not painful in the least.

19. Is the blood perfectly fluid?

20. Do not disturb it for some time, but closely observe any changes that may take place.

21. Note the clot that forms ; does the entire drop become solid ?

22. The matter that becomes solid in the clot is called *fibrin ;* the part that remains liquid is the *serum.* How does the serum differ in appearance from the blood ?

23. If the drop is large enough, transfer the clot to a clean piece of glass, and move it about with a pin in a little clean water ; does any of it wash away? In this way the solid fibrin may be separated from the red coloring bodies of the blood called corpuscles.

24. A large quantity of fibrin may be easily obtained thus : Catch a basin of blood in a butcher shop from a freshly killed animal, and with a bundle of twigs or wires whip it vigorously for a few minutes. The fibrin will collect in a stringy mass on the sticks from which it must be removed, and then thoroughly washed until freed from the red corpuscles. This may then be preserved indefinitely in alcohol for class use.

25. Is the clotting of blood of any importance to animals?

26. What effect does a brisk rubbing of the surface of the body have upon the circulation ?

27. How does a hot bath affect the circulation ? How does cold water affect it ?

28. In case of headache from over-study, which would be more apt to afford relief, a hot or a cold foot-bath? Why?

29. Why will cold water sometimes relieve a headache, and at other times hot water?

30. What animals can you name that you are sure have red blood? Do you know of any without it?

31. Examine the pulse of a young child, and also that of an old person; what differences do you notice? Compare with your own.

32. Compare your own pulse with that of your friend's, of about the same age; note both the rapidity and strength of the beat. At first you may not be able to detect any difference, but a practiced physician would probably find no two exactly alike.

33. Place the ear near the body of a dog; can you locate the heart? Does the rate of beating depend upon the size of the animal?

34. In the same way examine a cat, a horse, a cow, or any other animal you may have opportunity to observe.

The time has come when every teacher must make a demand upon his school board for a microscope for his school. No similar outlay will give the teacher such a vast increase in power to interest and instruct his pupils. Its use, within the past few years, has revolutionized our notions concerning the nature of most, if not all diseases, and it has done more to place the practice of medicine upon a scientific basis than anything else since the demonstrations of Harvey. Without its use it is absolutely impossible for the pupils to get any but the most vague conceptions of the extreme delicacy of those parts of the body that are concerned directly in the vital processes, and consequently need the greatest care.

Believing, therefore, that before the usefulness of this book is outlived, very many teachers will have one at their command, the following directions for showing the circulation of the blood are given. The manipulation of the microscope for school purposes can be learned in ten minutes from a book that is generally sent with the outfit, and no teacher should hesitate because he has had no previous instruction.

(*a*) Procure a small tadpole, and place it under a wet cloth on a strip of glass. Allow the end of its tail to project, and cover it with another thin piece of glass. Keep moist, and examine with an inch, three-quarter, or a half-inch objective. This observation is of historic interest. About two hundred and twenty-five years ago, by this means, the circulation of the blood became a demonstrated fact. This occurred ten years after Harvey's death.

(*b*) Procure a small water-newt (lizards the children will call them), having external fringe-like gills near the mouth. Place in a watch-glass of water, and, as he lies still, watch the pulsating currents through the looped vessels in the gills. It is indescribably beautiful. A *very young* tadpole will do as well for the purpose..

(*c*) Allow a hen to sit upon some eggs for four or five days. Perforate with a pin the large end of one of them. Break away the shell from the *upper* side, making a hole as large as possible without disturbing the contents. Remove the membrane and examine the delicate network of blood vessels that is exposed. Use direct light from above. Look for the pulsating heart. It is safe to leave the description of this beautiful sight to the observer.

(*d*) Procure a live frog and wrap it in a wet cloth, exposing one hind foot. Tie it to a thin strip of wood three inches wide. By means of thread tied to the toes, spread them so that the web will be somewhat stretched, and then fasten it over a hole in the board, that the light may be reflected upward through it from a mirror. Keep moist. This is a little more difficult to manage than those given above.

(*e*) In the instances above given the blood will appear colored. Procure a small spider with semi-transparent legs. Confine it lightly between two glass slips. You will be able to follow a single corpuscle clear down his leg to his "toes" and back again. It looks like a pebble being rolled and pitched along by a current. Can you detect color in the blood?

(*f*) A little later in the spring procure a very young crawfish. You can hardly fail to find a mother "craw" with hundreds of the little fellows clinging to her swimmerets. Confine him very carefully as directed above, and examine. You can see the corpuscles chasing each other all through the body, legs, and antennæ or feelers. A marvelous thing to behold!

REFERENCE. Humboldt Library : No. 48, Life in Nature.

Botany.

During this month the pupils should be alert for the first evidences of spring that appear in plants. If the observations indicated in the previous months have been made, they will be ready to notice the earliest changes that occur. The character and tendency of the lessons should be to lead the pupils in the end to a thoughtful consideration of nature's great miracle wrought in this spring-time renewal of life. The opening of a bud is a matter of common observation, and yet it cannot be said to be a simple or commonplace thing. It is the result of causes both near and remote, many of which are apt to escape unnoticed. The opening of the buds and the sprouting seeds that may soon be seen are a verification anew of every law in nature's code. The persistence for ages of certain plants, cultivated and wild, in different latitudes, furnishes strong proof of the uniformity of these laws in their operation. The distribution of the vine, olive and fig, for example, in Europe, would indicate that the climate has remained almost absolutely un-changed for a great length of time. It is said that a change of one-half of a degree in the mean annual tem-perature would seriously affect the growth of these plants, and render their cultivation difficult, perhaps im-possible, in regions where they now flourish. There could hardly be a finer illustration, either of the sensi-tiveness of the plants to their environment, or of the marvelous balance among those conditions which compose it.

The observations made on the waking plant should be accurate and systematic, within the capacity of the pupils, and a record of the changes ought to be kept. Each pupil should be required to select a tree conveniently located for daily study. In connection with this, a study of the wood, bark, mode of branching, etc., may be pursued before the buds are far enough advanced to require much attention.

1. Make a drawing of the tree selected for study, being careful to have the different parts in proper proportion.

2. Is the general figure of the tree symmetrical, as you view it from all sides?

3. Can you notice any difference between the north and the south sides? Between the east and the west sides?

4. Do trees that grow in the woods modify or change each other in shape?

5. Can you tell what determines the height above ground at which a tree begins to branch? Compare trees that are isolated with those of the same kind in forests.

6. What variation do you notice in the shapes of the tops of different trees?

7. What seems to determine the shape of the top? Compare the shape of a pine tree with that of an apple tree; all stems like the former are called *excurrent*, and all like the latter are *deliquescent*. Excurrent means, literally, running out; deliquescent means melting or dissolving; can you see the force of these meanings when the terms are applied to tree tops?

8. What peculiarities of growth give rise to these two forms of tree-tops?

9. Woody plants fifteen or twenty feet in height, or under, are called *shrubs;* above this height, trees. Will all shrubs become trees if allowed to grow?

10. Can you by examination determine the extent to which the roots of a tree spread? Compare with the spread of the top.

11. The main stem or trunk of a tree, and the root growing straight downward, are sometimes called the axis of the plant. The stem is the ascending, and the roots the descending axis. Is there a clearly marked plane of division between the ascending and descending parts?

12. Procure a piece of a branch two or three inches in diameter, and make a study of the wood. Can you tell in what part of the branch the oldest wood is to be found? When is the new wood added?

13. Make two drawings, one of a cross, and the other of a longitudinal section.

14. The wood may usually be distinguished as heart-wood, or *duramen;* and sap-wood, or *alburnum.* Can you distinguish the two kinds in your specimen? What are the differences between them?

15. What causes the circular markings that may be seen in a cross section? Are they alike on all sides of the branch? What will affect the thickness of the rings? Compare the upper and lower halves of a branch. The north and south sides of the stump of a tree. Which ring was formed last? Notice the soft spongy sub-stance in the center of the twig called pith; what is the shape of a cross section of the pith-tube? How does it differ from the wood? Split a twig care-

fully out to the terminal bud; does the pith reach the bud?

16. Notice any radial markings that may be seen in a twig; does any one cross more than one ring? Are they found in the bark? These lines are called *medullary rays*.

17. Split the twig, and try to discover the structure of the medullary rays. Compare the wood found in the rays with that about them.

18. Can you see these rays in any of the articles of furniture about you? How must the wood be cut to show them to advantage? How do painters imitate their appearance?

19. Can you see any pores in the wood? Wet one end of a dry piece, and try to blow through it from the other; is there any evidence that the air passes through? Are the pores openings into continuous tubes?

20. Compare the bark on the trunk of the tree with that found on the twigs; are there the same layers in both? What happens if the bark be removed down to the wood?

21. How does the bark differ from the wood? How is it joined to it? Is there a distinct division between them?

22. On the twigs, the layers usually found are the *cortex*, or *cortical layer*, which is the dark outer covering; the *green layer* immediately under it, and the *liber* next the wood. Are these all present in the older twigs and in the tree trunk? Find out why the name liber is given to one layer? What use is made of the cortical layer in some trees?

23. The specks often to be found in the bark of twigs

are called lenticels; how are they formed? Is their arrangement regular?

24. Make a careful examination of the entire tree this
month, and be ready to note the first changes that occur
in the spring.

Physics.

LIGHT.

In beginning the study of light, it is of first importance that an extended series of simple experiments be
devised which will clearly illustrate the fundamental
principles of the subject. The observations and experiments may be made in such a way as to arouse the deepest interest on the part of the pupil, and the best thought
of which he is capable. The principles underlying the
subject are comparatively few, and may be stated in the
simplest language ; but their application is so varied and
far-reaching that nothing but a great abundance of simple
illustrative experiments in the beginning will ever make
them clear. Teachers, here, if anywhere, are apt to make
the fatal mistake of supposing that a glib statement of a
principle implies mental possession of the concept it
embodies. Space will not admit of a sufficient number
of observations and experiments being described, in this
connection, to make the subject clear ; but such have
been selected as, it is believed, will best indicate to the
teacher the kind of work that should be done.

The apparatus needed is simple, cheap, and easily obtained. It is necessary to darken the room for some of
the observations, and the teacher should be able to do
this quickly. If the windows are provided with solid
shutters, there is no difficulty ; but if there be slats in

the shutters, the end can be attained by tacking over them light-proof paper of some kind. A small hole, half the diameter of a lead pencil, in an east, south, or west window, will admit a beam of sunlight that can be utilized in a variety of interesting ways. Where there are no shutters, curtains may be substituted with but little trouble. A small looking-glass and a lamp reflector, that may be obtained at any lamp store at small cost, will be needed in a study of reflection. For a lens, the magnifying glass used in botanical work will answer. Directions were given in the September work for making a suitable prism.

1. Why is it (without considering the eye) we can see an object, such as a book, in the room in daylight, but cannot see it in the darkness at night?

2. Why is it that we can see it after dark, if a lighted lamp is brought into the room? In seeing the book, does the light first pass from the lamp to the eye and then to the object, or first to the book and then to the eye?

3. Hide the lamp from sight, but place it so that its light falls upon the book ; is the book visible?

4. With the lamp in the same position, hold a thick piece of paper between the eyes and the book ; is it still visible?

5. What two things are necessary to enable us to see the book?

6. Why is it that we can see a lighted lamp when it is brought into a dark room, but cannot see a book, chair, etc. ? The lamp is said to be luminous and the book is non-luminous.

7. Give all the examples you can of each kind of body.

8. How can you make a non-luminous body be-

come luminous? How can you make it non-luminous again?

9. Heat a wire red-hot in a darkened room, using your alcohol lamp; can you see it from all sides? Why?

10. Take three pieces of cardboard six inches square. Place one on top of the other and cut a very small hole through all of them; place these upright several inches apart. Opposite the hole in one of the cardboards place a lighted candle; can you so place the other two pieces that the light will shine through the holes in all three? If so, what do you notice about the three holes with respect to each other?

11. Why is it the light will shine through all three only when they are in a certain position?

12. Arrange a lamp and book as in (3) and try to see the book by looking through the holes in the three cards; what do you notice about the position of the holes when the book becomes visible? What do these experiments show you about the lines or rays of light?

13. Where does the light come from in (3) which makes the book visible? Describe the path it must take from the lamp to the eye. In the same way, in daylight, describe the paths of the rays of light which make the different objects about you visible.

14. Instead of the book used in (3), place a small looking-glass, and, if a sunbeam can be substituted for the lamp, it will be better. What difference do you notice in the visibility of the two objects?

15. Can you see both the book and the glass equally well from all positions?

16. Explain why there is a difference in the visibility of the two objects. What difference do you notice in their surfaces?

17. The light from the book is said to be *irregularly reflected* or *diffused* light, and that from the looking-glass is *regularly reflected.* Compare the relation of the rays to each other as they approach the surface of the book and the surface of the mirror with their relation to each other as they leave these surfaces. By which kind of light do you see most of the objects about you? What is essential to a good reflector? Good reflectors are called *mirrors.* A mirror with a flat surface is called a *plane* mirror.

18. When rays of light strike a mirror, what happens to them? The rays from the object to the mirror are called *incident* rays, and those from the mirror are called *reflected* rays.

19. Conceal the book as in (3) from the eye, but place it so that rays of light will pass from it to a mirror: can you so place yourself with respect to the mirror that the figure of the book will appear? Do you really see the book? How can you prove that you do or do not see it?

20. Explain how the mirror brings the appearance of the book into view. To do this, recall (3), (4), and (5) relating to the visibility of an object. When is the object itself visible? The appearance of an object as seen in a mirror is called its *image.*

21. Which rays determine the direction in which the image is seen, the incident, or reflected rays?

22. Allow a small beam of light to fall upon a mirror and be reflected; make the beam more distinctly visible by striking two black-board erasers together near it. Erect a perpendicular line, called a *normal,* to the surface of the mirror at the point of reflection; note the two angles thus formed. The one between the normal and the incident beam is the angle of *incidence;* between

normal and the reflected beam, the angle of *reflection* Compare these two angles.

23. Support horizontally a light straight stick about two feet long on its ends eight or ten inches from the floor or table. From its middle point suspend a plumb line. A bullet partly split and then closed upon a small thread will do for this. Fill a goblet or pan with water blackened with ink, and place it under the line so that the weight will be below its surface. In the side and near one end of the stick, drive a tack or small nail, and standing at the other end, place the eye in such a position that its image will appear where the string touches the water. Compare the distance the eye is from the point where the plumb line is attached to the stick with the distance the tack is from it. Make a drawing of the apparatus, showing by a line the course of the incident ray from the tack, and the reflected ray to the eye. Point out the angles of incidence and reflection. What does this experiment show as to their relative size?

24. Can you see any reason why an image should appear to be *behind* the mirror? Can you by drawing a figure representing a mirror, an object, its image, and lines representing the rays of light, show how far behind the mirror the image must appear?

25. Is the image seen by means of the mirror a real one, *i. e.*, does it really exist behind the mirror? Such an image is called a *virtual* image.

26. Hold a printed page before a mirror; explain why the letters appear changed.

27. Can you explain why a surface which diffuses light does not give us images of objects?

28. Allow a beam of light to strike a concave mirror; what peculiarity do you notice about the reflected rays?

Explain why they form a cone of light, by using what was learned in (22) and (23). The point at which the rays meet is called the principal focus of the mirror. Measure its distance from the middle point of the mirror. The middle point of the mirror is called the *center* of the mirror.

29. In constructing a *normal* (see 22) to the surface, notice its relation to the sphere of which the mirror forms a part. Where in the sphere do all the normals meet? This point is called the *center of curvature.* A line drawn through the center of curvature to the center of the mirror is the *principal axis ;* all other lines through the center of curvature to the mirror are *secondary axes.*

30. Darken the room and hold a small lighted candle close to a concave mirror ; what are the points of difference between its image here and the one it forms in a plane mirror ? In what respects are the two images alike ?   .

31. Move the candle back from the mirror until it is between the principal focus and the center of curvature. Hold a sheet of paper, for a screen, back of the candle ; carefully compare the image here produced with the one seen in (30).

32. Make a diagram of the mirror and the candle. Draw two or more lines, representing rays of light, from the tip of the flame to the mirror ; show what will become of those rays when reflected. Recall what was learned in (23). At what place in the reflected rays do you find the image ? This point is called the *conjugate* focus.

33. The image formed in (32) is called a *real* image ; how does it differ from a *virtual* image ? See (25).

34. Move the candle away from the mirror ; what be-

comes of the image on the screen? As the candle is
farther removed, where does the image next appear? Is
it a real or a virtual image?

35. Again diagram, as in (32), and find where the reflected rays from the candle meet ; at what place along
the reflected rays do you find the image? Explain why
the image is inverted here, and why upright in (30).

36. Notice where the candle is, with respect to the
center of curvature and principal focus, when the image
appears on opposite sides of it ; that is, between the
candle and mirror, and beyond the candle. Try to explain why you can see a real image in either place.
Recall what was learned in (3), (4), and (5). Do not
confuse what is necessary to *see* an image with what is
necessary to *form* one.

37. Show by a diagram why the size of the image
varies with the position of the object.

38. Hold the candle before the *convex* surface of the
reflector ; in what respects is the image the same as that
formed by a plane mirror? In what respects is it different?

39. Explain the formation of the image in the convex
mirror by diagrams, keeping constantly in mind the laws
by which those formed by plane and concave mirrors
were explained.

40. It will be interesting to illustrate how light varies
in intensity with the distance from its source. Make
from cardboard three screens, one six inches square,
one a foot square, and one eighteen inches square
Draw lines across the last two, dividing them into areas
each six inches square. Fasten each screen in an upright
a few inches in height. This may be made by splitting a

stick, into which the card may be slipped and fastened with a tack. A small block will answer for a base.

41. Place the smallest card three feet from the flame; how far from the flame must the second in size be placed to be exactly covered by the shadow of the first? At what distance from the flame must the largest be placed to be exactly covered by the shadow of the second?

42. With the three cards in these positions, what do you notice as to the amount of light that each would receive from the flame? How much would each six-inch square on the second and third screen receive, as compared with that received by the smallest card?

43. How would the intensity vary at the points occupied by the second and third cards, as compared with that occupied by the first?

44. Does the edge of the card make a clear-cut shadow at its margin? Hold a pencil between a light and a screen; how does the edge of the shadow change as it is moved toward or away from the screen?

45. If possible, use a flat flame, and examine the shadows cast by the edges and by its flat surface. Make a diagram, drawing lines from the different parts of the flame to different parts of the object, and to the shadow beyond; can you account for the peculiarities noticed in the shadow?

46. The dark central part of the shadow is called the *umbra ;* the light border is called the *penumbra.*

47. Can you explain the difference that may be noticed between the shadow of an object cast in the moonlight and that from one illuminated by electric light?

REFERENCE. Humboldt Library : No 37, Six Lectures on Light.

Chemistry.

NITROGEN.

Nitrogen is less interesting than any of the gases that have been examined. On account of its abundance in the atmosphere and the important function it performs, however, it is thought best to make some study of it. The pupils should very early be taught about the constituents of air, and should know the chief properties of each ; also, as far as possible, by simple experiment, they should be taught about the origin, the cause of variation, and the effects of each upon themselves and other living things.

1. Nitrogen may be made in several ways, none of which are very suitable to be performed by young children. Two methods will be given, which are perfectly safe and present but few difficulties. The most instructive way is as follows : Take a piece of phosphorus half the size of a pea, and dry it with blotting paper. Place it in a small cup or upon a bit of porcelain, which may be floated upon a small block of wood in a pan of water. Ignite it, and immediately place over it an empty glass fruit jar. When the burning has ceased, allow the white fumes to clear away, and then invert the vessel, without allowing the water to escape, as directed in the experiments with oxygen.

2. The second method is to take two parts of bichro-

mate of potash (about one ounce) and ammonium chloride one part. Grind the two together until fine and well mixed. Heat in a flask arranged as directed in the experiment with oxygen, and collect in a jar over water. By the latter method the gas may be generated in a flask, and a test-tube full may be caught by each pupil as it forms. The cost of the material in either case need not be more than fifteen or twenty cents, to supply fifty pupils with two or three test-tubes of the gas.

3. Why does the phosphorus continue to burn after the jar has been inverted over it in (1) ?

4. What does the rising of the water in the vessel, as the burning ceases, indicate ?

5. Light a long splinter and thrust it into the jar of gas ; each pupil may do this with his test-tube. The gas may be kept until wanted by holding the thumb over its mouth.

6. What is the effect upon the blaze ? What other gas with which you have experimented has the same effect ?

7. Into another and perfectly clean test-tube full of the gas, pour a little lime-water ; does it undergo any change ? What gas causes lime-water to become milky ?

8. The gas formed in the above experiments is nitrogen ; compare it with the other gases that you have made in previous experiments.

9. When the phosphorus burned in the air in the jar, the oxygen combined with it and phosphoric acid was formed, which was then dissolved in the water, leaving the nitrogen in the jar ; why could we not get pure nitrogen by burning a candle in the jar instead of phosphorus ?

10. Note the amount of water in the jar after the phosphorus stopped burning ; how does it compare in bulk with the gas above it ?

11. What gas did the water, in rising, take the place of?

12. The air is a mixture consisting of one-fifth oxygen and four-fifths nitrogen ; what would happen if it were pure oxygen ? If it were pure nitrogen ? Recall the experiments with oxygen?

The Atmosphere.

13. Take a tumbler partly filled with lime-water and expose it to the air of the room for an hour or two ; can you see any change ? What else is proven thus to be in the air?

14. Fill part full a wide-mouthed bottle with air taken from near the floor of the school-room, and add half an inch of lime-water ; shake the water well in the bottle. Repeat the experiment, taking the air from near the point of influx ; does the lime-water indicate the presence of CO_2?

15. In the same way test a bottle of air taken from different points near the ceiling. (How can you get a bottle of air from any point in the room ?)

16. Is the CO_2 more abundant in one place than another ? Why is it ? Test a bottle of air taken from out doors.

17. What is the fruitful source of CO_2 in a school-room?

18. Fill a small vessel with snow and salt, and watch the outside surface of the vessel closely ; what does this experiment prove to be in the atmosphere besides the gases already shown to be there ?

19. Place a small amount of chloride of lime in a dish, and let it stand a short time ; can you notice any change ? Explain.

20. Look at a sunbeam as it streams into the room ; what does it prove the presence of in the air ?

21. What contrivance do animals have for straining the solid particles from the air before it enters the lung ? (See Respiration for April.)

Meteorology.

March is the fickle month of the year, and the approach is usually awaited with feelings of mingled hope and dread. To most people, all semblance, even, of natural law appears to be wanting in the spiteful play of the elements that are apparently uncontrolled. In the gales that generally blow, now from one direction, now from another, in the wintry days that are sometimes slipped in between those having the genuine touch of spring, and in the cautiously swelling buds that often come forth only to be nipped by the last lagging frosts, there is, indeed, good ground for the reputation that the month sustains. It will be no less instructive, however, to try to trace the sudden changes of this month to their causes, than it is in those months of more steady meteorological behavior.

1. In which one of the preceding months was the temperature nearest that of the present one ?

2. Compare the causes that combine in each month to produce the temperature noticed. In what way are the causes different ?

3. In what respect are the causes which operate now the same as those present in September ?

4. What influences give to March and September their different character ?

5. Compare the two months as to temperature; is there any correspondence in the average temperature or in the rate of change ?

6. Compare the rate of variation with that of each month since the lowest temperature of the year was reached ; is the rate increasing or diminishing ?

7. Make a similar comparison with the months preceding the date of the lowest temperature ; how does the rate during that period compare with the rate which follows the minimum point ?

8. Compare the barometric record with that of September ; what is the mean height and the greatest range of movement in each month ?

9. Compare, in the same way, with the record for December ; with which month does it most nearly correspond ?

10. Can you, from your record, determine. whether or not the height of the barometric column is affected by cold ?

11. At what temperature during the month has it stood highest ? At what temperature, lowest ?

12. Can you find any relation between the character of the weather and the height of the barometric column ?

13. What is the prevailing wind this month ? Is it generally cold or warm ?

14. What was the prevailing wind for September ? For December ?

15. What wind prevailed when the temperature was lowest ? When it was highest ?

16. What wind brings a cloudy sky ? Is it like the preceding months in this respect ?

17. Has the character of the clouds changed since December ? Compare with those months in amount of cloudiness.

18. Is the number of rainy days greater or less than in the winter months ?

19. From what directions do the heaviest rains come?

20. Are the rains followed by cooler or warmer weather?

STUDY OF THE WEATHER BUREAU MAPS.

21. In what quarter of the country have Low Areas most frequently appeared? Compare with September and December.

22. What has been the course of the great storms during the month? How does the path compare with that of previous months?

23. Can you tell what influence the Great Lakes have had upon their course? The mountains? The river valleys?

24. Where has there been the heaviest rainfall? Compare with September and December.

25. Is the amount of rainfall increasing or decreasing, as compared with the winter months?

26. What has been the lowest temperature recorded? Compare with September and December. In what region was it recorded in each case?

27. Compare the isotherms that cross the country this month with those of September. Is there any difference in general direction?

28. What is the most northern isotherm this month? In September? What does this indicate? In the same way compare the most southern isotherms.

29. Do the isotherms bend about the Great Lakes the same way in both March and September? Compare with December.

30. In the same way note the effects of the mountains and coast lines in the different months.

Astronomy.

March, the herald of spring, is a month in which observations under this head are fraught with especial interest and profit. The sun, mounting the meridian, as shown by the shortening shadow, and creeping almost stealthily northward around the horizon, more loth to close his eye at night, more eager to begin his labors in the morning, seems instinct with plans for a season which, though ten thousand times repeated, is ever new. The teacher who fails to seize the conditions presented at this time, loses one of the best opportunities of the entire year to broaden and strengthen his pupils' conception of the universe. It is wrong to suppose that the formation of the great conceptions which are necessary for an intelligent appreciation of nature is a matter that may be postponed till a definite time, and then be gained at once. They are never gained except through growth, and, whether physical or mental, that implies small additions through patient and prolonged observations.

1. Can you find any previous month in which the noon-marks correspond to those recorded during this one?

2. What suppositions regarding the movements of the earth can you make which will account for the observed facts? What is the correct one? Give the proof.

3. When did the noon shadow begin its retrograde or backward movement? Has the rate of movement been uniform since that time?

4. In what previous month was the rate of the advance

movement of the noon-marks the same that it is now in the retrograde movement? Using a globe, explain why it is so.

5. On what date this month do you find equality of day and night? For how much of the earth is this true? This is the Vernal Equinox.

6. How long since this was the case before? Count the days, using the almanac. When, between those two dates, was there the greatest inequality?

7. How many complete seasons have elapsed since the same equality was noticed before?

8. How many seasons yet remain to make a full year? Count the days; what do you notice about the relative length of the two parts of the year?

9. What suppositions can you make which will account for the observed inequality in the two parts of the year—that part including fall and winter, and that including spring and summer? Find out which supposition is correct.

10. What effect, if any, must this inequality in the two parts of the year have upon the seasons included in those parts respectively?

11. On the date when a day and night are equal, this month, note on the horizon the points of the rising and setting sun. In what previous month did they coincide with those of the present?

12. How long has it been since the sun rose and set in the same place that it does now? Explain the facts. If necessary, illustrate with a globe. How far has the sun moved along the horizon since the shortest day of the year? Since a day and night were equal before? Using a globe, explain. ·

13. When day and night are equal, measure the angle

that the sun's rays make with the earth ; can you determine, from what you observe, your latitude ?

14. Can you by the same means determine your
latitude on December 20 ?

15. What fact would it be necessary for you to know
in order to determine your latitude in the same manner
on any day of the year ?

16. In what latitude is the day longest in this month ?
Where are they increasing in length most rapidly ?
Explain this. (See April Astronomy for remarks on the
use of symbols.)

17. For whom does the sun rise for the first time in
some months, about the middle of this month ? For
whom does it set ?

18. It will be noticed that Jupiter has changed from an
evening to a morning star within the last month ; explain
how the change has been made. (See Astronomy for
September for the relative distances of the planets from
the sun.)

19. The period of revolution of Jupiter is twelve of
our years, lacking fifty days. Its time of rotation is four
and a half minutes short of ten hours. Its mean diameter
is eighty-five thousand miles, but there is a difference of
five thousand miles between its equatorial and polar
diameters. Its volume is over thirteen hundred times
that of the earth, but it weighs only three hundred times
as much. Its mean distance from the sun is four
hundred and eighty millions of miles.

20. Make as large a circle as possible, on the blackboard,
to represent Jupiter's orbit, and another to represent that
of the earth ; and upon the latter locate the earth at the
point where it is to be found this month ; in what position
must Jupiter be to appear as morning star ?

21. How long will it continue as morning star?

22. When a planet is seen in the same direction as the sun, or, in passing by it, approaches nearest to it, it is said to be in *conjunction* with the sun. It is *inferior conjunction*, if the planet lies between the earth and sun, *superior conjunction* if the planet lies on the opposite side of the sun from the earth. When a planet is on the opposite side of us from the sun, that is 180° from *superior conjunction*, it is in *opposition*.

23. In what positions will the earth and Jupiter be farthest apart? When will they be closest together? What will be the distance between the planets in each case?

24. Does Jupiter present to us the same phases that are shown by Venus and our moon?

25. Constellations same as preceding month.

REFERENCE. Humboldt Library : No. 20, Romance of Astronomy.

Geography.

EURO-ASIA. CLIMATE.

By consulting good physical maps, it will be found that the climatic conditions of Euro-Asia are vastly different from those presented by the Americas in corresponding latitudes, and that there are also marked contrasts in the same latitude in its own wide extent. The study should be supplemented by sand modeling as before, but the same precautions necessary in the use of devices in other subjects apply with equal force here. (See Astronomy for April.)

1. What is the general direction of the great air-currents over the northern part of Euro-Asia? Compare their direction on the eastern and western coasts; can you account for the variation that you notice?

2. Note the direction of the wind south of the Himalaya Mountains; how does its character differ from that on the northern slope?

3. What contrasts in climate are presented between that part of the continent lying north, and that part lying south of the great axis?

4. Contrast the two regions with those of the same latitude in North America.

5. In which of the two continents are the conditions more favorable for uniformity of climate? Why?

6. In what part of Euro-Asia would you expect the

greatest extremes ? What conditions are present to produce them ? Study the course of the isothermal lines.

7. Where would you expect the greater uniformity of
climate, north or south of the Himalayas ? Why ?

8. Compare the temperature of the eastern and western
coasts ; can you see causes for variation ?

9. Compare the coasts with the interior ; what cause
operates mainly to produce variation ?

10. Compare the variations mentioned in (6) and (7)
with corresponding regions in the Americas ; can you see
reasons for a difference ?

11. Contrast the climatic effects of the Gulf Stream
with the Japan current, and account for the difference in
climatic influence.

12. In what respect are the climatic conditions on the
southern coast of Euro-Asia different from those of the
Gulf coast of North America ? In what respect are they
alike ?

13. In what respect do the conditions differ on the
Mediterranean Sea from those on the southern coast of
Asia ?

14. What influences combine to produce the heavy
rainfall of southern Asia? Compare with southern
Europe.

15. Compare the region of heaviest rainfall with that
of North America ; what similarity do you notice in the
location ? Why is the amount less in the latter continent ?

16. Contrast the rainfall of the great area north of the
continental axis with that south of it ; why does it
diminish toward the north?

17. Consider the rainfall in the great peninsulas and

peninsular projections that extend south from the continent of Euro-Asia ?

18. Compare Arabia with Hindostan ; can you account for the difference ?   In the same way compare the Malay peninsula with that of Spain.

19. How can you account for the difference in rainfall in the British Isles and Newfoundland ?

20. Why is the rainfall north of the continental axis in Europe greater than that north of it in Asia ?

21. How can you satisfactorily account for the desert regions in the highlands of Asia ?

22. What reason can you assign for the desert of Arabia ?

23. The monsoons which blow from May to October toward the southern Asiatic coast from the southwest, and from October to May in the opposite direction, *i. e* , from the northeast, are the important climatic factors of this region.

24. Have you learned anything in physics about air which will help you to explain the monsoons and their change of direction ?

25. What climatic conditions favor the largest cities of southern Asia ?

26. Are there any cities that have prospered under adverse climatic conditions ?

27. How does the climate of a country affect the character of a city ?

28. Contrast the character of the people of southern with those of northern Europe ; to what extent may the differences noted be attributed to contrasts in climate ?

29. Are there any noticeable differences between the people that live in the mountainous regions and those of

low countries that are due to climatic contrasts ?   Compare those on the coasts with those in the interior.

30. Can you see any constant relation between the intelligence and thrift of a people and the climate, in a study of Euro-Asia?

Geology.

During this month observations on frost action should be continued. The effects of freezing and thawing will be shown in various ways. The manifestations of these forces are usually very slight, and they will possess interest and be instructive only as the pupil can be led to picture in his own mind what the results must be after a great lapse of time. The idea of time is one for which the teacher should work with the pupils unceasingly.

Geological pictures have not always presented themselves to the student of nature as they now do to those who are imbued with the more modern notions as to nature's way of doing. Formerly the pictures were filled with catastrophic action, which annihilated the old, and as suddenly established a new order of things. Then came a long time of absolute rest, or at least a period of trifling change. Now, one sees in the picture constant unrest, it is true, but modification so slight and so gradual, that nothing is destroyed except those things that, apparently through a loss of plasticity, fail to keep pace with the incessant change.

Thus far we have examined what may be considered some of the mechanical agencies which are at work molding and changing the face of the globe. There are others equally potent and certainly of no less interest, though they are not matters of such common observation. The agencies now meant are those called organic, and to gain some conception of these we will include in our study for this month a piece of coral. In many places, pieces of coral may be found in the common stones that are abundant—limestones. When they cannot be so obtained, it often happens that some of the pupils possess specimens of their own. At least, it will be comparatively easy to secure clam, mussel, oyster or snail shells, and these will give some idea as to how mineral matter may be deposited by animals, which is a necessary conception. From this, it should be the aim to have the pupils picture for themselves the history of the great beds of limestone.

1. Put a small piece of a shell of some kind into a test-tube and add a little acid. (See Mineralogy for January.) Does this recall any experiments previously performed?

2. What kind of stone does this remind you of? (See Mineralogy for January.)

3. Examine an oyster, clam, or mussel as it lies on the half shell ; also look carefully at the outer surface of the shell. Can you tell how the animal forms this shell?

4. Can you see the starting point of growth?

5. Can you tell whether or not the shell grows in thickness?

6. Can you find out from what part of the animal the material is secreted which increases the width of the shell?

7. Notice the thin membrane that lies closely against the inner surface of the shell ; this is the mantle of the animal.

8. Examine a piece of coral ; what kind of a substance does it appear to be?

9. In what respects does it differ from most kinds of stone?

10. Use the acid test ; what stones that you have examined before does it resemble ?

11. If you have a specimen of the branching coral, examine the curious little rosette like pits along the sides ; what similarity do you find among them ?

12. These little pits were once occupied by small jelly-like animals (not insects, as we frequently hear them named) called coral polyps. As they grew, they secreted the stony substance, not as the oyster does, in a covering, but in the lower part of the body. These minute animals can live only in the warm, clear waters of the tropical seas, and at a depth not exceeding one hundred and twenty feet. They are so small and delicate that one would almost at first think that they would have to live in the quiet places of old ocean, but the reverse is the case. Can you see why the dashing waves and the sweep of great ocean currents are necessary for their existence ? You can scarcely make a mistake in the answer. The myriads of these little polyps which live together, in the course of time build up great masses of stone. The waves break off the branches, which settle to the bottom, and in this way a solid wall is formed. These are often built out a little distance from an island, and coming to the surface form coral reefs. These great rock walls are sometimes thousands of feet deep ; what reasonable supposition can you make which will account for this, since the polyps can live only at the depth given above ?

13. Judging from the location where the polyps live, what would be the effect finally upon their stony structure ?

14. Look closely at the texture of the strong coral ; if it were to be worn away by the water, would it likely make a fine or a coarse material ?

15. What would become of the material thus worn off, as well as that which would be derived from the shells of dead animals such as the clam and oyster ?

16. Would this material retain any of the form of the original shells or corals ?

17. What property of the original shell or coral would still be retained by the material worn away ?

18. In the examination of any of the stones that you have seen, have you found any fragments of corals or shells ?

19. What would such fragments indicate as to the origin of the stones ?

20. In what kind of stones were such fossils found ? What does that tell as to their history ?

REFERENCE. Humboldt Library : No. 6, Town Geology ; No. 110 Story of Creation.

Mineralogy.

It will be useful at this time to begin a little closer study of the minerals that may have been collected during the year. They may be readily sorted and classified by very small pupils with respect to their structure, which in many cases is quite obvious to the naked eye. The external form of most of the minerals in their collections has, no doubt, been determined by forces which have had nothing to do with forming the mineral originally. That is, they are probably fragmentary and angular, or rounded as the water-worn pebbles. Here the external form is of no use in the description of the mineral. Sometimes, a few may be found whose form is not due to such causes, and attention should be given to them as they occur.

1. Look among your collection for stones that are seen to be hollow ; sometimes they are rounded pebbles so worn away as to expose the hollow within. Such a stone is called a *geode*.

2. Note the inner surface of the geode ; is it covered with crystals or is it smooth ? Sometimes its inner surface is covered with a layer full of *rounded* protuberances. This form of mineral is said to be *botryoidal*.

3. Have you any stones in your collection which were formed in rounded masses ? An examination of the surface will usually show at once whether they are water-worn or not. Such stones are called *concretions*, and are said to be *concretionary*.

4. Have you any specimens in which the material is arranged in layers, as in slate? This is said to be *stratified*.

5. Sometimes about springs of certain kinds the water deposits a porous incrustation of rock. It is very light, and often sponge-like in appearance, and is called *tufa*. It is said to be *tufaceous*.

6. In caves, sometimes the water which drips from the roof leaves hanging an icicle-like mineral deposit which is called a *stalactite*. The rock is described as *stalactitic*. The water dripping to the floor there heaps up a mound-like rock which is called a *stalagmite*. Such a rock is *stalagmitic*.

7. Can you find in your collection any distinct crystals? Are they perfect? How many faces have they?

8. Examine some specimen that clearly shows a granular structure, and by carefully tapping it separate some of the grains. Are they crystals? Are there any perfect crystals among them? Such minerals may be described as coarsely or finely granular, according to the size of the grains.

9. When the grains are too small to be detected by the naked eye, the mineral is *compact*.

10. Procure a piece of mica; it is sometimes used in stove-doors. What is the peculiarity of structure? It is *foliated*.

11. If possible, procure a small piece of asbestos; such a mineral is *fibrous*.

Zoology.

During this month, usually, great abundance of material for outdoor study appears. The calendar started in the previous month will rapidly fill up, and as the days go by will prove to be an interesting and instructive record. Collections of every kind should be encouraged, and informal talks and discussions should be permitted as often as time and the disposition of the pupils will warrant.

GENERAL OBSERVATIONS.

1. Watch for the first appearance of earthworms ; why are they so abundant after a rain ? Do they come down in the rain ?

2. Let the pupils each select and measure off a square yard of ground in different locations and count the number of entrances to burrows that are found. What is the average ?

3. In what locations are they most numerous ? Where are they fewest ?

4. What is the meaning of the small heaps of earth at the entrance of a burrow ?

5. How do they bore their way through the ground ? Put one or more in a glass of damp earth for a few days and watch it.

6. Carefully clean away the little heaps of earth from about the burrows in a square yard, and the next morning gather all that has been cast up during the night.

Dry, and weigh it ; at the same rate how much would be brought to the surface on an acre in one night ?   In three months ?

7. Do they bring up as much in day-time as they do at night ?   What kind of weather seems to suit their work the best ?

8. What must be the effect of their work upon the soil ?   How must it affect objects lying on the surface of the ground ?   Notice stones and flag pavements that have begun to sink.

9. Follow out a burrow and find its depth, and make a diagram of it.   Is there more than one worm to a burrow ?   The burrow may be followed by using a small wire probe, the ground being dug away as it is pushed carefully into the hole.

10. Does the earthworm eat ?   If so, what is its food and when does it feed ?   What are its enemies ?   Does it fight or seek safety in flight ?   Upon what does it depend as means for concealment ?   How do birds find them ?

11. Why is it so much alike on all sides?   Why is it not exactly alike all around ?

12. In what respect does it resemble a snake ?   How does it differ from one ?   Can you see why it differs ?

13. Why are its two ends so much alike?   Are they exactly alike ?   Why are they at all different ?

14. Compare its movements with those of a snake ; can you find any scales or legs ?

15. Draw it gently backward through the fingers and examine its sides under a lens.   Count the segments of the body ; do they vary in different specimens ?

16. Does the earthworm breathe ?   Look for respiratory movements along the body.

17. Can it live in water? Expose a worm on a piece of paper to the sun; is there any evidence of distress? Can you tell what ails it? Put it into a dish with a little water in it and expose again; does it seem as uncomfortable as before?

18. Examine the worm in a good light with a lens; can you see any trace of a circulation? Lying along the back is a pulsating tubular organ which assists in keeping the circulating fluid in motion. The true blood is not red, but rather milky in appearance, and does not circulate in closed vessels as in our own bodies.

19. Can the earthworm see objects? What plan can you devise which will fairly test this? Does it distinguish between light and darkness?

20. Can it hear? What evidence can you gather on this point?

21. Test it for the sense of touch. Also for the sense of smell.

BIRDS.

1. What influences bring the birds north in the spring?

2. What do those that arrive this month have to feed upon?

3. Are there any that feed entirely while on the ground? Are there any that never feed on the ground? Have you noticed any taking food while in flight?

4. Why do some birds hop while others walk or run? Why do certain birds climb trees? Why cannot they all do it?

5. Compare the flying of different birds; what things determine the character of the flight? Notice shape of body, wings, etc., and the proportion of the different parts.

6. What enables a bird to have such speed in flight?

Compare the line of flight of different birds ; is there any
uniform difference between those which fly great distances, and those that fly but a short distance at a
time ?

7. Does the size of the tail affect the character of the
flight ? Is the tail used for any other purpose than that
of assisting in flight ?

8. Are there any good flyers that have very short
tails ? Is there any substitute for the tail in such cases ?

9. How do birds dispose of their legs when flying?
Compare those of widely different kinds.

10. How do birds manage to cling to a small twig
when asleep ? Have you found any that do not roost in
trees?

11. How do birds seize their food ? Are there any
that use both claws and beak ? Are there any that use
but the beak ?

12. Do you know of any birds that live upon the flesh
of other animals ? How do they differ from those that
live on insects and seeds ?

13. At what time do birds sing most ? Why do they
sing ? Which sings the more, the male or female ?

INSECTS.

In the study of insects, it is necessary to collect them
in some way in which they may be speedily killed, and
yet not be spoiled for examination. This may be done with
a cyanide bottle, prepared as follows. Drop into a wide-
mouthed bottle three or four lumps of cyanide of potassium the size of a small marble. Pour in half an inch of
water and then sprinkle evenly with plaster of Paris, until
a dry cake is formed. Wipe inside and outside with a
dry cloth and close with a tight cork or cap. Any drug-

gist will prepare one for a few cents. A wide-mouthed morphia bottle is a very convenient size.

Insects dropped into this bottle will be quickly killed and yet preserved in a perfect state for examination.

Insects may be mounted and preserved thus: slice ordinary bottle corks into pieces one-fourth of an inch thick and glue them to the bottom of a box or tray. A cigar-box answers the purpose very well. Pass a pin through the insect, in beetles through the right-hand half of the abdomen, in butterflies, etc., through the center of the middle division of the body, and set it upright in the cork. Keep a small camphor ball in the box, to kill the pests that attack them.

Some insects, such as butterflies, etc., must be dried with wings spread before being mounted permanently in a tray. Take two strips of smooth, soft wood three inches wide and about two feet long. Leaving a space one-fourth inch wide between them, nail them side by side to two blocks of wood, one on each end. The upper surface of these blocks should be cut slightly slanting toward the middle, so that the strips when nailed on will be somewhat trough-like. Tack underneath the space between the strips a piece of soft wood, card-board, or cork. Pass a pin through the body of the insect, as directed above, and pin it fast to the cork, placing its body in the space between the strips. Draw the wings forward to the natural position, and fasten by pinning narrow strips of paper across them.

1. Collect and sketch the insects that first appear ; when are they to be found ?

2. Are they young ones, or have they lived through the winter ?

3. What is their food? Of what are they the prey ?

4. What means of escape and defense have they ?

5. When are they more frequently abroad, in daytime or night ?

6. What modes of concealment have they ?

7. How does their flight differ from that of a bird ?

8. Do any insects possess wings without having the power of flight ?

9. How does the number of wings vary in different kinds ? How are they used ?

10. How do they walk or run ? Make a sketch showing the order in which they move their legs.

POND LIFE.

1. Secure a mass of frogs' eggs from a pond or ditch and place them in a jar of water. Toads' eggs are distinguished by their being in long strings.

2. What are the earliest signs of life ? Can you discover movements before the eggs are hatched ?

3. As soon as hatched, examine one of the tadpoles closely ; how does it swim ?

4. Has it any appendages? Look closely about the mouth for gills ?

If a microscope can be obtained, place one of the little creatures on a piece of glass with a little water (a watch glass is best) and examine the gills. The blood flow thus revealed is a thing of rare beauty.

5. It is difficult to preserve the same specimens through all the changes, and new ones must be obtained as needed.

6. What becomes of the external gills ? How do they breathe? Look just behind the mouth for a small opening ; this leads to internal gills.

7. What is their food ? Is the number of tadpoles

which develop into frogs relatively large or small?
Why?

8. Do you notice anything different in the early life of
a toad from that of a frog?

RESPIRATION.

1. Standing erect, inhale slowly a full breath. Through
what openings does the air enter?

2. Can you close the mouth and inhale through the
nostrils? Can you inhale equally well through the mouth
alone?

3. What muscles of the trunk seem to be most concerned in inhaling air? In exhaling?

4. What changes occur in the shape or size of the chest
in breathing? With a string or tape measure find out
how many inches the chest varies in size.

5. In what part does it change most?

6. Is the air filling the lungs the cause or effect of
the expansion of the chest? Close the mouth and nostrils and try the movements of inhalation.

7. What experiments in Physics will explain the process
of inhalation?

8. How do the ribs move in inhalation? In exhalation?

The chest cavity is separated from that of the abdomen
by a dome-shaped muscular partition called the diaphragm. By contraction, the diaphragm is somewhat
flattened, and the chest cavity is enlarged vertically, thus
assisting in inhalation. When relaxed, the contents of
the abdomen, which have been compressed during its
contraction, force it back into its dome shape, thus assisting in exhalation.

9. What position is best for full breathing?

10. What is the meaning of the occasional long breath we take? Of yawning?

11. Why do sad thoughts cause us to sigh?

12. Do the common animals, dog, cat, horse, cow, etc., breathe through the mouth or nostrils?

13. What advantages in taking breath through the nostrils?

14. How do people who snore breathe, through the mouth or nostrils? Open the mouth and make full inspiration through both mouth and nostrils. Can you tell where the snoring sound is formed?

15. With a mirror examine the back of the mouth. Note the fleshy flap hanging down toward the throat. The air passes on both sides of this to and from the throat when the mouth is open, and causes it to flutter more or less rapidly, thus producing the peculiar sound of snoring.

16. Can you make the snoring sound with the mouth closed?

17. Count the number of respirations to the minute; take average per minute for five minutes.

18. How do your movements affect the number of respirations? Take the number after vigorous exercise.

19. How do the movements affect the general character of the respirations?

20. In ordinary breathing are the lungs filled to their utmost capacity? Try breathing in additional air after a quiet inspiration has ceased.

The extra amount thus taken into the lungs is called *complemental air.* That which passes in and out in ordinary quiet breathing is called *tidal air.*

21. After an ordinary expiration, can you still force outward an additional amount? This is called *supple-*

mental, or *reserve*, air. After all has been forced out that is possible, some air still remains in the lungs; this is called *residual air*.

22. Prepare a small amount of lime-water and breathe into it through a tube. Does this recall any other experiment?

23. What was it that changed the lime-water in the former experiment?

24. Try stirring fresh lime-water with a glass rod, so as to mix it with pure air. Does it show the same change?

25. Is the air, when it leaves the lungs, of the same composition it was when it entered them?

26. What are the effects you have noticed upon yourself when in a poorly ventilated room containing several persons?

27. Fill a jar with water and invert it in a pneumatic trough, as directed in lessons on oxygen. Take full breaths and by means of a tube fill the jar with air from the lungs.

28. Test the air in various ways; note the odor. Try burning a splinter in it. Can you tell what the air lacks? What has become of the missing part? What has it gained from the body?

29. In what respect are our bodies like a burning stick? (See Chemistry for March and also previous lessons in Physics.)

REFERENCE. Humboldt Library : No. 1, Light Science for Leisure Hours. See " The dust we have to breathe." No. 92, Formation of Vegetable Mold by Earthworms.

Botany.

During this month much attention should be given to germination, as the young plantlets appear. It is impossible to cast in any single outline a set of directions which will exactly suit the environment of every teacher. The time has come, however, when teachers should cease trying to follow some one else step by step; no one has ever risen in his work by following, no matter how perfect the leader. An outline, at best, can only furnish a teacher with hints and suggestions as to how he may utilize his own conditions. It adds immensely to the vitality of the work with the pupils, if the plants that come up at random outdoors be used as specimens for study. It is surprising how small a spot will furnish an abundant supply for an entire school. That the whole process of germination may be observed from the beginning, however, it is well to have seeds planted in some manner in the school-room also. There are many devices that may be used successfully for this purpose, but, on the whole, there is perhaps nothing better than some suitable vessel filled with clean sand.

A pan that has proved useful and convenient is one made of galvanized iron, thirty inches long, eight inches wide and four inches deep. By filling it two-thirds full of sand, space enough is left above to admit of glass being placed over the young plants if the weather be very severe; but this precaution is rarely necessary. By allowing to one pupil a space of three inches, such a pan will accommodate eight persons, and there will be a six-inch space left as common ground in which odd or curious forms may be grown, such as bulbs, underground stems, etc. Five pans of this kind will equip, at a trifling outlay, an ordinary school-room with a useful outfit that will last for years. No trouble or time is required beyond what is necessary to keep the sand moist and the pan near a window. The pans when well made are water tight, without being soldered, and will be found very useful in other seasons in many experiments in physics and chemistry when pneumatic troughs are needed. The development of buds may be observed by placing small twigs in bottles of water. A few wide-mouthed bottles, such as may be easily procured by the pupils, will enable them to watch without trouble the development of the buds of every different kind of tree and shrub in the neighborhood. Some of the twigs start their buds, when treated thus, quite slowly ; others develop almost at once, and not a few not only put forth leaf and flower, but plenty of roots too. The twig should not be more than six inches long and should have a terminal bud, that its functions may be studied.

GERMINATION.

1. Plant some of the seeds that were gathered last fall. (See September Botany.) With beginners use large seeds of some kind first. Plant carefully, placing the seeds in different positions and at different depths.

2. Make the conditions different for the same kind of seeds. Place some in the dark, or cover with a tin cup or flower pot. Plant some in dry sand. Keep some cold and others warm.

3. As the seeds begin to grow, write a list of what appear to be the most favorable conditions for development.

4. Do different seeds, under the same conditions, grow equally well ?

5. Where does the plant get its first food to give it a start before it has either leaf or root outside the seed coats ?

6. When the seed coats burst, as growth begins, closely examine what is inside ; what parts of a plant can you recognize ?

7. As growth proceeds, watch daily what becomes of the different parts of the seed ; what parts do not continue with the growing plant ? What parts develop as the plant grows ?

8. Are the seeds you find sprouting outdoors near the parent plant ? Can you tell how they came to be planted where they are ?

9. Scrape away the surface of the ground from some spot and take up a box of earth that has been buried several inches. Put this in a suitable place and watch for the sprouting of any seeds it may contain. Take up a small box of earth from the surface in another place ; how many different kinds of plants grow from it ?

10. In some place not likely to be disturbed, mark off a square yard of ground and count the different kinds of plants it produces. Can you tell where the seeds that sprout in this space came from ?

11. With what adverse influences do the sprouting seeds and young plants have to contend ?

12. Look for plants of the same kind in different locations ; compare the growth of those under trees or in the shade of buildings with those away from such influences Compare those growing in sand with those in soil.

13. Do they grow alike on different sides of a house?
14. Compare the chances of those that start early with those that sprout later.

A SEED.

Synopsis of the terms that may be used at the teacher's discretion, in a study of the seed.

I. OUTER PARTS.

Hilum or scar ; the point where it was attached to the pod.

Micropyle ; minute opening near the hilum.

Seed coats ; outer, testa ; inner, tegmen.

II. INNER PARTS.

Cotyledons ; the thickened leaves in which nourishment is stored. When there are two cotyledons, the plant is a *dicotyledon ;* when but one, it is a *monocotyledon.* Find examples of each.

Plumule ; small terminal bud lying between the cotyledons, or embedded in it when there is but one.

Caulicle or Radicle ; small stem within the seed coats.

Embryo ; the plantlet within the seed coats.

DEVELOPMENT OF BUDS.

1. Which seems to be in advance, the sprouting of the seeds, or the unfolding of the buds?

2. Which is the more serious loss to a plant, the destruction of a seed, or the loss of a bud? Which are destroyed in greater numbers, seeds or buds?

3. Compare, as well as you can, the ratio of the seeds that are destroyed to those that produce plants with that of the buds that are destroyed to those that survive. In

the production of which does nature seem to be the more extravagant?

4. Are the buds all equally advanced in all parts of the tree? Compare the opposite sides and the top of the tree with the bottom.

5. Are they all equally advanced on the same branch? On the same twig? Try to account for any irregularity in development you find.

6. Do all of the buds develop? What is the location of those that remain dormant, if any are found?

7. Is there any advantage to the plant in having dormant buds?

8. Cut off the outer end of a few twigs and watch the effect on the development of the buds that remain. Pick off all the buds from a few twigs and watch the result.

9. What is the function or use of the terminal buds? Look for the former positions of the terminal bud on the same branch; why does it leave a scar each year?

10. What is a bud? To answer this, examine as large a one as you can find (a lilac will do) that is just beginning to swell. Dissect a bud and find in the center the tender *growing point.* What is the difference between a bud and a seed?

11. Can you find any buds on the trunk of a tree? What evidence can you find that they are there?

12. Do roots produce buds? How do you account for sprouts that sometimes come up from the roots of trees?

13. Examine some of the fruit trees for flower buds; which unfold first, flower or leaf-buds?

14. Do you find any buds growing about the same point in pairs or clusters? Do all of such buds develop?

15. Are these buds always arranged in the same way

in the group? Does the arrangement differ in the same plant?

The following synopsis of the terms needed in the study of buds is appended to assist the teacher. The proper name should be given when it is needed in description.

BUDS.

I. As to position.
  1. Terminal; at the end of the twig.
  2. Lateral; along the sides of the twig.
    (*a*) Axillary; in the leaf-axil; that is, the upper angle between the leaf and the stem.
    (*b*) Accessory; buds clustered about the axillary buds.
    (*c*) Adventitious; buds that are produced irregularly on the branch or trunk. Often develop when the regularly arranged buds are destroyed.
    Nodes are the points on the stem at which the buds are produced; *internodes*, the spaces between the nodes.

II. As to activity.
  1. Active; those that develop.
  2. Dormant; those that form, but do not develop. Note the effect on these of destroying the active buds.

III. As to covering.
  1. Scaly; covered with dry, tough, bark-like layers.
  2. Naked; without scaly covering.
  3. Hidden; those buried under or in the bark.

IV. As to arrangement.
  1. Opposite; two at the same node and opposite.

2. Whorled ; three or more arranged around the same node.

3. Alternate; in ranks along the stem, not being opposite or whorled.

UNDERGROUND FORMS OF THE PLANT AXIS.

This season of the year is an appropriate. time in which to study underground stems and those roots which, preserved through the winter, are now ready to send forth vigorous growths and make woodland and meadow gay with early flowers. As great a variety as possible should be collected.

1. If they grow in the neighborhood, gather the underground part of the common blue flag (the iris), or calamus (sweet flag), Solomon's seal, or blood-root. Are these roots or stems ? What evidence can you find on either side ? Can you find any evidence as to how long they have been growing ?

2. Compare these with the common potato ; what differences do you find ? What are the eyes of the potato ? Plant some of these and watch how and where the young potatoes are formed. What becomes of the old potato ? The potato and all underground parts like it are called tubers. Those like the blue flag are called rhizomas.

3. Examine the thickened underground part of an Indian turnip (Jack-in-the-pulpit). How does it differ from a tuber or a rhizoma ? It is called a corm.

4. Examine the underground part of a lily or an onion. Cut it so as to make various sections ; what part of a plant does it most resemble ? What part of the plant forms the overlying scales of the onion? What forms its solid base from which roots are produced ? Under-

ground parts like the lily and onion are called bulbs. How do they differ from the forms previously examined ? What have they in common with them ? An onion is called a tunicated bulb ; in the lily bulb and others, where the layers are small, it is said to be scaly.

5. Examine the underground parts of the hepatica or buttercup ; how do these differ from those first examined ? Are they roots or stems ? Where they are clustered in this way they are said to be fascicled. Where they are thickened they become tuberous.

6. Can you find any plants with a main root growing straight downward ? This is called a tap root. These become thickened sometimes so as to become conical, spindle-shaped, napiform, or turnip-shaped. What examples of these can you find among our common vegetables ?

7. Do stems ever produce roots above ground ? Under what conditions and for what purposes ?

8. Can you see what features distinguish a root from a stem ?

9. Can you understand why such plants as many of those mentioned above can produce early flowers?

Physics.

In continuing the study of Light this month, we shall find that images may be formed in a very different way from that by which they were produced with mirrors. In their explanation, however, it will be seen that nothing is involved that has not already been considered in previous lessons, except the fact of refraction and its laws. If the work indicated for the preceding month has been well illustrated, no difficulty will be found here.

1. Through a small hole in the window shutter admit a beam of sunlight into a darkened room; allow it to strike the side of a glass vessel filled with water. A useful tank for this purpose can be made by any tinner for a few cents. It should be about six inches long by four in depth and width. The bottom and ends should be made of tin, with edges turned in so as to admit of glass sides being slipped in. Putty well on the inside. A large square bottle of clear glass will answer the purpose of the tank very well.

2. Hold the vessel so that the beam will strike the sides perpendicularly; can you trace the path of the beam through the water? Can you trace it after it leaves the water on the opposite side?

3. Notice the kind of a line it follows from the point where it enters the room to the place where it should strike the wall or a screen beyond the vessel of water.

4. Hold the vessel so that the beam will strike the sides at an acute angle; follow its course through the water and to the screen. Do you notice any change in

its course? Compare its course with that which it follows in the air.

5. Turn the tank around on a vertical axis and watch the path of the ray; upon what does its variation from a straight line depend?

6. A beam of light thus bent from a straight course when it passes into or through different substances is said to be *refracted.* What difference do you see between refraction and reflection?

7. The *direction* in which a beam of light is refracted is always referred to a normal (see 22, Physics for March) drawn (within the refracting substance) to the point on the surface where the beam enters it. When the beam enters the water in the vessel, is it refracted toward or away from the normal?

8. Draw a normal to the point where the beam enters the air again; in what direction is the beam refracted? Turn the tank or vessel in different directions; can you find a position where the refracted beam does not take the same direction with respect to the normal?

9. Is there any position in which the beam is not refracted at all?

10. Place the end of a pencil or stick in a vessel of water; what do you notice at the point where it enters the water?

11. Make a drawing of the vessel, the water and pencil, and, by lines, show the course of the rays of light that passed upward through the water from the pencil. Do you see the pencil, or its image, below the surface?

12. In a tin cup, place a penny and hold it so that it cannot be seen when looking across the rim into the vessel. Cautiously add water, and watch for the appearance of the penny. Is it the penny or its image that appears?

13. As in (11), make a drawing showing the course of a ray of light from the penny to the eye.

14. Is it the reflected or refracted part of the ray from the penny that brings what we see into view?

15. Hold an ordinary lens or magnifying glass between the sun and a sheet of paper; move the paper back and forth until the light spot is brightest and smallest.

16. How large in diameter is the beam of light from the sun that strikes the surface of the lens? Why should it be conveyed to a point by passing through the lens? Before trying to answer this, examine the lens; what do you notice about its surfaces? Draw a veitical section so as to show the curvature of both surfaces; construct lines which will be normals to different parts of the surface; are they parallel? If not, where would they meet?

17. Is any line that is normal to one surface, normal also to the other?

18. In a drawing similar to the one above, draw a line on one side, representing a ray of light to the lens somewhere between its center and circumference; construct normals and show what its path would be on entering and leaving the lens. To another point on the same side of the lens draw a line representing another ray, and in the same way show its course through the lens and beyond. What is the relation of the two lines after leaving the lens? Can you now account for the bright spot observed in (15)?

19. Take a thin strip of wood three inches wide and two and a half feet long. Mark off one side in inches. In any convenient way mount a common single lens magnifying glass so that the light will pass through it horizontally and fall upon a screen. The latter may

consist of a piece of card-board six inches square. A low block with a groove sawed in it to recive the card-board, which may be fastened with glue or a tack, will make a support.

20. Place the lens and screen on the strip of wood. On the opposite side of the lens from the screen, place a small lighted candle, and move it into a position where it will throw an image on the screen. With which kind of mirror was a similar image formed ?

21. Make a diagram of the lens, object, and image, and trace (see 32, Physics for March) lines showing the course of the rays of light from the object to the image.

22. Place the lens so that the size of the image is the same as that of the object ; draw lines showing why this is so.

23. Place object and lens in such a position that the image is less than the object ; can you show by lines why it is smaller ? Is the image formed in each of these experiments real or virtual ? In what ratio does the image vary with the distance of the object from the lens?

24. Look through the lens at a letter or other small object ; do you see the object, or an image ?

25. Prove by lines which it is. If it is an image, is it real or virtual ? Why is it enlarged ? Prove by drawing lines showing their path of light from the object to the eye.

26. Admit a beam of light through a small hole in the window shutter. Hold a screen so as to catch the spreading rays ; can you see the image of any objects outside ?

27. Compare the image in position, size, etc., with the

object ; how does moving the screen backward and forward affect it ?

28. Why should an image form under these conditions ? Make a diagram showing by a vertical section the position of the object, the shutter, and the image on the screen ; recall what was learned in March about reflection and the visibility of objects.

29. Allow a small sunbeam to pass through a prism (for directions for making one, see Physics for September).

30. Note the rays that fall upon the screen, and compare with the sunbeam. How many colors can you distinguish ? In a diagram, show the course of the beam through the prism.

31. Catch all these colored rays on a concave mirror, and reflect them to a screen ; what color is the light at the focus ? What does this prove as to the sunbeam before it strikes the prism? Which rays are most refracted as they leave the prism ? Which the least ?

32. Hold some white object in the red rays ; what color does it appear to be ? Try in the same way the different colored rays ; what is it in this case that seems to determine its color ?

33. What colored rays are carried to the eye in each case? When the sunbeam, not refracted, falls on the object, what color does it appear to be ?

34. In ordinary daylight look at some red object ? what kind of light strikes it ? What kind must be diffused from it ? Try in the same way objects of different colors. The rays not sent to the eye from the object are absorbed by it.

35. What colored rays are absorbed by an orange ? What ones are absorbed by a white surface ? By a black surface ?

36. Is color something belonging to the object itself?

37. Can you apply what you have learned about refraction of light by a prism, to show how a rainbow is formed? Under what conditions is it seen? Make a diagram showing the relative position of the bow, the sun, and the observer.

38. What is there in the atmosphere to break the sunlight up into the colored rays? How are these rays directed to the eye of the observer?

39. Can you give a reason why the colors in the rainbow stand in the order in which you see them?

40. Why is the rainbow in the form of an arc of a circle? Did you ever see one in form of a circle, entirely above the horizon? Why? Have you ever seen one at noon? Have you ever seen one in the west?

41. Can you, from what you have learned, give any satisfactory explanation of rings around the sun and moon?

Chemistry.

WATER.

1. Dissolve a small quantity of salt in a bottle or test-tube of water ; when the salt disappears, is it destroyed ? Is it changed to anything else ? Proof. Has it united with the water ?

2. Fit a bent tube through a cork that will fit the flask or test tube and gently heat it over your lamp. Hold the vessel in such a position that the steam that comes through the tube may be caught in a cool receiver. Taste the drops of water that soon appear ; are they fresh or salty ? Does this enable you to answer the last question in (1) ?

3. What is this process called ? (See Physics for October.)

4. Take a small piece of perfectly clean glass ; place upon it a large drop of hydrant or spring water, and hold it over the lamp until it has evaporated. Is there any deposit left on the glass? What is it ? Can you burn it in the flame ? What does the burning or the failure to burn prove ?

5. Take a drop of the purest filtered water you can get and evaporate it as in (4) ; is there any solid matter left ?

6. What is removed from water by filtering it ? What still remains in it ? Try filtering a salt solution, using filter paper. (See 19, Chemistry for February.) Can you taste the salt in the filtrate, that is, in the filtered part ?

7. Distil some hydrant or spring water as directed in (2) and evaporate on your glass some of the drops formed from the steam ; is there any deposit left? What did distillation do for the water ?

8. How and where is distillation of water carried on in nature ?

9. When it rains, catch in a perfectly clean vessel some rain water ; evaporate a drop of this in your glass. Is there any solid matter left? Compare it, as to purity, with hydrant water filtered.

10. How does spring water gather its solid matters? What parts cannot be filtered out ?

11. Powder a small lump of gypsum, and add it to a bottle of rain water, or distilled water. Shake it thoroughly and filter ; are there any traces of the gypsum visible in the filtrate ?

12. Dissolve some soap in hot water and keep the solution in a bottle labeled Soap Solution.

13. Add a little of the soap solution to a test tube of distilled, or rain water, and shake it. Add, also, some of the soap solution to the filtrate obtained in (11) ; what difference do you notice in the two tubes? The first is called *soft* water, the latter *hard* water.

14. Boil some of the filtrate, and then add soap solution ; does boiling affect the hardness ?

15. Take a tumbler of lime-water and blow your breath into it through a tube ; recall an experiment in Chemistry for November. (See 24, Chemistry for November.)

16. Continue blowing until the water clears ; this may take some minutes. Filter.

17. Divide the filtrate, and test one part with the soap solution ; is it hard or soft water ?

18. Boil the other part of the filtrate, and test with

soap solution; compare with what you observed in (17).

19. The hard water containing gypsum is said to be permanent hard water; that containing limestone or chalk, is temporary hard water.

20. The explanation of the formation of hard water in the second instance is this : the carbon dioxide from the breath unites with the lime in the water and forms carbonate of lime. By continuing the blowing the excess of carbon dioxide dissolves the carbonate, and the water containing this in solution is hard.

21. Can you see why boiling temporary hard water renders it less hard ?

22. Add to some of the filtrate obtained in (16) some clear lime-water ; when the mixture clears, test a little of the clear part with the soap solution ; is it soft or hard ? Explain.

23. Which requires the greatest amount of soap to be used in washing, hard or soft water ? What difference do you notice in the feel of the two kinds of water ?

24. An interesting test for a small quantity of salt in water may be made as follows : Put a ten-cent piece into a small amount of dilute nitric acid ; when it is dissolved, evaporate the solution. Redissolve the crystals formed in distilled water. This is silver nitrate, which also contains some copper which gives the bluish tinge. Bottle, in a clean dark-colored bottle, or else keep in the dark. Label it properly.

25. Thoroughly wash and rinse two bottles or tumblers, and partly fill each with pure distilled water. In one, dissolve a piece of salt about the size of a pin-head.

26. Add a drop or two of the silver nitrate to the beaker of pure water ; can you notice any change ?

27. Add a drop or two to the vessel containing the grain of salt ; what change do you notice?

28. With the silver nitrate test the hydrant water, rain water, spring water, and well water. if it can be obtained.

Meteorology.

The meteorological influences of April are usually of a very different kind from those of the preceding months. For six months they have been negative in character, but from now forth they are positive ; they no longer play the part of a destroyer, but rather that of a creator. These benign influences are to be seen and felt by all, and the pupils, properly guided, will be interested in tracing them to their cause.

1. Can you notice any difference in the character of the wind this month ? To what is the difference due ?

2. What is the prevailing direction of the wind ? Has it changed within the last month ?

3. In what month studied has the wind been most variable ?

4. Is the prevailing wind accompanied by wet or dry weather ? Can you give a reason for the observed facts ?

5. What wind usually accompanies a clear sky ? Compare with previous months.

6. Are the clouds changed in their character this month ? Notice their height and compare with previous months.

7. Compare the fogginess of this month with that of preceding ones ; can you account for the difference noticed ?

8. Under what conditions are the heaviest fogs formed? What conditions about you are especially favorable for

their formation? When fogs disappear, what becomes of them?

9. What difference do you notice between April rains and those of the winter months?

10. How does the amount of rainfall now compare with that of October? With December?

11. Compare the number of rainy and clear days with that of previous months.

12. Compare the temperature of this month with that of March.

13. In what autumn month did the earth occupy the same relative position with respect to the sun? Compare the temperature for the two months. How does the rate of change correspond?

14. Compare the rate of change in temperature this month with that for March.

15. What wind accompanies the highest temperature? The lowest? Compare with March and December.

16. What is the greatest range in the movement of the barometric column? Compare with March and October.

17. Has there been any uniformity in the barometric record just before storms?

18. Does the movement of the barometric column correspond in any way to that of the thermometer?

19. Have there been any mornings without either frost or dew?

20. Can you find any places where the ground is still frozen?

STUDY OF THE WEATHER BUREAU MAPS.

21. What isotherm crosses nearest where you live this month? Is it changing its position in either direction?

22. What isotherm crosses the Gulf States ?   Compare with March.

23. Compare the position of the isotherms that cross the country this month, with those of the month referred to above in (13).   Try to explain any difference noticed.

24. Where have the Low Areas generally been formed this month?   Compare with March.

25. What has been the direction of the great storms ? Can you notice any difference from that of preceding months ?

26. Compare the temperature of the Low Area with that of the High Area ; does it bear the same relation that it did in preceding months?

27. In what quarter of the country has there been the heaviest rainfall?   Compare with the autumn month referred to above in (13).

28. In what place does the heaviest rainfall occur with respect to the Low Area ?

29. What is the uniform direction of the wind about the Low Area ?   Have you found any exceptions to the rule ?

30. Do the Great Lakes appear to affect the course of the storms ?   Note the effect of the mountains, valleys, and coast lines.

Astronomy.

In view of the importance of the point to be enforced, it will not be considered out of place here to speak specifically of what has been hinted at before concerning the proper use of symbols and diagrams in illustrating this subject. The teacher should sharply discriminate between the pupil's ability to comprehend an illustration, a mere device, and his power to grasp or form a concept of the real thing to be taught. A pupil, pointer in hand, may glibly explain a diagram on the blackboard which illustrates the various movements of the heavenly bodies and their mutual relations, without having the faintest glimmer of those great educative conceptions of space, time, and force, which are the true outcome of the study when properly conducted. Specific rules of procedure which will suit all cases cannot be given ; it should be constantly borne in mind, however, that the true ideas must come from small beginnings, but, if properly started, they will be of perennial growth. Something which falls within the bounds of the pupil's experience should be seized upon, and from it his mind, unaided, should be led outward toward the source of the phenomenon to the very limit of his power of thought, and then, only, may a device be relied upon to safely perform its proper function of illustration.

1. Compare the movement of the noon shadow with that of last month ; what do you notice about the rate of movement ?

2. With what previous month do the marks most nearly coincide ?

3. How does the rate of movement correspond with that of the same month ?

4. Is the rate of movement of the noon shadow increasing or diminishing ?

5. What angle do the sun's rays now make with the earth ? Compare with December.

6. If the apparent path of the sun could be traced across the heavens daily, what kind of a line would be formed ?

7. Can you determine from a measurement of the angle of the noon shadow how high the sun would appear to one at the North Pole ? How high would it appear to one on the Arctic circle at noon ?

8. Where on the globe is the longest day at this time ? Explain why it is so.

9. Where is the shortest day ? Are the days and nights equal in length anywhere ?

10. How many degrees on the horizon has the sun moved since the vernal equinox ? How many degrees has it climbed the meridian in the same time ?

11. How many degrees has it moved on the horizon since the winter solstice in December ?

12. Is the rate of change in the day's length increasing or diminishing ? Explain why this is so.

13. Is the increase of the day's length made by equal additions morning and evening ?

14. When are the variations at morning and evening most nearly equal ? When are they most unequal ?

15. In what part of the year is the variation greatest in the morning ? When is the variation greatest at evening ?

16. To what causes are the differences noted in (15) due?

17. About the middle of this month it will be noticed that Mercury appears as evening star. How have the earth and it changed in relation to each other since it was seen as morning star? (See Astronomy for February).

18. Additional constellations : Crater ; Berenice's Hair.

REFERENCE. Humboldt Library : No. 14, Wonders of the Heavens.

Geography.

EURO-ASIA. PRODUCTIONS.

1. Where are the greatest differences in productions between the northern and southern, or eastern and western divisions of this great continent? Why?

2. What contrasts are presented in the productions between those of the coast and the interior?

3. Does the eastern or western coast differ more widely from the interior in productions. Why?

4. Are the river valleys important in their bearing upon the productions? Which ones are most important?

5. Where is the most important grain region? What conditions favor it? What cities lead in grain exports?

6. Is the grain region found in the same latitude in the different parts of the continent?

7. Compare the latitude of the grain districts in Euro-Asia with that of North America.

8. Where are the timber regions of Euro-Asia? What varieties are to be found? What are the climatic conditions found in a timber region?

9. How does the character of the forests in the northern latitudes differ from that of those in the southern?

10. Compare the latitude of the northern timber-line in Euro-Asia with that of North America; how can you account for the difference noticed?

11. What differences are there between the produc-

tions of the Mediterranean countries and those of southern Asia ?   What influences combine to give them some
similarity ?   What is the difference in latitude?

12. In what regions are the fruits of the temperate
zone grown ?

13. Where are the vine, the olive, and fig cultivated ?
Compare with the same latitude of North America.   To
what is the great contrast chiefly due ?

14. Where are the great meadow-lands of Euro Asia ?
Which do these more closely resemble, those of North
America or South America ?

15. In which of the three continents mentioned in (14)
is the character of the productions mostly dependent upon
latitude ?

16. Compare the effects of the great mountain ranges
in these continents upon the productions.

17. Locate the chief mineral regions of Euro-Asia.
What minerals are of most importance ?

18. What ones of value in the Ural Mountains ?

19. Where are precious stones found ?   Where are
gold and silver found ?

20. Where are the valuable iron mines ?   Coal mines ?
Where is tin found ?

21. Does the character of the productions of a country
make its impress upon the people ?   Compare the agri-
culturists of Europe with those that work in mines ;
what differences in their character are due to their different occupations?

22. Where are the most thrifty peoples of Euro-Asia
located ?   Is their thrift due to any extent to the kind of
productions in their countries ?

23. What is the character of the vine-growers ?   Of
the grain-raisers ?

24. Is the intelligence of a people in any great measure dependent upon the productions of the countries in which they live ?   Illustrate the point in Euro-Asia.

25. Are the conditions of the present tending to reduce or increase the importance of the relation which exists between the character of a people and the productions of their country ?

Geology.

Last month we considered the geological importance of an organism which has done, in connection with other creatures of the same character, a work almost inconceivably vast in making the earth's crust what it is. This month we must consider the work of another class of organisms, which is of less extent, perhaps, but hardly less interesting. The study relates to the work that plants are doing, and have done, when under certain conditions, at building on the earth's surface. The work should be preceded by a visit to a swamp, and as close a study of it as the age and experience of the pupils will warrant.

1. What are some of the conditions which have caused the swamp?

2. Is it the result of a stream or a lake? Is it being filled by sediment that is washed in from the adjacent land?

3. Examine some of the mud; what is its color? Does it consist of sand grains?

4. Is it like clay mud found in drier places in times of wet weather? Dry some of it, and compare with clay and sand.

5. Using a pole as a probe, can you tell how deep it is?

6. Where does the soft material come from that is not washed in from adjacent higher ground?

7. Can you find the remains of either animals or plants in the mud? Do they seem to be decaying?

8. In some of the great bogs of the world, some marvelously well preserved specimens have been found. " In

1747, in an English bog, the body of a woman was found, with skin, nails, and hair almost perfect, and with *sandals on her feet.* In Ireland, under eleven feet of peat, the body of a man was found *clothed in coarse hair-cloth."* (Le Conte.)

9. Can you tell what effect the vegetation that now covers the swamp has upon it ?

10. Can you tell whether the vegetation ever differed from what it now is ? Was it a swamp when the vegetation differed ?

11. Does the vegetable matter decay as it falls to the earth each year?

12. When the black material of which the swamp is composed is dried and ignited, will it burn ?

13. If it burns, what does this show its history to be ?

14. Peat swamps are found in Ireland, France, and many other parts of middle and northern Europe. They are much more abundant in the north than in the south. They are rarely found south of 36° latitude.

15. The Great Dismal Swamp of Virginia is an exception. It is forty miles in length, north and south, and twenty-five miles wide. There is a depth of fifteen feet of vegetable matter.

16. Why is it that peat bogs are much more common in the north than in the south?

17. What kind of climate would be best for them ? Why ? The peat formation in the Dismal Swamp is rendered possible by the large trees with dense foliage which grow there. Can you see a reason ?

18. What happens to vegetation that falls to ground in the southern or very warm countries ?

19. Can you picture to yourself how it would be possible for a peat bog to be transformed into a coal bed ?

20. Where is peat now used largely as fuel?

Mineralogy.

Pupils are always greatly interested in making those tests which produce some mysterious changes in the substance used. It is often not possible for them to understand what those changes really are (who does understand them?), but such work is stimulative of thought and inquiry, and is perfectly legitimate with those pupils who can handle the material and apparatus themselves. Through this kind of work will be acquired the habit of carefully examining such things as come under their notice, and also the skill necessary to enable them to do so. The outcome of the habit is self-reliance, a factor of inestimable worth in the make-up of character. The apparatus needed for certain instructive flame-tests is so simple that no pupil, even in remote country districts, need be without the means of informing himself of important and interesting properties of all the different minerals in his locality. Directions for making an alcohol lamp are given under Chemistry for November.

A small pair of sharp-pointed steel forceps or tweezers, such as are in common use by jewelers, will be useful, it may be said, a necessity. In addition, there should be provided two pieces of hard glass tubing, each about three inches long, one closed at one end and the other open at both ends. A few small pieces of red and blue litmus paper will also reveal interesting facts about some minerals when heated in the tubes. Enough may be obtained of any druggist, for five cents, to supply a whole class.

1. Select from the minerals, collected by the pupils, a number of different kinds, and break off some very small pieces or splinters of each.

2. Take up one of these with the forceps—it should not be larger than a pin's head—and hold it steadily in the tip of the flame just below the bright part. Does it melt? Look sharply at the thin edges of the points of the piece. When melted thus it is said to be *easily fusible*. When minerals cannot be melted, they are *infusible*. Some minerals, here infusible, might fuse in a flame with blowpipe.

3. In the same way hold a small lump of salt. Does it melt? What becomes of it? Minerals which fly to pieces when heated are said to *decrepitate*.

4. Can you detect any odor when the mineral is heated? Heat a small piece of sulphur and note the odor. Note the odor from a small piece of soft coal.

5. Some minerals color the flame. To get this color, hold the mineral in the edge of the blue part of the flame. The wick should be new and clean and the alcohol pure, so that the flames may be as nearly colorless as possible.

6. Hold a small piece of salt in the flame; what is the color? This is called the *sodium* flame.

7. Try a small piece of calcite in the same way; what difference in tinge is noticeable?

8. Try a piece of copper wire. What is the color? Dip the wire into hydrochloric acid and hold in the flame. What is the color?

9. Take a small piece of potassium chlorate that was

used in making oxygen. (See December.) What tinge has the flame ? This is the potassium flame.

10. Place a very small amount of the powdered mineral, not more than half the size of a pea, in the closed tube and heat gradually over the lamp ; watch closely the sides of the tube. Are there any drops of moisture ?

11. Try a small amount of marble ; does it undergo any change ?

12. Try a little powdered gypsum ; what change noticed ?

13. Separate those minerals which contain water from those which do not have it, as shown by this test.

14. Try a little sulphur in the tube ; what collects on the sides of the tube ?

15. Use a little powdered iron pyrites ; note the sides of the tube. Is there any odor ?

16. The substance formed on the sides of the tube is called a *sublimate.* This process is called *sublimation.* Compare with distillation.

17. Repeat the experiment, using the open tube. Place the mineral some distance within the tube and hold it but slightly inclined, so that the mineral will not slide out.

18. Note the odor. Does sublimation take place as before ?

19. Moisten a small slip of the litmus paper in clean water and hold in the tube so that the vapors will strike it. Which color is affected ?

20. To get the meaning of this, moisten each kind with a little acid ; which color is affected ? Try, in the same way, moistening each with a little ammonia. The blue litmus paper is thus a test for acids, being changed

to red by them, and the red is a test for alkaline substances, the color being changed to blue by them.

21. Do all of your minerals give off acid vapors ?   Try the above tests with quartz.

22. These exercises with minerals may be extended so as to include all the specimens in their collections.

Zoology.

Some one has said that the child is a natural born sav-age. Whether this savagery is due to inherited traits that root far back in his remote ancestry, or to a gross ignorance concerning the creatures about him, the result of criminal neglect on the part of his teachers, is a question that will bear discussion. Both sides may, perhaps, contain a half-truth. Certain it is, however, that as the child learns more and more of the habits of the living things about him he becomes less cruel in his treatment of them. Cruelty to animals and their wanton destruction is the concrete, as well as the most pronounced, hateful, and brainless expression of that worst of all traits of human character—selfishness. The teacher of natural science fails in a most important function of his work if the pupils that pass from under his care are not ever afterward entirely humane toward the lowly members of creation. If the teaching of elementary science in the public schools could accomplish no other end beyond that of making the children more thoughtful, tender, and considerate toward the brute creation, it would be well worth all the time and attention its most enthusiastic advocates claim for it.

The robbing of birds' nests by the "bad boys" of every community is a pastime that is as common as it is, unfortunately, destructive. The natural timidity of the birds is a thousandfold increased, and many a bush, tree, or thicket that might become the abode of a family of feathered songsters is rendered silent, tenantless, and dreary by the untimely raids of juvenile vandals. It is only because the misgivings, which naturally arise about the propriety of giving such directions in an elementary work, are outweighed by the hope that the teacher's constant supervision and humane judgment will at all times prevail in properly directing the pupils, that instructions are here given as to the collection and preservation of nests and eggs. Whatever collections are made by the pupils should be for the school of which they are members. Taking nests and eggs for mere pastime or by individuals who have neither the means nor the intention of permanently preserving them should not be permitted at all. The birds can well afford to spare a nest and a set of eggs of each kind for the school, and in the end they will be the gainers through the greater consideration in treatment which they will receive at the hands of the pupils who thus learn about them.

No nest or eggs should be taken unless it is certainly known to what kind of bird they belong. Nests near dwellings and schools should not under any circumstances be disturbed, as they afford easy opportunity for the study of the habits of the birds. A nest should not be taken until it is certain that the full set of eggs has been laid. To preserve a nest, remove it carefully, without displacing any of the materials, and sew it through and through with a very fine wire. This may be done so that the wire will not be visible except on very close examination, and yet all the parts will be held firmly together. Do not draw the wire tightly enough to change the shape of the nest. Make a stand as follows: Take five pieces of annealed iron wire, about six or eight inches long and about fifteen gauge. Twist them together for three

or four inches from one end to make a stem, and spread
the wires apart at the other end so as to form in basket-
like support to receive the nest.   Make a hole of suitable size in a block one inch thick and four inches square,
and insert the end of the stem formed by twisting the
wires as directed above.   Put the nest in position and
bend the wires about it so as to hold it in place.   Attach
a label bearing the name, date, location, and other data
regarding the nest.   Nests thus mounted will bear a great
deal of handling in class use.

To preserve the eggs, they must be blown.   Break a
large sized knitting needle in two in its thickest part and
file the thick end down to a tapering three-sided point.
This makes a serviceable drill.   Draw a small glass tube
to a fine point, and at about an inch from the pointed
end bend it to nearly a right angle.   In the side of the
egg, drill a single hole, twirling the drill rapidly and
lightly between the thumb and forefinger, the size being
dependent upon the size and freshness of the egg.
Place the tip of the blow-pipe described above, at the
entrance of the opening (it need not be thrust into the
egg), and, by blowing gently, the contents will be forced
out.   Fill the mouth with clean water, and by means of
the blow-pipe inject it into the egg and thoroughly rinse
it out.   Do not wet or smear the outside, and do not
wash off the mud or any other matter adhering to the
outside of the shell when the egg was found.   After
rinsing until the water comes out clear, inject, by means
of a small glass syringe (a medicine dropper will do), a
little water in which a very little corrosive sublimate (a
deadly poison ! !) has been dissolved.   After draining
it out, the eggs may be put away in the nests or trays
prepared for them.   When the eggs contain embryos, as

is frequently the case, a large hole must be drilled and the contents be cut to pieces with a pair of sharp pointed scissors and either rinsed out or removed with a hooked pin.

If the egg is large enough, with a fine pointed pen write the name of the egg on the shell with ink and also number it. If too small, then use the number only. In either case, record the name and number in a check book, and also note the conditions under which it was found. A brief history of the nest and eggs and their environment is interesting, and in the end very valuable. Place the number and name on the same side through which the hole is drilled and make it the under side as the egg lies in the tray.

BIRDS' NESTS AND EGGS.

1. Make a study of the materials found in different birds' nests; what points of similarity and contrast do you find between those that build on the ground and those that build in trees?

2. Which class of birds build the more elaborate nests, the ground or arboreal?

3. Where are the materials for the ground nests obtained? What objects does the bird appear to have in view in selecting a site?

4. Are the materials uniformly of the same kind in the arboreal nests?

5. By what devices are different nests held in place? Are they the same in nests of the same kind of bird in different places?

6. Where is the material obtained? Do the birds prepare it in any way before building it into the nest?

7. How do they carry the materials ? Do both sexes engage in the work ?

8. Note and compare the different locations selected. Can you see the advantages of each ?

9. Do the birds display intelligence in building their nests, or can you account for all you see through inherited instinct ? What would be a fair test as to whether blind instinct or intelligence guides the bird ?

10. Can you find any odd or new adaptations to the surrounding conditions in any of the nests ?

11. What are the devices for concealment, natural and artificial ?

12. Is there any correspondence between the color of the bird and the character of the nest ?

13. Compare the nests of the brightly colored birds with those that are dull colored. Is there any attempt made to simulate the surroundings in any way ?

14. At what time in the day are the eggs laid ? Aa what intervals ?

15. Can you see any reason for the coloring and peculiar marking of some of the eggs ? Can you see why some eggs are pure white ?

16. Is the number of eggs laid uniform with the same kinds of birds ?

17. Note the time when the female begins to sit ; what does the male do during this period?

18. How long before the young birds appear ? Note the date.

PARTS OF AN EGG, AND THE EMBRYO.

(Use a hen's egg.)

Some teachers will have opportunity at this point to suggest and conduct a series of most interesting observa-

tions on the incubation of the hen's egg. Among the
pupils there will doubtless be some who are the owners
of a flock of chickens. If so, it is not difficult to find
one or more hens that are willing to do their part of the
experiment by sitting upon a nest of eggs. Start with
about twelve eggs in the nest and replace those taken out
until the total number reaches twenty-one or twenty-two.
Mark each new egg put into the nest with the date so that
they may be removed in proper succession. When the
egg is removed, always keep that side uppermost which
was so in the nest. With a knife point or pin puncture
the large end. Can you see why this is done? Then
tap lightly on the upper side of the shell until enough is
broken to make, when it is removed, a hole about the
size of a penny. Carefully remove the membranes, and
look for any changes that may have taken place within.
If a compound microscope be at hand, there may be seen,
within a few hours, most wonderful evidence of a new life
that has just begun. (See Zoölogy for March.) Even
to the unaided eye the changes are very soon well
marked. Examine an egg every twenty-four hours, and
note the progress of development. It is well to remove
the embryo chick and preserve the series for further
study. To do this, immerse the egg, the opening uppermost, in a vessel of strong salt water. With fine-pointed
scissors cut around the area, plainly visible, occupied by
the embryo chick and let it float out of the shell. Catch
it on a bit of cork or smooth soft wood and keep it
spread with pins. Sink this in weak alcohol. As the
development proceeds, less trouble will be experienced
in removing the embryo. Small wide-mouthed ointment
bottles are excellent receptacles in which to preserve the
specimens. Each bottle should have a label bearing the

date when the embryo was removed and its age in days.

1. Note the general shape and size ; what is the ratio of the length to the breadth ?

2. Carefully remove the shell from one side ; how many linings inside of it ?

3. Note the clear white called the albumen. Also the yellowish center, called the yelk.

4. Observe the small white spot on the upper side. This is called the germinal spot. Observe this spot when the process of hatching begins. Did you ever see it anywhere except on top of the egg ? What advantage in this ?

5. Remove the shell from a hard boiled egg ; do the contents entirely fill the shell ? What reason can you assign ?

6. What is the very first evidence of life in the egg ? In what length of time did it appear ?

7. Can you find any evidence of internal organs ? What ones appear to be the most necessary ?

8. Which appears first, the outline of the body, the skeleton, or the internal organs ?

9. Where does the nourishment necessary for growth come from ? Does the embryo chick eat ? How does it get its food ? Does it need air ? Does it breathe ?

10. How soon can you notice the formation of any external organs ? What are they ? Which part of the body is most conspicuous ?

11. Notice very carefully the first appearance of the legs and wings ; can you observe any differences ?

12. How soon do bodily movements begin ?

13. When do feathers first appear ? In what parts of the body are they found ? How are they arranged ?

14. What becomes of the contents of the shell ?

15. Why is it that the chick has no use for its beak while developing in the shell? Does it use its stomach? Why?

16. What is the first use it makes of its beak?

17. After what length of time does it leave the shell of its own accord?

18. What changes take place in its mode of living when it leaves the shell?

19. Compare its feathers with those of the mature bird; do the feathers themselves change?

20. Compare the new-born chick with new-born animals of other kinds in vigor, intelligence, and self-dependence.

THE CRAWFISH.

1. Collect some crawfish and place them in an aquarium or jar of water for daily observation.

2. Note the character of the places where they are found; is the water clear or muddy, still or running?

3. How many ways have they of moving. Contrast these ways. Study the flexible part of the body; it is called the abdomen. Make a drawing of it.

4. What is the chief means of propulsion in swimming? Compare the parts and form of the tail-fin during the stroke with that during the return. By what contrivances is the resistance reduced during the latter movement?

5. Do the legs perform any function in swimming? What is their position when it swims?

6. Study how the animal walks; are all the limbs used in performing this movement?

7. Can you see the use of the short limbs under the hinder part of the body? These are called *swimmerets*.

8. Can the animal see where he is going when swimming tail foremost? What peculiarity do you notice about

the eyes ?   Examine the eye under a lens ?   Is it sensitive to the touch ?

' 9. By what means does he move his eyes?

10. What is the food of the crawfish ? How does he seize it ?

11. How do his prehensile organs differ from those used most in walking ?

12. What advantage do you see in the great number of joints ?   How do we manage to execute even a greater variety of movements with fewer joints ?

13. Note the different parts concerned in bringing the food to his jaws.   Is the food cut, crushed, or ground by the jaws ?   What can you see of the movements ?

14. How does the crawfish breathe ?   Does it come to the surface of the water for air ?

15. Lift slightly the shell-like covering of the forward end of the body by taking hold of its edges ; note the little brush-like gills lying close to the side of the body.

16. Can you discover the means by which fresh water is continually furnished to the gills ?   Put the animal into a shallow pan of water and watch carefully with this in view.

17. Which way does the current of water flow ?

18. Can the crawfish live when removed from the water ? Why is this ?   Why can we not live long if placed under water ?

19. Has the crawfish the sense of touch ?   By using a pencil or any other means find the organs of feeling.

20. Has it the sense of hearing ?   Do not try to answer this question until you have made a proper test.   Invent some way by which a test may be applied.   Can you locate his ears ?

21. Try to find a crawfish with eggs or young ones at-

tached.   If one with the eggs be found, note the movements of the swimmerets.   Why is this?

22. How does a crawfish fight or defend himself?   If
any should have a limb torn off in combat, put it in a
small tank by itself and observe what takes place in a few
weeks.

23. How is it possible for a crawfish to grow, since the
stiff, hard covering is on the outside of the body?   Have
you any proof that the shell is shed sometimes?

24. How many distinct things are done by the various
appendages of the crawfish?   How many are devoted to
each particular kind of work?

25. The following synopsis of the external characters
is appended to assist the teacher :

> Cephalothorax ; the anterior inflexible part of the
> body.   Note its covering, the *carapace*, and its pro-
> jecting spine in front, the *rostrum.*
>
> Abdomen ; posterior flexible part of the body.
> Eye-stalks ; appendages carrying the eyes.
> Antennules ; pair of small feelers.
> Antennæ ; pair of large feelers.
> Mandibles ; jaws.
> Maxillæ ; two pairs next behind mandibles.
> Maxillipedes ; three pairs next behind maxillæ.
> Great chelæ ; largest claws, one pair.
> Legs ; remaining pairs on the cephalothorax.
> Swimmerets ; abdominal appendages.
> Telson ; middle piece of tail fin.   Compare it with
> the other abdominal segments.

SEEING.

1. Try reading from a book, standing in the following different positions : Facing the light, with the back

to it, and with it at one side. Which enables you to see most clearly? Try to give a reason. (Recall lessons in Physics for March.)

2. Try to read holding the book at different distances from the eye; what is the best distance for you? If you are compelled to hold this book at much less than fifteen inches you are probably near-sighted.

3. Can you see near and distant objects distinctly at the same time? Look at the window sash and then at some object beyond. Can you account for the fact that a little time intervenes before the latter becomes distinct? Why is it bad for the eyes to read while on a vehicle in motion?

4. What is the effect on one's vision to pass from a light room to a dark one? From a dark one to a light one? To understand this, stand facing a strong light. Hold a mirror to one side toward a dark wall or surface. Suddenly turn and look into the mirror; watch narrowly the small black opening in the eye called the *pupil*. How does it change?

5. Turn quickly toward the light and hold the mirror in front; what change is noticed? The curtain which by contracting and relaxing alters the size of the pupil, is the *iris*. Note its color.

6. Watch the changes of the pupil in a cat's eye and compare with your own. Observe the pupil in an owl's eye. Can you see a reason for its great size?

7. Can you give a reason, from what you have seen, why one should have a steady light and not a flickering one? What precaution would you suggest when going from a dark room to a brilliantly lighted one?

8. Why are objects less distinct at first when there is a sudden change in the intensity of the light?

9. Of what use are the eyebrows ?   Of the eyelashes ?

10. Why do not the eyelashes interlock when we wink ? Can you see a good reason for winking?   Can you stop winking if you so will it ?

11. Examine a cat's eye when she winks.   Close it quietly with the hand and allow it to open slowly ; do you notice anything different from your own eye ?   Examine your eye carefully.

12. Examine the eyes of other animals for the same thing ; the dog, the frog, the bird, the turtle, for example.

13. Can you see why we shed tears when a cinder gets into the eye ?   Why do we do it when hurt severely in any part of the body ?   Why, when we feel extremely sad ?

14. What becomes of the moisture in the eyes under ordinary circumstances?   Standing before a mirror, pull the lower lids out slightly and look for a hole on the small elevation at the inner end ; this is the opening into a tube which leads to the nose.   Can you find a similar opening in the upper lid ?   Through this tube the water is drained off as fast as secreted under usual conditions.   The tear gland is situated above the eyeball, about midway between the outer angle of the eye and the middle of the bony arch.

15. Note the thickened but flexible edges of the lids ; they are kept smooth by oil, which is poured out at the roots of the lashes.   Sometimes this is in such quantities that the eyes are glued together in the morning ; if so, slightly moisten the edges with saliva.   To prevent this, wash the eyes well with warm water, and then bathe freely with cold water before retiring.   Use them less at night.

Botany.

May is a month of flowers. At no season of the year do they seem so beautiful and so fresh as now. Where a few weeks ago there was naught but the bare earth or brown leaves, the relics of a past season, the magic of the sunshine has now brought forth the delicate blossoms as the harbingers of a new life. Botany, in the past, has meant largely a rending to pieces of these flowers in an endeavor to find their name by means of an artificially arranged key. The key has its place and is useful, but it is not designed for children or beginners of any age. It is not likely to lead to an intelligent study of plant life. To secure this, much attention should be given to the habits of plants—for plants as well as animals have habits, one is tempted to say, likes and dislikes—and it is through these that easy entrance is made to the study. The flower, however, is but one part of a plant, and its study should not be separated from the study of the plant as a whole.

Since children are so universally attracted by flowers almost from the dawn of existence, it is frequently a matter of great astonishment to teachers to find how dull a subject the study of the flower sometimes becomes to their pupils. It must ever be kept in mind that children are most deeply interested in objects through their functions. Now the only function which the child can see for the flower is to make woodland and meadow beautiful for his own pleasure ; and since it can perform this function only in its entirety, he cannot be expected to en-

357

thusiastically pick it to pieces for the purpose of study. Whether the flower has five petals or ten stamens or a compound pistil is a matter of no consequence to him whatever ; and in the early stages of observation, therefore, he should not be troubled with such things. But instead, let him gather as many as possible, and drink in their separate and combined beauties, and then project the treasures of his soul, by means of brush and pencil, until his firm and loving companionship with them is fully established. It is this growing bond of union between child and flower, alone, which can later lead to deeper study that is honest in its purpose, intelligent in its character, and fruitful in its results.

The classes should in all cases, where practicable, visit the flowers in their native haunts. The younger pupils may gather all within their reach and the.more advanced may be limited more or less to those of a particular kind or to those growing in a certain prescribed area of peculiar conditions. In all cases attention should be directed to the relation of the surroundings to the plant and its adaptation to its environment.

1. Why is it that some plants can blossom so early in the season and others must wait until fall ? In trying to answer this, examine, if possible, such plants as Spring Beauty, Hepatica or Liver-leaf, Dutchman's Breeches, Bloodroot, Dentaria or Toothwort, and Trillium.

2. Have any of the seeds which you planted last month produced flowers ?

3. Have any of the flowering plants mentioned above come from the seed this spring ?

4. What advantage do such plants have over others in the spring ?

5. What differences have you observed among those

mentioned in (1)? Compare the Hepatica with the Spring Beauty.

6. Do you find them growing in exactly the same locations?

7. What appears to be the favorite place of the Hepatica? Of the Spring Beauty?

8. Do you find one growing in any location where the other is not to be found? Examine wet, dry, cool, warm, wooded, and open places?

9. In what respects is the Hepatica adapted to woodland? Is it equally well adapted to open places? Why?

10. Can you see why the Hepatica can bloom even earlier than the Spring Beauty?

11. What do the early flowering plants do the remainder of the season?

12. How many different arrangements of the flowers on the plants have you observed? The arrangement of the flowers is called the *inflorescence* of the plant.

13. Compare the inflorescence of the plants mentioned above in (1); which ones are clustered? Which are single? The latter are said to have *solitary* inflorescence.

14. Where are the oldest flowers in the clusters? The youngest? When the flowers open from the outside of the cluster inward or from below upward, the inflorescence is *centripetal* or *indeterminate.* When the reverse is true it is *centrifugal* or *determinate.*

15. What is the most common color of flowers that you find? Which color is least common? Can you see any reason for this?

16. Can you see any advantage to the plant in the color of its flowers? Do the flowers remain open day and night? Are there any that bloom only at night? Are there any that bloom only during the day?

17. Can you find any that bloom for a day only ?

18. Do any of the flowers that you have found have odor ? Where is this located ?

19. Why do the bee and other insects visit flowers ? Where are the sweets (nectar) stowed away ? To answer this, watch an insect very closely and taste the different parts of the flower. Where does the odor come from ?

20. How does the insect know where to look ?

21. Why is it that the flower so kindly feeds the insect ?

22. Do the insects carry away anything besides nectar from the flower ? How do they get it ?

23. How many different sets of parts do you find to a flower, the Spring Beauty, for example ?

24. Each set is called a whorl, even though it consists of but a single part. In the Spring Beauty, for instance, is the single central part called the *pistil*. Surrounding this is a whorl or circle of *stamens ;* next outside is the delicately colored *corolla,* and still outside of all is the *calyx.*

25. Are there four whorls present in all the flowers that you have found ? Which whorls have you found absent ? When *any one* or more of the whorls is absent, the flower is *incomplete.* When all are present it is *complete.*

26. Can you see any use for the pistil ? Note its enlarged basal part called the *ovary;* what does it contain ? The undeveloped young seeds are called *ovules.*

27. Note the slender stalk on top of the ovary called the style and the three-lobed tip called the *stigma.* Is there any evidence of a whorl of parts united in the pistil of the Spring Beauty ?

28. Examine the stigmas of different flowers very carefully ; do you find anything adhering to them ? Use a magnifier.

29. Shake a flower over a clean piece of paper; where does the dust come from ? The stamens have two parts, usually, the slender *filament* and the enlarged knob-like *anther*. The yellowish powder from the anther is the *pollen*.

30. The parts of the corolla are called *petals*. Are they present in all flowers that you have seen ? Of what use to the flower is the corolla ?

31. The calyx, as seen in the Spring Beauty, is composed of parts called *sepals*. What appears to be their use ?

32. The stamens and pistil together are called the *essential organs* of the flower. Can you see why the pistil should be classed as an *essential* organ ?

33. Taken together, the corolla and calyx are called the *perianth*. When the perianth consists of colored parts only, it is usually the calyx. The whorls of the perianth are sometimes called the *floral envelopes*. Why ?

34. Note the whorl of green leaves just at the base of the flower in the Hepatica. Is it a calyx ? Compare with the Spring Beauty.

35. Note the position of the flowers on different plants. Can you understand why some droop while others are upright ? Does the position seem to affect the growth of any of the whorls ?

36. Compare the stamens and pistil in drooping flowers with those habitually erect. Can you find any prevailing contrast ?

37. Compare these with flowers that project sidewise from the stem ? Is there any constant difference in the shapes of flowers that grow in different positions ? Can you see any reason for it ?

38. Flowers in which the different parts of the same

whorl are not of the same size or shape are said to be *irregular*. Can you see anything in the growth of the plant which would tend to produce irregular flowers?

39. Carefully compare the number of parts in the different whorls of the flowers ; where there is not the same number of parts in each whorl, the flower is *unsymmetrical*.

40. Can you find any ruling number in the parts of the flower? What is the most common number? The next prevailing number?

41. How are the parts of one whorl arranged with respect to the adjacent whorls? Are all flowers alike in this particular?

42. Are the petals separate in all the flowers you have examined? When separate, they are said to be *distinct* and the corolla is *polypetalous*. When united entirely or in part they are said to *cohere*, and the corolla is *gamopetalous*.

43. Note in the same way the calyx ; it is either *polysepalous* (distinct sepals) or *gamosepalous* (cohering sepals).

44. Can you find a flower when one whorl grows fast to another? It is then said to be *adnate*. Examine apple or cherry blossoms.

BUDS.

1. Procure a branch on which the buds are unfolding. Do all of its parts develop into leaves?

2. What do you find inside the bud? Cut one of the buds lengthwise and another crosswise and examine the arrangement of the parts inside. Make drawings to show it.

3. Are the small leaves all packed away in the bud

in the same manner? Pick a bud to pieces and notice how each leaf is wrapped or folded. The folding of the leaf in the bud is called the *vernation* of the leaf. Is there any relation noticeable between the shape of a leaf and its vernation?

4. As the young branch grows, can you see any indications of new buds being formed on it? In what positions do they grow?

5. Is there any growth in the last year's branch which is now putting forth the new ones?

6. What is the difference in the texture and general appearance between the new and the old branches?

7. On some rapidly growing branch make some measurements and determine the daily rate of growth. A lilac, poplar, or willow will be a good one to observe.

8. Can you tell where the new material is deposited which elongates the branch?

9. Watch closely the time when the twigs on the tree selected for study in the spring stop growing; has the tree any work to do during the remainder of the season after the growth of the twig stops?

10. On what part of the tree are the strongest growths produced? Can you give a reason for it?

FERNS.

For beauty and gracefulness of appearance the ferns rival any of the flowering plants. The field lesson will reveal the fact that they are as attractive to the pupils as any of their more pretentious neighbors, and they should, therefore, receive their share of attention.

1. Can you find anything about the fern that resembles a flower?

2. Does it produce a stem as other plants do? Examine the part under ground.

3. In what locations are ferns to be found? Do they seem to have anything in common with other plants in the same location?

4. Notice the small brown dots called *sori* (singular sorus) on the back of the fern-leaf or frond. Such fronds are called fertile, for it is from the fine dust-like *spores* that come from the sori that the young ferns are produced. These are much too small to be studied with the unaided eye.

5. Are all the fronds fertile? Can you find any ferns that do not produce the sori on the back of the fronds? Are they all arranged the same way when they do grow on the back of the fronds?

MOSSES.

1. In what locations do you find mosses most abundant? How do the locations differ from those of most plants?

2. Do you find them growing in dry as well as moist spots?

3. Does the moss found growing upon the trunk of a tree derive its nourishment from the tree?

4. Do those which grow upon rocks, use the rock as other plants use the soil?

5. Do mosses have roots? Do they have flowers?

6. Can you find any moss that is sending up delicate, thread-like stems salled *setæ*, which bear small spore-cases on top? The lid-like covering of the latter is called the *calyptra.*

7. Remove the calyptra and shake the moss over a clean sheet of paper. These minute dust-like bodies are

called spores, and from these the young plant is produced.

8. Do you find any resemblance in the mosses to the ferns? To flowering plants? What are the chief differences from the latter?

Physics.

SOUND.

In the study of sound there are many interesting experiments which may be performed that will properly open up the subject for young beginners and lead them to further observation. Experiments may be performed by the pupils which will enable them to see something of the relation of sound to vibrating bodies ; but it is not so easy to devise those which will show directly that air is a conducting medium ; nor is it possible, by actual experiment, for them to understand very clearly the nature of the sound waves in it.

Initial interest in the subject may be gained by taking up some sounds with which the pupils are familiar. Nothing will more certainly assure this than some simple instrument, such as an Æolian harp, which may be constructed by the pupils as follows : Take a dry pine board, about six or eight inches wide by one-half inch in thickness, and cut it so that it will slip easily into the window when the sash is raised. Drive about ten tacks or small nails in each end, opposite each other, letting the heads project about one-eighth of an inch. If small screw eyes instead of nails are used in one end, the strings may be keyed up or loosened as desired. Beginning at one side stretch from the first nail in one end to the one opposite it in the other a single silk thread, which has been well waxed. Then twist two threads together tightly and wax them and stretch between the second pair of nails, and so on increasing each cord by one thread of silk. Next, make two bridges of hard wood of the same size and shape. Their length should equal the width of the board, and they should be about one and one-half inches wide at one end and three-quarters of an inch at the other. The upper edge which supports the strings should be beveled to a sharp edge. Slide the bridges on their sides under the strings near the middle of the board and then turn them up properly and slip them along toward either end of the board until the strings are all quite taut. Raise the sash high enough to clear the bridges and place the board in the window. A very slight breeze will start the music, which will continue to be produced while the wind blows, with almost infinite variation.

1. What is the cause of the sound that comes from the Æolian harp?

2. Can you discover how it is produced? Fold a few very light, narrow strips of paper half an inch long, and drop them across the middle of different strings ; what do you notice when the wind blows across the string?

3. Lay a small stick of wood across the middle of the strings ; what effect does it have upon the music?

4. How are the low tones produced? Place a stick upon different sets of the strings and note the result.

5. What produces the high tones? What is there about the strings of the harp which affects the pitch of the tone?

6. What causes the loud tones? Do loudness and pitch depend upon the same thing?

7. Why is it that sometimes very soft tones are pro-

duced? Are all the strings capable of producing soft tones? Test, as before, with a stick.

8. What is the difference between a low tone and a soft tone?

9. Compare a loud tone with a high tone; may both tones be produced by the same string?

10. Can both a high tone and a low tone be produced by the same string?

11. Does the board have any influence upon the tones produced?

12. Move the bridges a little closer together; what difference in sound is noted? To what is this due? If screw eyes are used in one end of the board, as suggested above, the strings may be readily tightened with the bridges in any position.

13. What effect is produced by placing the bridges farther apart? To what is the effect due?

14. What is the best size for the window opening? Would the harp play as well in a similar opening at the top of the window?

15. Can you see a reason for using silk thread? Why should it be waxed?

16. Can you, when out of doors, hear any sounds which are produced in a way similar to the manner in which they are made by the Æolian harp?

17. What sounds can you distinguish that come from a different cause?

18. In the sounds that you hear about you on all sides, can you distinguish those of the same varieties that were produced by the Æolian harp?

19. What produces high tones? Low tones? Can you distinguish soft tones? By what are the loud tones produced?

20. Are there any sounds produced that are not musical? What difference do you notice between musical and non-musical sounds?

21. Fasten a stiff wire (a knitting needle answers the purpose), eight or ten inches long upright in a vise, or drive it into a board or block of wood. Pull the free end to one side and suddenly let it go; describe what takes place. Make a drawing of the wire, showing its range of movement.

22. For convenience, certain parts of the course traversed by the swinging wire are named as follows: The motion from one extreme position of the wire to the other is called a *single vibration;* from one extreme position to the other and back again is a *double vibration* or a *complete vibration.* The distance from the middle point of a single vibration to either extreme is called the *amplitude of vibration.* The time occupied in making a complete vibration is called the *period* of vibration.

23. Fasten the same wire used in (21) in the vise so that but half its length shall project; what differences do you notice? Did you secure a pure tone in the first instance? Compare with the vibrations in the second position.

24. In which position does the wire have the *greater period* of vibration? This can be shown if you place two wires in the vise, one double the length of the other.

25. How does changing the *period* affect the tone?

26. Cause the wire to vibrate with different amplitudes; how does it affect the sound?

27. Strike one edge of a small bell with a stick or a pencil; hold a small cork or a bead suspended by a thread so that it rests lightly against the opposite side of the bell at the edge. What does the cork tell you?

28. Strike a tuning fork against something, and while

it is giving out a tone dip it quickly into a glass of water ; what do you learn from this ?

29. Strike it again and set the end of the fork against your closed teeth. Try again and hold one of the prongs just touching the tip of the nose or ear. Can you tell what is producing the sound in the fork.

30. Drive a small nail nearly to the head into one end of the table. Stretch from it across the table a fine wire or violin string. The wire may be obtained at any hardware store for five cents a spool. Place under the string two bridges similar to those in the harp, and from its free end suspend a small pail with shot enough in it to make a weight of about a half pound.

31. Pluck the string with the finger; can you follow the vibration with the eye ? Make a drawing of the string with its attachments and mark the different things described above in (22).

32. Add shot until the pail weighs one or two pounds, and pluck the string again ; can you get a tone from it ?

33. Add shot to the bucket until the octave is reached ; how much does the pail and shot weigh ? Compare with the weight with which the lower note was attained.

34. How does the increased weight affect the period of vibration ? How does it affect the tone ?

35. Place a third bridge under the string, so that the part of the cord on one side of it will give the octave above that given by the whole cord ; what is the length of that part of the cord compared with the entire string ? Why should the third bridge be no higher than the others ?

36. How does the period of vibration of the segment compare with that of the whole cord ?

37. Stretch another string, heavier than the first, by the same weight ; pluck with the finger and compare with

that obtained from the smaller cord. Compare its period of vibration.

38. What changes could you make by which the same note could be obtained from both ?

39. What things have you discovered which affect the pitch of the tone ? What things affect the period of vibration ?

40. Pluck the strings so that each will produce both loud and soft tones ; can you discover what determines loudness of tone ?

41. Support in a horizontal position a pane of glass, about eight or ten inches square, upon a block of wood half an inch square. Hold a glass rod or piece of tubing, eighteen inches or two feet long, upright on the glass plate immediately over the block. Dust a small cloth well with powdered rosin, and holding the rod firmly with one hand, rub the cloth up and down it with the other until a sound is produced. Sprinkle fine dry sand evenly over the surface of the glass and rub the rod as before.

42. What causes the sand to move? Note the different effect upon it of the shrill and deep notes.

43. Why does it lie still along certain lines ?

44. If convenient, draw a violin bow over the edge of the glass. What effects are produced by drawing it over different parts ?

45. The lines along which the sand gathers are called *nodes*. Strike a tuning fork and turn it round slowly near the ear ; can you account for the intermitting sounds ?

46. Can you see any relation between the periods of silence noticed with the fork and the lines of rest on the glass plate as are indicated by the sound ?

47. Hold a light piece of paper across one of the strings

mentioned in (37) and cause it to vibrate ; can you see any nodes ?

48. Why is it that when you grasp the cord, the tuning fork, the bell, or the glass plate in any of the foregoing experiments you produce silence ?

49. Recall the singing flame that was studied in Chemistry for January in the experiment with hydrogen ; can you account for it ?

50. Why did changing the length of the tube affect the sound ? What causes the sound when you blow across the mouth of a hollow key ?

51. What causes the sound in a steam whistle ?

52. Where is the sound of the human voice produced ; Place the finger on the throat on "Adam's apple" and prolong the sound of O, then change to the octave above ? can you feel any movement?

53. Try in the same way the long sounds of all the vowels ; do you notice any difference in the throat movements in making these different sounds?

54. The vocal sounds are produced by the air passing over the edges of membranes that are so stretched across the larynx as to form a narrow slit-like opening. The larynx, also called the voice box, is the chamber-like modification of the upper end of the windpipe. The membranes across it are called the vocal cords.

55. Can you tell what probably takes place with the cords when the voice is raised in pitch? When it changes from soft to loud ?

56. By what means do we mold words from the sound produced by the vocal cords ? Practice many different sounds until you understand how this is done.

57. Of what importance is full, perfect breathing in using the voice ?

58. In observing a workman using a hammer some distance from you, can you hear the sound as soon as you see the hammer strike ? Can you hear a distant whistle as soon as you see the steam issuing from it ? Why is this ?

59. Sound travels about eleven hundred feet per second through air. Suppose you hear a peal of thunder ten seconds after you see a flash of lightning ; how far distant is the cloud ? Suppose five minutes afterward you hear the peal in five seconds after the flash ; how long will it be before the storm reaches you ?

60. Do loud, soft, high, and low sounds travel with equal rapidity ? How does it happen that you can hear at the same time the music of many different instruments playing in a band at some distance from you ?

61. What difference can you detect between a musical tone and mere noise ? Why does the tuning fork give a musical tone, while a stone against which you strike it makes only a noise ?

62. Can you account for an echo ? Note the conditions which are always present when an echo is heard.

63. Hang a watch at the focus of a concave mirror ; facing the mirror, but at a sufficient distance from it for the ticking to be inaudible, place another concave mirror. Place a small funnel in the end of a rubber tube, and with the other end of the tube held to the ear, place the funnel at the focus of the second mirror.

64. Can you hold it so that the ticking of the watch can be heard ? Why place the watch in the focus ? Why hold the funnel in the focus of the second mirror ? Why use the funnel ? Why use the rubber tube ?

65. The following table shows the number of vibrations

per second of each tone in the octave below middle C, and the relation of the numbers in any octave.

C_2	D_2	E_2	F_2	G_2	A_2	B_2	C_1
1	$\frac{9}{8}$	$\frac{5}{4}$	$\frac{4}{3}$	$\frac{3}{2}$	$\frac{5}{3}$	$\frac{15}{8}$	2
128	144	160	170	192	214	240	256

66. If there were no ear in the world, would there be any sound?

67. When a bell strikes, where does the sound *seem* to be? Where is it really?

68. Suppose a person were to be born deaf, and after growing to adult age were suddenly to acquire the power to hear; what troubles do you think he would find in his new experience?

69. What enables us to properly locate the source of a sound? Why cannot the child do it so accurately?

70. Can you get an idea of sound by any means except through the ear? Place a watch at first loosely between the lips and then clasp it firmly between the teeth; do you notice any difference in the loudness of sound?

71. Do you see any use for the external ear? Why do we not have the power to move the ears as many other animals do? Of what advantage to them are the ear movements? What different expressions are possible with them by means of their ear movements?

Chemistry.

Following the studies of the previous months upon the different gases, it will now be a matter of both interest and profit to study flame, with a view to seeing how it is produced and of what parts it is composed. An ordinary candle will serve the purpose, though a gas jet would be better in some respects for part of the work.

1. Trim the tallow away from the wick, leaving it projecting half an inch, and light it at the tip ; what happens as the flame increases in size ?

2. Shield it from draughts from doors or windows ; is there any part visible outside the luminous cone of flame ?

To discover this, hold a sheet of paper close to the flame so that the luminous part is obscured ; what do you notice when you look past the edge of the paper toward the outer edge of the flame ?

3. Take a short glass tube that is drawn to a point and hold the large end in the blue center of the flame with the pointed end upward ; can you detect any odor at the tip ?

4. Hold a lighted match at the tip of the tube. What does this indicate ? What comes up the tube ?

5. Hold a sheet of writing paper horizontally above the flame and lower it steadily down in the flame to the wick and quickly remove it ; what does the scorched part indicate ?

6. Hold a small splinter across the blaze for an instant and note the scorched spots; what does their position indicate concerning the different parts of the flame?

7. Approach the flame with a splinter and notice when it takes fire; is it necessary for it to touch the luminous part of the flame to ignite?

8. Does the wick burn? Is it the burning wick that makes the large bright flame?

9. What use can you discover for the wick? What do you find around the base of the wick?

10. How does the oil or melted tallow reach the blaze? What change does it undergo when it reaches the blaze? See question (3) above.

11. From what you have seen can you tell which is the hottest part of the flame? The coolest?

12. Hold a piece of a dish or glass for a moment in the luminous part; what proves to be in this part of the flame?

13. Why is the center of the flame cooler than the outer part? Why is the carbon not entirely consumed in the luminous zone of the flame?

14. Lower a wire gauze over the flame; does it burn above the gauze?

15. Hold a lighted match above the gauze; can you produce a flame then that comes from the candle? What does that show? Look down upon the flame through the gauze.

16. Roll a little piece of gauze around a lead pencil and then lower the tube over the flame; can you explain what happens? Read about safety lamps used by miners.

17. Examine, in the same way as you have the candle, the flame of your alcohol lamp and note the differences.

18. In the same way, also, if possible, examine a gas flame.

19. Are we burning gas when we use candles? What gas is it? What forms as a result of the burning of this gas in air? Hold a cold plate above the flame. (See Chemistry for January.)

BOOK OF REFERENCE. Humboldt Library : No. 99 ; chapter on Flame.

Meteorology.

There is no month in the year whose meteorological influence is more potent for good or ill than May. Upon its influences hang the prosperity and comfort, if not the fate, for the rest of the season, of almost every living thing, both plant and animal, in our latitude. A dry, windy, warm May so thoroughly checks and stunts the growth of all sprouting seedlings that hardly any amount of favor for the rest of the season will enable them to make good their loss. At this time the germinating plants are just trying to learn how to take their nourishment from the soil, and they need no end of encouragement in rains and friendly clouds that shield them from the direct rays of the sun. The meteorology for the month should, therefore, be studied with interest.

1. How many frosts, if any, have you noted in May?

2. Compare May with the autumn months; which one is it most like in this respect?

3. What inference can you make respecting the temperature during the night of each of these two months?

4. How do the daily records of the two months compare as to temperature?

5. Have you noticed any change in the amount of cloudiness this month? Compare with the autumn months; with the winter months.

6. Is a cloudy May favorable or unfavorable?

7. How do the clouds differ in character from those of winter months? Can you explain?

8. Compare the temperature before and after rainfall; does it vary uniformly?

9. Do the movements of the mercurial column in the barometer seem to be associated in any way with the storms that have occurred?

10. Compare the direction of the prevailing wind with that for January.

11. What wind has been accompanied by rain? What one with clearing weather? Compare with preceding months.

12. Under what circumstances has dew been formed this month? Have there been any fogs?

13. Compare the rate of change of temperature this month with that of April and March.

14. What have been the extremes of temperature? Compare with the autumn months.

15. What are the extremes in the barometric record?

STUDY OF THE WEATHER BUREAU MAPS.

16. In what quarter of the country has the Low Area appeared most frequently?

17. In which quarter has there been the heaviest rainfall?

18. Trace the isothermal line 60 degrees; compare with its course and location in April.

19. Is the isothermal 60 degrees more or less regular in its course this month than last month?

20. Compare in this particular the course of all the isotherms this month with last.

21. Where are they turned most widely from the normal east and west line?

22. Do the coast lines affect them now as in the winter?

23. Can you see any change in their course about the Great Lakes?

24. Do the great river valleys, the St. Lawrence and Mississippi, seem to affect their course?

25. What effect upon them have the Rocky and Appalachian mountains? Compare with previous months.

Astronomy.

1. How much change in the length of day and night during this month?

2. Is the *rate* of change increasing or diminishing?

3. How does the rate of change compare with that of last month?

4. In what other month of the year was the rate of change near what it is now?

5. Compare the positions of the earth in its orbit during these two months.

6. Try to explain, using a globe when necessary, why the *rate* of change in the length of day and night varies as it does this month.

7. Is the day gaining in length more in the evening or morning?

Can you explain this? Compare with the amount of change during the winter and fall months.

8. How is the position of the sun on the horizon, morning and evening, changing? Explain why it is so.

9. How much has it moved on the horizon since March? How much since December?

10. Compare the *rate* of change in the noon shadow with that of last month; can you see why it varies?

11. During what other month in the year was it nearest its present position?

12. What angle do the sun's rays make with the earth this month? Is the angle increasing or diminishing?

13. How does the change of this angle affect things upon the earth ? Does it in any way affect us ?

14. At what place or places about the middle of the month on the earth is the sun on the horizon all day ?

15. It is said that in the polar regions, before the sun appears, and after it sets, there is a long period of twilight ; can you explain why it is so ? Compare our twilight now with that in winter ; can you see any difference ? (See Physics for April.)

16. Does the twilight period increase or diminish toward the equator ? Can you explain this ?

17. Have you noticed any change in the position of the constellations that were observed last month ? In what way can that be accounted for ?

18. How have Jupiter and Venus changed position as morning stars since last month ? Explain why this is so.

19. Can you tell how much of its orbit each has passed through since it became morning star ?

20. How much of its orbit has the earth traversed since then ?

21. Additional constellations : Hercules, Lyra, Arcturus, and Northern Crown in the east in order from the horizon to the meridian.

Geography.

AFRICA. RELIEF, DRAINAGE, CLIMATE, AND PRODUCTIONS.

It will be noticed that the structure of this continent combines to some extent the physical features of both the eastern and western continents. Its structure is not so simple as that of either of the American continents, nor is it, as yet, nearly so well known. As before, the study should be based upon good physical maps, and should be accompanied by modeling and drawing.

1. Which ocean receives the largest rivers? What is the direction of the greatest highland?

2. Compare the direction of this highland with that of North America. With South America.

3. In what respect does the northern part of Africa resemble the continent of Euro-Asia?

4. In what respect does the southern part resemble the Americas?

5. Where is the highest point in the principal highland?

6. Where are the secondary highlands? Compare their position with respect to the main highland with that in the other continents previously studied.

7. The navigation of the rivers is greatly hindered by rapids and waterfalls; can you see a reason for this?

8. Compare the direction of the great rivers of Africa with that of the greatest rivers of other continents.

383

9. Compare Africa with respect to its lakes, both in size and number, with the other continents.

10. From what region do the great rivers derive their waters?

11. Compare the rivers of Africa with those of America with respect to tributaries ; can you account for the contrasts observed ?

12. Where are the fertile regions in Africa? Can you account for them ?

13. What influences tend to make the coasts fertile and the interior barren ?

14. Note carefully the boundaries of the Sahara Desert ; can you understand why they are fixed when you find them ?

15. What causes can you assign for the position of this desert ? Note the direction of the winds as indicated by the arrows on a good physical map.

16. Compare the region in the same latitude in America ; do you find a desert ? Can you see a reason ?

17. Compare with the different parts in Asia in the same latitude ; what contrast do you find ?

18. Do any rain-bearing winds reach Africa from the Atlantic Ocean ? Why ?

19. Can you see any reason for desert regions in the southern part of the continent ?

20. Compare with South America in the same latitude ; is there similarity or contrast ?

21. Compare the equatorial regions of Africa and South America ; which region has the more luxuriant vegetation ? In which is animal life more abundant ?

22. What has determined the location of the cities in Africa ? Contrast their location with that of the cities of other countries.

23. Can you see what things have contributed to give

Egypt so conspicuous a place in history? Compare and contrast its natural advantages with Italy and Greece.

24. What are the natural obstacles in the way of African exploration? What physical features stand in the way of trade?

25. What are the valuable productions in the tropical interior? How are they carried to the cities?

26. Why is it that there are no cities in the centers of these productions as in other continents?

27. Where are the mining regions? What minerals are found?

28. By whom are the mines worked?

29. What contrasts are found in the continent of Africa and South America in the same latitude?

Geology.

FIELD LESSONS.

The importance of doing a great deal of field work with beginners in geology cannot be overestimated. In fact, there is but one way to begin, and that is by going into the field. Such lessons are often less fruitful than they might be because of a lack of system in the plan for it. From the beginning of this month on to the end of the school year, the season is likely to be suitable for outdoor work, and a few hints as to the mode of conducting a field lesson will be found useful.

As a rule it is best to have a definite thing to look for or to study each time a field lesson is undertaken. Sometimes all hope of good results is lost by calling it a picnic. This term has a distinctive meaning of its own in the minds of the children, and it has but little in common with serious study. The pupils should be provided with baskets or bags in which they may carry the specimens gathered, and there should be a number of good hammers in the class. A small pocket compass will also be found useful in getting the exact direction of the *dip* and *strike* of rock. For getting the angle of the dip use the instrument described under Astronomy for September, on page 61. If a lake or stream is visited, a small wide-mouthed bottle will be needed in which some water may be obtained and allowed to settle to show the amount of silt in suspension. It should be definitely understood at the outset that each pupil will be held responsible for a description of what he has seen, to be expressed in writing, a drawing, a painting, a clay or sand model, as may best be adapted to the particular circumstances of the case. All true education must develop three great ideas—those of space, time, and force, and the field lesson gives capital opportunity to broaden all three. A few suggestive questions are appended.

1. What is the size of the area you wish to study? Its length? Its breadth? Its area in square miles or acres?

The area selected must not be too large. Take only so much as will be needed to illustrate the point it is desired to study.

2. What forces have given the surface its chief character? Are they still at work? Have the organic or inorganic agencies done most of the work?

3. Has the work within the selected area been one of building or tearing down? If tearing down, what counter forces have retarded it? If building, what counter forces have opposed?

4. Which of the inorganic agencies, rain,-snow, ice, frost, etc., have been the most active?

5. Have any forces acted here in the past which are now quiescent?

6. Note the work of running and standing water, if there be any; is it destructive or constructive?

7. Note the soil and subsoil, and compare both with the underlying rock, if any is to be found. How was the soil formed?

8. Are the underlying rock strata horizontal or inclined? What is the amount and direction of dip in different places?

9. Are there fossils in the rocks? Are they fossils of animals or plants? Land or water? Fresh water or

marine ?   Are there any forms like them living at present ?   What present forms do they most closely resemble ?

10. If a stream is studied, consider the course of the
channel ; is it changing at present ?   How far has it in
the past deviated from its present course ?

11. Does the water contain silt in suspension ?   Test
by allowing a bottle full to stand until it settles.   Is the
water soft or hard ?   Why ?

12. Are there any springs?   Are they constant or intermittent ?   Are they greatly and suddenly affected by a
heavy rain ?   Have you any means of telling whether the
underground reservoir is deep or near the surface ?   Does
the water form a deposition near the outlet ?   What
is it ?

13. If a standing body of water is present, can you tell
what the source of the water is ?   What hollowed out the
basin that holds the water ?   Why does the water not sink
into the earth ?   Is there an outlet ?   Did it always occupy the spot it now does ?   Is it changing its limits now ?
What is the cause of it ?   Is there silt suspended in the
water ?

14. For suggestions as to the study of a marsh, see
Geology for April.   See, also, Geology for September.

15. On the ground make necessary measurements and
sketches, and on returning make (*a*) drawings showing the
outline of the area studied, the course of the streams,
etc.   (*b*) A model in clay or sand, showing the chief
features of relief, direction of elevations, valleys, depressions filled with water, springs, etc.   (*c*) Drawing or
painting, or both, showing the rock strata, their colors,
dip, fossils, etc.   (*d*) A written description of the special
features of the lesson ; this may include description of

the soil, of the characteristic vegetation, and the probable geological history of the region. Any or all of these modes of expression should be required at the discretion of the teacher as the age of the pupils and the demands of the lesson may seem to require.

Mineralogy.

EXAMINATION OF SOILS.

One of the most obvious things to any one who makes a study of plant life is the close relation which exists between the growth of a plant and the character of the soil that produces it. For this reason something should be done in the course of the season to lead to a more or less close examination of the different soils in which plants are found growing. The work must of necessity be mostly of a qualitative nature, and even in this line only the simplest things can be noticed. It is well to keep in mind during the study that the fertility of soil depends upon its physical and chemical nature. A knowledge of these properties is of great practical value in determining what plant food, if any, should be added to it, and also what classes of plants are best adapted to it. Some care should be used in selecting a specimen for examination. Try to secure a block of it a few inches square and as deep as the soil is to be found. Portions of it may then be examined in the order in which it actually occurs in the ground.

It is thought best to briefly outline the entire process for the mechanical analysis of soils, though the wise teacher will decide whether it is best to have his pupils go through with it all at once. Problems may be given at different times as occasion requires, such as:

To find the amount of clay in a certain soil ; or, To ascertain the amount of gravel, or coarse sand, etc.

1. What depth is the soil where you have examined it ? What kind of subsoil is underneath ? Subsoil is the layer immediately below the surface soil.

2. What depth is there to the subsoil ?

3. How has the soil been formed ? Is it made by the rotting away of the underlying rock, or has it been carried to its present place from a distance ?

4. What part have plants played in forming the soil ?

5. How does the subsoil differ from the soil ?

6. Has the slant or position of the field had anything to do with the formation of the soil ?

7. Has the soil ever had any fertilizers added to it artificially to increase its productiveness ?

8. Dry a small amount of the soil, rub up finely the earthy lumps, and pick out the small stones it may contain ; are they of one, or different kinds ? Use some of the tests mentioned in the previous lessons to determine some of their properties.

9. Weigh about three or four ounces of the dried soil and pass it through a small sieve made from gauze in which the meshes are one-tenth of an inch apart. Rub up the earthy lumps so that all the fine material will pass through.

10. Wash the part too coarse to pass through until thoroughly free from dirt, and dry and weigh it. How much *coarse gravel* do, you find in the soil ? What per cent. of its entire weight ?

11. Take that part of the soil which passed through the sieve and rub it through another, the meshes of which are one-fifteenth of an inch apart.

12. Again take the part that is too coarse to go through,

and wash, dry, and weigh ; this will give the amount of *gravelly sand* in the soil.   What per cent. is there ?

13. Weigh a small amount of this gravelly sand and heat it red hot for some time in a small crucible and weigh again ; does it lose weight when burnt thus? Why ?

14. Take an ounce of the fine material that has passed through the second sieve and boil it in a flask until all the particles are completely separated.   When cool, rinse it out into a tall jar or bottle with a wide mouth. By means of a funnel and long tube reaching nearly to the bottom pour a gentle stream of water into the jar so as to agitate the sediment.   Set the jar in a larger vessel and catch the overflow.

15. When the water runs away clear, pour off the water and dry the remainder ; this will give the *coarse sand* in the soil.   What per cent. of the soil is it ?

16. Weigh a small amount of it after it is dried and then heat it red hot in a crucible ; does it lose weight? Why ?   What kind of substances burn ?   What kind cannot be consumed in the fire ?

17. Repeat the process described above with the overflow from the jar ; this will give the *fine sand.*   Do not agitate so strongly as in the first instance.   Does it lose weight by being burned ?

18. Subtract the weight of the coarse and fine sand from the weight taken in the beginning and it will give the amount of *clay* in the soil.   What per cent. is it of the whole amount ?

19. Where does the sand come from that you have found in your sample of soil ?   Was it derived from the underlying rock ?

20. Can you account for the presence of the' gravel that you found ?   Are the pebbles all of the same kind ?

21. Where did the clay come from ?

22. How was that part of the soil formed that was consumed in the fire when heated ?

23. Which element found in the soil is best for vegetation ? Which is the poorest ?

24. Why is gravel poorly adapted for plants ? Does its presence add or detract from the fertility of the soil ?

25. What are the advantages and disadvantages of sand for vegetation ?

26. Which is better for plants, clay or sand ? Why ?

27. What properties of loam make it valuable for plants ?

Zoölogy.

At this season of the year, the material which might be taken up in this subject for study has become so abundant that it is difficult to make a selection. The decision as to what shall be studied may be left, partly at least, to the pupils themselves, due regard being given to the ease with which specimens may be obtained.

Insect life presents great variety, and, also, abundance of interesting material upon which many profitable lessons may be given. Enough work should be done along this line to lead the pupils into inquiry concerning the habits of the various kinds found, their relations to plants, and the structures by which they are adapted to their modes of life.

It will be possible during this month to observe the newly hatched birds and the treatment they receive from the old ones. The work of the earthworms may be followed up according to the suggestions offered for the previous month and, in fact, any of the work begun in the spring may be continued now.

BIRDS.

1. Upon what kinds of food are the young birds fed? Do the old ones prepare it in any way for the young birds?

2. What feathers appear first upon the young birds?

3. Do the feathers grow evenly over all parts of the

body ?   Can you see any reason why certain spaces are left bare ?

4. How long after hatching is it when the young birds attempt to fly ?   Do the old birds render the young ones any assistance ?

5. Which parent do the young ones resemble more closely ?   Can you see a reason for it ?

6. What dangers threaten the young ones at this time ?

7. What evidences do you have that bear upon the chances of the young birds for life ?   Compare with the chances of infantile human life.

8. What are the most active destroyers of bird life ? What means of escape have they ?

9. Select feathers from different parts of the body and compare them.

10. In a large quill-feather selected from the wing, note the following points : (*a*) the central *shaft* bearing on both sides, (*b*) the *vane ;* (*c*) the *quill,* that part of the shaft below the vane.   The small branches making up the vane are called *barbs ;* these are interlocked by means of the *barbules.*   Note how this is done.   Why is it so ?

11. Compare a *down* feather with a *quill ;* where is the chief difference ?   What difference in use is there between the down and quill-feathers ?

12. Are the feathers waterproof ?   Explain.

13. Note the arrangement of the feathers in the wings ; what form do they give to the wing ?

14. Do you know of any long legged birds that have long tails ?   Have you seen any short legged birds with very small tails ?   What have you noticed about the flight of such birds ?   When a bird is flying, is its neck stretched out or drawn back ?   Can you see a reason ?

15. Can you see what determines the line of flight of

a bird ?   Note the form and relative size of the body, wings, tail, and legs.

16. Try to count the strokes of the wings of different birds while they are flying ; can you move your arms for five minutes with equal rapidity ?

INSECTS.   (*See, also, Zoölogy for September.*)

Bees.

1. Watch closely a bee, either bumble bee or honey bee, in its visits among flowers ; can you tell why its visits are made ?

2. Do they visit different flowers promiscuously or only those of the same kind ?

3. Do honey bees and bumble bees visit the same flowers ?   Examine the bees closely for a reason for what you observe.

4. By what means do they cling to the flowers ?   How do they examine a flower ?

5. Do they injure the flowers by their visits ?   Can you see what they carry away ?   Examine their legs and backs.

6. Can you see any use for the hairs that are found on the bee's legs and body ?

7. How do they manage to reach the nectar of the flower ?   Can you see how they carry it ?   The nectar is stored up in the crop—one of the divisions of the alimentary canal—and is then elaborated or changed into honey by a process not yet fully explained.

8. How do bees hum ?   Is it always on the same key ? Can you tell how rapidly the wings vibrate? (See Physics for May under Sound.)   Compare the wings with those of the butterfly and beetle.

9. Can you find any evidence of sight or hearing? If so, can you locate the organs?

10. When a bee has secured its load, notice its flight; is a " bee-line " a straight line?

Ants.

Suggestions have already been made as to how ants may be confined for the purposes of indoor observation. (See Zoölogy for October.) But it is of great interest to observe them at work at this season outdoors. Ant-hills are to be found in almost every field or bit of woodland where the soil is rather light and dry. Along paths and roadsides the work of a small red ant may be observed.

1. Do ants and earthworms work together in the same soils? Can you see any reasons for the difference in the locations that are chosen?

2. Look into the nests and secure if possible some of the small, almost cylindrical bodies usually to be found, which most people call eggs; are they eggs? Can you find eggs?

3. Do the ants move them regularly? When do they bring them out? When do they take them back? What is accomplished by this care?

4. How do they carry their burdens? Can you trace any resemblance to the crawfish?

5. Can they see or hear? Can you find either eyes or ears?

6. What do they eat? Can you tell from their mouths which they prefer, solid or liquid food?

7. If you can find a densely populated ant-hill, place in it or near it a dead mouse inclosed in a box. Leave entrances for the ants, and you will not only feed the

ants, but; by and by, you will have a nicely prepared mouse's skeleton for yourself.

8. Can you find any small plant lice on plants near the ants' home? If so, watch closely and try to find out whether or not the ants take any notice of them.

9. Do the ants store up food as the bees do? How do they employ their time? Have they honestly earned their reputation for industry?

10. Do ants of different sizes live together; are they the same or of different kinds? Do ants living in different hills communicate with each other? Are they friendly or hostile? Try placing strangers in one of the hills.

Spiders.

1. In what locations do you find spiders? Select one or more places for observation, and, if possible, try to observe one spinning a web.

2. How is the silk obtained for the web?

3. What feet do they use in fastening their silk as it is spun? How do they place their long guys which suspend the web? Do they repair old or broken webs?

4. Where do they begin to spin the circular threads, in the middle or at the circumference of the web? At what time do they spin the web?

5. Examine some of the filmy webs that may be found on the roadside; how do they differ from those that are suspended? where do you find the spider? To discover his whereabouts drop a fly on the web or shake it slightly.

6. In what position does the spider place himself in one of the suspended wheel-like nests? Why?

7. Do they eat solid or liquid food? Do they make any use of plant food?

8. Where do they lay their eggs? Sometimes the mother spider may be seen carrying a large white ball ; what is it ?

9. In what way is the use of the spider's cocoon different from that of the moth ?

10. Can you discover the way in which the mother spider cares for her young ?

11. How does the spider differ in its structure from the bee and ant ? Compare as to the number of legs, parts of the body, etc.

The House-fly.

1. Place a grain or two of moistened sugar upon a table and notice how a fly takes it up ; does it eat it as a solid ?

2. How do its mouth parts differ from those of the ant ?

3. Does it make any use of its feet in eating ? By moving a magnifying glass up cautiously, the mode of managing food may be clearly made out. It is an interesting observation. Can you account for various movements it makes with its legs and wings at intervals while eating.

4. What evidence have you that it can see ? Can you determine whether it can hear ?

5. Does it move its legs in the same order as the ant ?

6. Examine its foot ; can you account for the way by which it clings to a pane of glass or the ceiling ?

7. Can you find any evidence that it breathes ?

8. Has it the sense of smell? Do not guess at the answers, but find actual proof from close observation.

9. Where do they lay their eggs? What comes directly from the egg? Compare with the ant, the bee, and the spider. A small piece of meat exposed to the warm sun

will very soon enable the pupils to see the early stages of a fly's life.   Is it the house-fly that lays its eggs upon meat ?

10. Can you tell how many vibrations the wings make in a second ? (See Physics for May.) Compare with a bee.

Beetles.

1. These are at once recognized by the hard shiny coats and wings.   Where are they most abundant ?

2. Can you see a good reason for the contrast between the beetle and bee in regard to their wings ?

3. How are the wings employed in flying ?   Can you find any beetles that do not fly ?

4. Can you find any beetles that do not spread or open the outer wings ?

5. What is the food of beetles ?   Examine the mouth parts ; compare with the fly, the ant, and the spider.

6. Can they see or hear ?   Where are the organs of seeing and hearing ?

7. What enemies do they have ?   How do they escape ?   Have they means of attack or defense ?

8. Can you find any insects that are injurious to plants ?

9. Have you found any that are beneficial to plants ?

10. Have you found any insects that are either beneficial or injurious to man ?

REPTILES.

It would be nothing less than wonderful for the season to pass by without one or more members of this group of animals being found and brought in by some of the pupils.   Turtles are abundant in streams, usually, and are easily kept in an aquarium or even in a pail of water. A small piece of raw meat now and then is all the food they require. A snake, repulsive as it is to most people, is nevertheless an interesting object for study. The teacher should rise above his unnatural prejudices against this creature for the sake of the children who are dependent upon him for the truth concerning nature, and try to have them grow up with less of the unnatural horror than he has himself.

Snakes.

1. A snake may be kept in a box with a glass cover over it. There should be a little dried grass or other material in the box to afford at least partial means of concealment.

2. Can you discover any signs of intelligence? Does it show signs of fear?

3. What is the meaning of the frequent darting out of the tongue? Many people have an idea that this is a weapon of defense or attack; is it so?

4. It is interesting to see the small striped garter snake capture its prey; put a mouse in the box and watch the operation. If you can find a poisonous snake compare the two in this respect.

5. Turn the box upside down so that the snake will lie on the glass; can you see from beneath how the snake moves?

6. Compare its motions with those of the earthworm.

7. Do the scales on the under side play the same part that the spines of the earthworm do? How do the scales on the sides differ from those on the under side?

8. Is the snake propelled by means of the scales alone?

9. Does the snake wink? Compare with the turtle.

10. Are the upper and under sides of the snake more

or less unlike than in the case of the earthworm ?
What reason can you give ?

Turtles.

1. How does the turtle compare with the snake as to
intelligence ? As to activity ? As to expressions of
fear ?

2. Does it have any actions or habits in common
with snakes ? What differences ?

3. What would seem to be the use of the hard shell ?
Compare the shells of water turtles with those found
on dry land ; can you see a reason for the differences ?

4. Do turtles chew their food ? How do they seize it ?

5. By what means do they swim ? Compare the
swimming powers with a fish and a frog.

6. Has it any advantages over either ? Are there any
disadvantages ?

7. Does it wink ? Are you reminded of any other
animal examined in this respect ?

8. What modes of attack have they ? What are their
enemies ?

9. Turtles lay their eggs at this season in the sand on
the shores of streams and ponds ; try to find a nest.

10. Note their breathing, and compare with the snake,
frog, and bird.

Botany.

In elementary work in the subject of botany, usually, comparatively little is planned in any practical manner for a study of plant physiology. It is not difficult, however, for the pupils to perform a number of experiments which will do much in illustrating plant action. By similar means, some notion of the chief constituents of the plant may be gained.

1. Carefully remove from the soil any small vigorous plant having a number of leaves. Gently wash away the adhering earth and dry with a cloth or blotting paper, and weigh it as accurately as possible.

2. Place in an oven or near the fire and dry it completely without scorching, and then weigh it again ; how much loss by drying ? What per cent. ? What part of the plant's constituents remain ?

3. What caused the plant to lose weight ? Let different pupils try different plants. Try the same plant in different locations ; how does the location affect the loss per cent. ?

4. After finding the loss of weight, cut or break the dried plant into small pieces and heat them in a test tube or crucible until no further change takes place ; what now remains ? What was formed before the final residue was obtained ? What became of this as change took place ? (See Chemistry for December and February.)

5. Weigh the residue found in (4) and find what per

cent. it is of the fresh plant. What per cent. is it of the dried plant ?

6. Test the residue with a little hydrochloric acid ; is there any action ?

7. Stir up a little of the residue with distilled water and test with litmus paper. (See Mineralogy for April.) Can you determine anything regarding the character of the residue after burning?

8. In the same way tests may be applied to different kinds of wood, leaves, bark, etc. ; what part of the plant has the most dry, solid matter ? Which part the most carbon ?

9. Remove from the ground any small healthy plant and cleanse the roots as before. A seedling maple or ash, or any woody plant is to be preferred. The top of the plant should not be too large to be covered by a tumbler or small glass jar.

10. Cut a piece of cardboard large enough to support an inverted tumbler, and through a hole in the center pass the roots and part of the stem of the plant. Seal the opening about the stem with tallow or wax and suspend the roots in a wide-mouthed bottle of water. Invert over this another tumbler and seal it around the edge. Arrange two tumblers thus and place one in sunshine and the other in the shade.

11. What do you observe in the two inverted tumblers ? Note the effect of different temperatures.

12. What does this experiment show you about the roots of a plant ? About the stem ? About the leaves ?

13. Prepare another plant in the same way but use a cork instead of the cardboard (the inverted tumbler not being needed). Dry the plant and weigh it. Suspend the roots in a small bottle of water. Bore a hole through

the cork, and then cut into it a lengthwise slit from the side, through which the stem may be passed without injury to the root. Seal the bottle tightly and weigh carefully. Place in the sunshine for two hours and weigh again.

14. Can you notice change in weight? How do you account for it?

15. Place it for the same length of time in a dark closet and weigh again ; what is the result?

16. Compare the amount of change during the day with that during the night.

17. Compare the amount of change during a cloudy day with that during one of sunshine.

18. To what part of the plant is this passage of water chiefly due? Prepare another plant in the same way, but remove the leaves. Also another plant with the stem cut off above the roots ; which bottle loses most in weight?

19. Estimate the square inches of leaf area of one of your plants. Count the leaves on a branch of the tree you have selected for study and estimate its entire leaf surface. How much water could it, under the same conditions, lift in one day?

20. When done with the foregoing experiments, remove the plant and carefully remove the adhering wax and water and weigh it ; has the plant lost or gained since you prepared it? If scales are not convenient, ask any druggist or grocer to do the weighing for you.

21. The passage of water through the plant is called transpiration. What conditions outside the plant do you find most favorable for it? What is the chief cause? What parts of the plant promote it?

22. Fill a good sized test tube with water and immerse in it a small stem with the leaves of some water plant ;

place in the sunshine and observe closely.   Are there any signs of plant action ?

23. Remove to the shade ; does it affect the action ? If possible try different temperatures.

24. Use boiled water ; any change in the action?

25. Blow the breath into the water by means of a small tube ; can you notice any effect ?

26. What is it likely the water must contain, judging from the above experiments, in order that plant action may take place ?

27. By placing plants and leaves of different kinds in a similar manner in small bottles of water, try to collect some of the gas given off and test it to find out what it is. (See Chemistry for preceding months.)

LEAVES.

1. On what part of the tree are the leaves most vigorous ?   Where least so ?

2. On what part of the branch are they most thrifty ? Can you account for this ?

3. Do you observe any regularity in the arrangement of leaves ? Can you account for it? Is there any constant relation between the distance the leaves are apart and the size of the leaf ?   Compare different plants.

4. Are they arranged equally on all sides of the branch ? Does their arrangement depend in any way upon the direction that the branch grows? Compare different kinds of trees.

5. How many ranks or distinct rows of leaves can you count upon your twigs ? Wind a string around the twig across the nodes ; how many times does it pass around the twig until it crosses a bud over the one started with ? How many ranks are crossed in reaching this point ?

6. The ranking arrangement is expressed by a fraction whose numerator is the number of times the string passes round the stick, as suggested in (5), and whose denominator expresses the number of ranks.

7. What is the size of the angle between any two ranks? What part of the entire circumference is it? Compare with the fraction found in (6). The size of the angle between two successive ranks is called the angular divergence of the leaves. Study the twigs on a number of different trees and determine the number of ranks, angular divergence, etc.

8. Can you see any reason why the leaves of any particular kind of tree take the shape they have?

9. Why should they all be approximately the same shape on the same tree?

10. Can you find any two of exactly the same shape? What is the cause of the variations noticed?

11. Of what advantage is the petiole, *i. e.*, the leaf stalk? Such leaves are said to be *petiolate*.

12. Compare a plant with petiolate leaves with one that has *sessile* leaves, *i.e.*, those without foot stalks; can you see any advantage to the plant in the sessile leaf?

13. Note the two common varieties of netted venation, the *pinnately-veined*, *i.e.*, those having a mid rib with diverging veins, and *palmately-veined*, or those having several ribs of equal size radiating from a common point.

14. In the pinnate leaf do you find both sides alike in any specimen? What causes the difference? Note the relation of one leaf to another and to the branch that bears it.

15. Can you find any leaves that appear to be transitional between the two leading types?

16. Note the leaves borne by the ash tree or locust tree;

these are compound leaves. Also the leaves of the
poison ivy, or Virginia creeper; compare these two types
of compound leaves with the two classes of simple leaves.
The ash leaf is *pinnately compound* and the Virginia creeper
is *palmately compound.* Can you find intermediate forms
between compound and simple leaves?

17. What is the real difference between the pinnate
and the palmate type of leaves?

18. Compare the venation of the above mentioned leaves
with that of grass blades, and flags, and all lilies ; what
difference do you find? The latter are *parallel-veined
leaves.*

19. Which kind of plants are most numerous, those with
netted or *parallel* veined leaves?

20. What kinds of seeds produce those plants that bear
netted veined leaves? (See Botany for April.) Do you
find any exceptions?

21. What kind of seeds produce plants with parallel-
veined leaves? Look for exceptions.

22. Compare the stem of a woody plant, as the ash, maple,
or oak, with a stalk of corn ; how is the new material which
goes to thicken the stem added in each? Compare the
leaves of the woody plants mentioned with those of the
corn. Compare the seeds from which they grow.

23. Carefully remove the bark from any twig or branch
that is alive and note the different layers ; compare with
what you observed in early spring. (See Botany for
March.)

24. Can you tell why the bark has become more loosely
attached to the wood? Is it entirely separated?

25. Scrape up a little of the sappy layer and rub between the fingers; is it pure water? Compare with the

watery substance which you find in young leaves and twigs.

26. This sappy layer is called the *cambium*, or the *cambium layer ;* can you see what it does for the plant? You must watch the growth carefully before trying to answer this question.

27. Can you find a cambium layer in the cornstalk ?

28. Plants whose stems grow in thickness by means of the cambium layer are called exogens, and are said to be *exogenous*. *Exogen* means growing on the outside. Plants whose stems thicken by general growth throughout the stem are called *endogens*, and are said to be *endogenous*. *Endogen* means growing within.

29. Which are more abundant in our latitude, exogens or endogens? Compare the two kinds as to their buds and branches. Compare the locations where the two classes of plants are found.

30. Look in pictures of tropical scenes for endogenous plants, conspicuous among them being the palms. Note the branches. In some kinds the whole life of the tree is dependent upon the life of the terminal bud : when that is destroyed the plant dies.

31. Compare the flowers of the parallel-veined leaved plants with those having netted-veined ; what is the ruling number in the parts of each whorl in the former? (See Botany for May.)

32. What contrasts do you observe between exogens and endogens ? Compare as to seeds, stems, leaves, and flowers. Have you found any plants that form exceptions to the rule ?

THE GRASSES.

The best material, perhaps, which can be used in the
beginning of the study of grasses is wheat or rye in blossom. This may be obtained almost anywhere during
this month.

1. What peculiarities distinguish rye from other plants
studied thus far ?

2. Can you see a reason why its flowers are not
colored ?   Have they any odor?   Have they nectar?

3. Do insects visit these flowers ?   Why ?

4. What is most conspicuous about the flower ?   Compare in this respect with other flowers previously examined.   Can you see a reason for the difference ?

5. Compare the stem in point of size with that of other
plants.   How does it compare in strength?   In weight ?
Is the slender stem of any advantage to the plant ?

6. The hollow jointed form of stem is called a *culm.*
The form of inflorescence is a *compound spike.*   The different parts borne upon the axis of the flower-cluster are
called spikelets.

7. The outer husks in the spikelet are called the upper
and lower *glumes.*   Inside of these, look for the floral
whorls.   The chaffy scales are the *palets*—inner and outer.
At the base of these look for two minute scales called
lodicules.   What whorl of the flower do they represent ?
Note the feathery (plumose) stigmas.

8. Compare the amount of pollen produced by grains
and grasses with that of other plants ; can you see why
a great quantity is needed ?

9. Compare some of the common grasses with the
grains that have been examined; do the parts correspond ?

10. What resemblances and differences do you find between wheat, rye, oats, etc., and Indian corn? What constitutes the tassel in corn? What is it that forms the ear?

11. When are the different cereals planted or sown? How long does it take them to mature?

ꟍbysics.

ELECTRICITY.

There is no more interesting department of physics than that of electricity, and certainly there is no one of greater practical importance at the present day. Owing to the fact, however, that to get much out of the subject in an elementary course that is of practical value, considerable apparatus of some complexity is required, not much beyond a few simple experiments, showing something of the nature of electricity, can be attempted in the common schools at present. As an offset to the difficulties in the way regarding apparatus, there is the deep interest which pupils almost invariably show in the subject, which will impel them to greater efforts in the preparation of needed materials.

MAGNETISM AND FRICTIONAL ELECTRICITY.

1. Dip a common magnet (see Physics for September) into a pile of iron filings or small carpet tacks; will they stick equally well all round the bend in the magnet?

2. Magnetize a large knitting needle, as directed in September, and test it with iron filings. Enough filings may be obtained by filing a piece of soft iron or a nail for a few minutes. Place them on a sheet of white paper. Do the filings adhere equally well along its entire length? Break the needle in the middle and try again.

3. A straight magnet like the knitting needle is called

a bar magnet ; one that is bent, like those used in September, is a horseshoe magnet. In what respect are the two kinds alike in the attraction of filings ?

4. Procure some pith, such as may be found in an elder or cornstalk and thoroughly dry it. Make two small balls from it about the size of a pea, and suspend them an inch apart by a fine silk thread, eight or ten inches long. Fasten the upper ends of the threads to a wooden support by means of a drop of sealing wax.

5. Rub a stick of sealing wax briskly upon the sleeve or with a dry piece of flannel for a minute, and then bring the wax near the balls. At what distance do you notice the influence of the wax upon the balls ?

6. What happens after they have clung to the wax for a short·time ? After they have left the wax rub it again and bring it near ; it is now said to *repel* the balls, while a moment before it *attracted* them.

7. Rub a glass tube or rod instead of the sealing wax and bring it near the balls ; are they attracted or repelled ?

8. When they are repelled from the rod, again bring the sealing wax near ; are they attracted or repelled ? When they are repelled from the sealing wax, bring the glass rod near ; are they attracted or repelled ?

9. Instead of the sealing wax, use a gutta-percha penholder or comb ; do the balls behave toward it as they do toward the wax, or as they do toward the glass ?

10. Bring the wax, the glass tube, and the comb, after rubbing vigorously, close to some bits of paper or cotton ; are they attracted and repelled in the same way ?

11. Bring the excited wax and glass near your magnetic needle ; is there any effect.? Does it repel either end ?

12. Rubbing the glass and wax produced *electricity by friction.* When the pith balls flew to either they re-

mained until charged. The silk thread prevents this from escaping very rapidly, if the air is dry.

13. That received from the wax is called *negative* electricity ; that received from the glass is called *positive* electricity.

14. Rub both the glass and the wax and bring them close to the pith ball on opposite sides ; what takes place ?

15. What do you notice when the ball becomes charged with *negative electricity?* What happens when it becomes charged with *positive electricity ?*

16. When two bodies are charged with the *same kind* of electricity how do they behave toward each other ? How is it when they are charged with the *opposite kinds* of electricity ?

17. Any contrivance like the pith ball which will show the presence of electricity is called an *electroscope.* Use it to test whether electricity may be obtained by rubbing silk, paper, and other substances.

18. Charge the pith ball with electricity from the glass tube, as above described. Now bring near to it a piece of silk ribbon which has been briskly rubbed ; can you tell whether the silk is charged with *negative* or *positive* electricity ? How may the electroscope be used to tell the *kind* of electricity developed in any substance?

19. By rubbing a stick of sealing wax vigorously for some time with dry flannel, a slight crackling sound will be heard when it is brought near the knuckle ; in the dark a tiny spark may be seen. The same kind of sparks may be seen when a cat's back is rubbed, and the same crackling sound will be heard.

20. Can you develop electricity by rubbing an iron rod as was done with the glass and sealing wax ?

21. Wrap one end of the iron rod well with a silk

handkerchief, rub thoroughly, and test with the pith ball for electricity ; anything which prevents an object from losing its electricity is called an *insulator.*

22. Rub one end of a long stick of wax and bring the other end close to the pith ball or a bit of cotton ; does it show the presence of electricity ?

23. In the case of the iron, in the first instance, the electricity passed over the iron to the hand and through the body to the ground as fast as formed, but not so with the sealing wax. Any substance like the wax in this respect is called a *non-conductor;* when like the iron, it is called a *conductor.*

24. Lightning is a large spark of electricity passing from one cloud to another cr from a cloud to the earth ; can you see a use for lightning rods? Why are they usually fastened to the roof and sides of the house by being passed through glass rings ? What is the proper name for the rings ?

VOLTAIC ELECTRICITY.

1. Place a piece of zinc, about three inches long and two inches wide, in a glass of water to which half a teaspoonful of sulphuric acid has been added ; what takes place? Is it a chemical or physical change ?

2. Place in the same vessel a strip of copper of same size. Punch a small hole through the ends of the copper and zinc not immersed, and pass through each a small copper wire a foot long. Bend the outer ends of the copper and zinc over the edge of the tumbler so that they will remain in place without touching.

3. Put, first, the end of the copper wire from the zinc in the mouth, and then that from the copper ; is there any taste noticeable ?

4. Place the ends of both wires in the mouth without allowing them to touch ; do you note any difference in taste ? Note what is taking place in the tumbler.

5. Procure several feet of insulated copper wire, such as is used for door-bells, and wind two or three feet of it lengthwise around a block, two inches long and one inch wide, in an even coil. Place this coil beneath your magnetic needle and close to it, with the wires running parallel with the needle.

6. Bring the wire from the copper strip into contact with one end of the wire in the coil, and, watching the needle sharply, place the wire from the zinc in contact with the other end ; does the needle give any evidence of disturbance ? Which way does it turn ?

7. Touch the ends of the coil with the opposite wires from the copper and zinc ; what changes in the behavior of the needle ?

8. Such a coil with a needle attached is called a *galvanometer*.

9. Another form easily made may be constructed thus. Take a block of pine wood five inches square and two inches thick. Saw each corner off, making it octagonal in shape. Cut a hole through the middle about two and one-half or three inches in diameter. Within the ring of wood thus formed suspend a magnetized sewing needle (see Physics for September) by a single fiber of a silk thread. The thread is easily attached to the wood by a drop of sealing wax. Wrap around the ring on the outside, smoothly and evenly, eight or ten turns of the insulated copper wire. A groove should be cut on the under side of the ring to receive the coil of wire so that the ring may be fastened to a block about the same size for a base. No iron should be used in the construction of this

instrument. Why? It is more convenient to have the ends of the wire in the coil near each other. Place the ring in such a position that the wire in the coil will be parallel with the needle when it points north and south. Bring the wires from the copper and zinc strips in contact with the ends of the coil and observe the needle. Change the wires to the opposite ends of the coil and note the difference.

10. The needle is turned, deflected, by what is called a current of electricity which is generated by the action of the acid and water on the zinc and copper. Anything which will thus generate electricity by chemical action is a battery.

11. The *direction* of the current is also determined from observation of the needle. If the current passes from *north to south above the needle,* or from *south to north below it,* the north pole of the needle is deflected toward the *east.* If the current passes from *north to south below the needle,* or from *south to north above it,* the north pole of the needle is deflected toward the *west.* Do you see any way by which the needle may indicate the *strength* of the current?

12. Another way to make a battery is as follows: procure about fifteen copper cents and an equal number of pieces of sheet zinc, cut in squares, the edge of each being equal to the diameter of the cent. Cut, also, thirty squares of cloth or blotting paper of same size of the zinc. Of these make a pile: first a piece of zinc, then a square of cloth, then a cent, then a square of cloth, then zinc, and so on. When finished, bind them together tightly with a strong cord. Two copper wires must either be soldered, one to the zinc and one to the copper at the opposite end, or else tied tightly against the two pieces.

This is called a Voltaic pile, from a man named Volta, an Italian, who first used this means of producing electricity.

13. The acid and water may be used with this battery, but a better fluid may be made as follows for a few cents : Water, one pint ; bichromate of potash, two ounces ; sulphuric acid, two ounces. Powder the bichromate and dissolve in the water ; afterward add the acid in a fine stream, stirring all the time, and allow it to cool. When the battery is not in use remove the pile and rinse thoroughly, and it will last for some time.

14. Another battery, easily and cheaply made, and which will give a current of sufficient strength to ring a door-bell, may be made thus : Procure two sticks of carbon, each about eight inches long, such as are used in electric lights, and two pieces of zinc of same length, and about one-fourth of an inch square. Any dealer in electrical supplies can furnish them, provided with binding screw, for ten cents each. Cut a strip of wood six inches long, an inch wide, and half an inch thick. One inch from each end bore a hole sufficiently large to let the carbon sticks pass through, and fasten a carbon in each one, allowing about an inch to project above. To the side of the stick next the carbons bind or clamp the zincs. Connect the zinc at one end with the carbon, at the other with a wire. Attach a copper wire to the other zinc and another one to the other carbon for the *poles* of the battery. Use wide-mouthed morphia bottles for jars for the battery fluid. The zincs should be amalgamated before using by first washing perfectly clean, using a little dilute acid if necessary, and then rubbing them with a little mercury until bright. An amalgamating fluid may be made thus : Mix one part nitric acid and three parts hy-

drochloric acid by measure ; to about one pint of the mixture add an ounce of mercury. When dissolved, clean and immerse the zincs until bright. Keep the fluid in a glass-stoppered bottle. It may be used over again as long as the mercury lasts.

15. Test the battery with the galvanometer. Wrap a wrought nail or piece of soft iron wire with a coil of insulated copper wire. Test the nail or wire with iron filings for magnetic properties. Connect the ends of the wire in the coil with the poles of the battery, and test again ; what result ? Break connection, *i. e.,* open the circuit and note the effect on the filings.

16. If possible, study the mechanism of an electric bell and note the battery connections. The nail with wire around it, described in (15), is called an electro-magnet. The electric bell is rung by means of an electro-magnet which is rapidly magnetized and as quickly demagnetized. How is this accomplished ?

17. In how many ways can you prove the presence of the electric current in the wires ?

18. How can you decide as to its direction ? Since the needle in the galvanometer tends to place itself in a position at right angles to the course of the current along the wires, can you from that fact make any inference as to the force which causes the needle of the compass to point north and south ?

19. How can you test the strength of an electric current ?

Chemistry.

CHLORINE.

The study of this gas will present several noteworthy contrasts with those considered in the preceding months. The materials needed are cheap and easily obtained. The experiments are all perfectly safe, but to avoid some disagreeable effects on breathing, the gas should be made where there is a good draught. The properties of chlorine are interesting and useful.

1. Place in a test tube half an inch of manganese dioxide and pour upon it a little hydrochloric acid. Warm gently over the alcohol lamp. What evidence have you of a gas being formed? Can you detect any odor? The gas formed is *chlorine*. Symbol, Cl.

2. Hold in the tube moist strips of litmus paper; what takes place? Moisten pieces of calico and hold them in the fumes. Is there any change produced if the articles are not moistened?

3. Place a few small crystals of potassium chlorate in a test tube, add hydrochloric acid, and test again as in (2). Have you the same gas formed?

4. Place in a test tube a small quantity of manganese dioxide mixed with an equal weight of common salt. These should be well mixed and pulverized. Mix together a small quantity of sulphuric acid and water, equal weights of each, and pour upon the mixture in the tube. Warm gently and test as above for chlorine.

5. Is chlorine heavier or lighter than air? To collect

this gas fit the test tube with a cork and bent tube as in former experiments, and so arrange the latter that it may pass through a piece of cardboard to the *bottom of the collecting* jar, the cardboard being used as a lid for the jar. Why is it possible to collect the gas in this manner? Could you collect it as you did oxygen or hydrogen?

6. Moisten a piece of paper with turpentine, a little warm, and hang it in the vessel of chlorine; does it re-call any previous experiment?

7. In a fresh jar of chlorine insert a candle or lighted taper; does it burn? Does it support combustion?

8. Place in a fruit jar a tablespoonful of sulphuric acid. Sprinkle into this a tablespoonful of bleaching powder, or chloride of lime, as it is also called. Cover the jar with a plate or piece of glass.

9. Moisten some rose leaves and hang them in the jar; what change do you notice?

10. Write a sentence upon a piece of paper, and, after moistening it, hang it within the jar. Try a moistened bit of paper with printing upon it.

11. Chlorine has a strong affinity for hydrogen. In the experiment with turpentine it united with the hydro-gen and left the carbon. Printers' ink being made of carbon, the chlorine does not affect it.

12. Chlorine is now much used in bleaching cloth, paper pulp, etc. It is prepared in the form of the bleach-ing powder that may be bought at the shops.

13. Bleaching powder is also used as a disinfectant in sick rooms and other places. Exposed to the air the Cl is set free and unites with the hydrogen of the offensive substances, breaking them up. The process is hastened by the addition of a little dilute sulphuric acid. It is much used in hospitals.

Meteorology.

The meteorological influences of this month are usually benign. If the past month has supplied a liberal amount of moisture, the warm sunshine, now almost assured, will produce most wonderful results.

1. How many thunder showers have you noticed during the past two months?

2. From what direction do they usually come?

3. In what part of the day have most of them occurred?

4. What is the ratio of rains without thunder to those with it?

5. Is there any uniformity in their effect upon the temperature?

6. How long do thunder storms usually last?

7. Have any of the storms been accompanied with hail? What was the effect upon the temperature? Examine a hailstone.

8. Has the prevailing wind been cool or warm? What is its direction?

9. What wind accompanies a clearing sky? A cloudy sky? The heaviest rains?

10. What is the rate of change in temperature? Compare with May and April.

11. Are there any fogs this month? When are they formed?

12. Have you noticed any frosts this month? Any dews? Any nights with neither frost nor dew? Can you explain the latter?

13. Which are cooler, clear or cloudy days ? Why ?

14. Which are cooler, clear or cloudy nights ? Why ?

15. Compare the barometric record with that for May.

16. Use the following suggestions for a summary for the year : What month had the greatest number of rainy days ? The largest number of clear days ?

17. Which was the warmest month for the year ?

18. Which was the coldest month ? How far apart are these extremes ?

19. Which season has the most cloudy days ? Can you explain this ?

20. Do the rains of summer occur mostly in the fore-noon or afternoon ? In daytime or night ?

STUDY OF THE WEATHER BUREAU MAPS.

21. Compare the isotherm 60 degrees this month with its course and direction in May and April. Can you account for any variation.

22. In what quarter of the country have there been the most Low Areas ? In what quarter has there been the heaviest rainfall ?

23. Are the isotherms more or less regular in their course this month than last ?

24. Compare the temperature of the plain between the two great mountain systems with that indicated along the coast. Can you see any reason for any differences noted ?

25. Which isotherms vary most from their normal course, those in the north or in the south ? Why ?

26. What isotherm this month crosses where you live ? Compare with last month,

27. Does the temperature of the Low and High Areas still vary as in the preceding months?

28. Where is the region of lowest temperature in the country during this month? Why is it so?

29. Where is the region of highest temperature? Can you explain?

Astronomy.

In this month, the last of the school year, as much as possible should be done by way of comparison with the different seasons. At this time another mile post of the year is reached at the summer solstice, and the effects should be traced as far throughout nature as the children can comprehend. Children naturally seek for causes of the results they see around them, and it is the principal duty of the teacher to impress them with the fact that the immediate causes will always be found if skill and patience are observed in the search. It too often happens that teachers, either through ignorance or neglect, directly or indirectly impress the pupils with the notion that the phenomena of nature either have no important bearing upon themselves, or that they happen at random, without direct cause. In either case the result is a grown up man or woman who has not the slightest knowledge of nature, or interest in the very things about him on which his life depends. That the possibility still exists for the public schools to produce such deformities in character is a fact much to be deprecated.

1. How does the rate and direction of change in the noon shadow compare with that in May?

2. Compare the length of day and night in the two months. Is the *rate* of change the same?

3. When is the greatest variation in the day's length made, at morning or evening?

4. What angle do the sun's rays make with the earth the

first of the month ?   What is the greatest angle they make during the month ?   What do you notice about the length of day at that time ?   June twenty-first is called the summer solstice, a word meaning the sun standing still. Consult your noon marks for a reason for this.   Can you explain why the sun seems to move slowly at this time ?

5. At the same date note the points on the horizon where the sun rises and sets ; how far have they moved since March ?   Since December ?

6. Why are the days and nights unequal at this time of year ?

7. At what point in the United States is there the greatest inequality in day and night?   Where are they nearest equal ?

8. Compare the length of day and night in the places found in (7) with that of the same places in December ; explain why the case appears to be reversed at this time.

9. Is there a corresponding variation between places remote from each other but on the same parallel ?   Can you see a reason for this ?

10. In what month during the year did the shadow travel farthest along the shadow-stick ?   In which the least ?

11. Through how many degrees did the slant of the rays, as indicated by the shadow, travel during the year ?

12. In what months did the shadow stand at the same place on the stick ?   How did those months compare as to temperature and rainfall ?   Explain why the shadow stands at the same place, and why the effects as observed in temperature and rainfall are different.

13. Can you now explain why we have four seasons in a year? Is it the same all over the earth? Why?

14. At what date was the lowest temperature reached this year? What has caused the gradual rise in temperature since then?

15. In what region is the greatest heat during the year? Where the greatest cold? Why?

16. In what region is there the greatest extremes of heat and cold? Why?

17. Compare the plant and animal life, including man, in the three regions referred to in (12) and (13); in which region does the greater amount of land lie?

18. In which region is the highest civilization to be found at present? Was it always so?

19. Suppose the earth's axis were inclined less than it is, or not at all—how would it affect the climate of the earth?

20. Suppose it were inclined more than it is; how would the three regions mentioned in (14) be affected? How would the length of day and night compare with that at present?

21. Mercury appears June fifth in 1891 as a morning star; how have it and the earth changed position with respect to each other since it last appeared as morning star? (See Astronomy for February.)

22. How have they changed relatively since Mercury appeared as evening star? (See Astronomy for April.)

23. How does it happen that Mercury only appears thus periodically as morning and evening star?

24. Additional constellations: Cygnus in the east; southeast, Scorpio; south, the Crow and the Crater.

Geography.

WINDS.

In the study of climate as suggested in many of the preceding lessons, it has been necessary to refer to the winds that are found in the different regions. Taking these together, now, it will be seen that there is a similarity between those of certain areas, though they may be remote from each other. Proceeding from such generalization, keeping in mind what has been learned and illustrated in Physics, pupils may in time be led to trace the winds to their causes and thus get a connected view of the great atmospheric movements of the earth. In the same way, also, the subject of ocean currents should be developed. Consult a good physical map which shows the direction of the winds and currents.

1. In what portions of the globe are the great wind currents the least turned from the normal course? Compare the land and water areas.

2. Observe the direction of the winds, as indicated by the arrows on the map, over the Pacific Ocean within the tropics ; what contrast do you find north and south of the equator as you approach the tropics?

3. What seems to be the prevailing direction at the equator?

4. Trace these winds around the globe ; where are they most interrupted? Compare the Atlantic with the Pacific Ocean.

5. Which coasts receive these winds? This belt of westerly moving winds is called the *Trade Winds*.

6. What is the direction of the winds within the polar circles ; does it appear to be uniform ?

7. Which coasts of the continents must receive the polar winds? How are these winds turned from their normal course ?

8. Note the direction of the arrows between the polar and equatorial winds ; follow this belt around the globe and notice the countries included in it.

9. These arrows indicate the place of meeting and conflict between the polar and equatorial winds ; how will this interference of winds affect the climate of this region ?

10. From what you have learned heretofore (see Physics for October) can you see what the great disturbing cause of the atmosphere is ?

11. Under what conditions would there be no atmospheric movements ? How do existing conditions differ from this ?

12. What movement of the atmosphere must occur under the vertical rays of the sun ? What is the shape of this area under the vertical rays on the globe ?

13. Is the position of this belt the same throughout the year ?

14. How must the movement of the air in the belt under the vertical rays affect the air lying outside of it ? How far north and south will the disturbance extend.

15. Will the air that comes from the poles be a surface or an upper current ?

16. What will determine the height to which the air under the vertical rays will rise ? When it ceases to rise what will become of it ? What forces are acting upon it ?

17. How will its elevation change as it moves away from the equatorial regions? Why?

18. Can you now account for the line of conflict noticed in the temperate regions? See (9) above. This region is called the belt of *Variable Winds*.

19. What influences will tend to make it change its position during the year? At what season or seasons is the wind most fickle and changeable in our latitude? Where are the rays of the sun vertical then?

20. At what season or seasons are the winds least variable? Where is the belt of vertical rays at such times?

21. When do the warm winds prevail? Why? The cold winds? Why?

22. The winds blowing from the equatorial regions toward the poles are called the *Return Trade Winds*. They descend to the surface at about latitude thirty degrees. What coasts receive these winds? What is their influence upon those coasts? Compare the eastern and western coasts of North America; also, eastern North America and western Europe.

23. What features on the surface of the globe tend to change the course of the winds? Study the course of the arrows near the great mountain ranges. Also near the coast lines.

24. Can you see how the presence of both land and water tends to deflect the winds from the course they would take if only one were present?

25. Which heats more rapidly under the rays of the sun, land or water? Which cools more rapidly when the sun is removed?

26. How would the winds be deflected near a continent or ocean in winter? In summer? In the daytime? At night?

27. Study the effect which the earth's rotation must have upon the atmosphere. Turn a small hand globe rapidly and hold a thread or other light substance near it ; is there any evidence that the air surrounding the globe is in motion ?

28. The circumference of the globe is twenty-five thousand miles and it makes a rotation in about twenty-four hours ; what is the rate of movement of a point at the equator ?

29. Would a point in our latitude have the same speed ? Why ? How would it be with a point on the polar circles? At the poles ?

30. When the cold air starts toward the equator from the poles what rotary velocity does it have ? As it moves into regions having greater rotary velocity, what must be the effect ?

31. Will it at once acquire this increased velocity ? What must happen, then, as it advances toward the equator ? What direction will it have in the northern hemisphere ? In the southern ?

32. When the air in the upper equatorial regions (see 16 above) starts toward the poles, what will be its rotary velocity ? As it advances to higher latitude how will this change ? Will it acquire this less velocity at once ? What will be the effect, then, upon its direction ?

33. What is the direction of the return trades in the northern hemisphere ? In the southern ? Where are they most interrupted ?

34. What causes can you see for the oceanic movements ? Are they in any way dependent upon the winds? Have you ever seen currents started on the surface of a pond or lake by the wind ?

35. Where would the winds have the strongest effect ?

36. Note the width and direction of the great equatorial current and compare with the winds of the same region.

37. Note how the continents affect the direction of this current ; would the earth's rotation affect currents of water as it does the winds? What shores receive the warm currents? Which receive the cold currents?

38. Can you now understand why Europe and North America have such contrasts in climate? Compare the eastern and western shores of North and South America?

39. Is the character of a nation in any way determined by the winds and currents that sweep upon its shores?

40. What nations can you cite as illustrations?

Geology.

SPRINGS AND WELLS.

One of the chief features of a country which will always tell for or against it is the springs it affords. Abundance of pure spring water! It is a recommendation for a place which will outweigh many very disagreeable things in surface, soil, or climate. Its mere mention brings up visions of health, and it is indeed one of the strongest barriers against pestilence and death. From earliest times, springs of pure water have been objects of veneration to mankind, and they have inspired a literature, both poetry and prose, that can be appreciated only by those who, having once enjoyed their refreshing, have afterward been compelled to depend upon the warm, turbid supply of cities that has, too often, a doubtful origin. Common as springs are in many places, they are always interesting to the student, and their ceaseless flow, year after year, is shrouded in something akin to mystery.

1. What becomes of the rain water that falls to the earth? What does the fog that rises after a shower mean? What does the moistened earth after the water has disappeared from the surface mean? Where does the water come from that causes a stream to suddenly overflow its banks?

2. Why does the water which comes down in a shower stand longer on the surface in some places than it does in others?

3. In what kind of ground does it disappear soonest?

4. What determines the depth to which it must sink ?

5. Can you imagine any conditions under which the water would start to flow underground ?

6. Why is it that water stands in a swamp ? Can you think why it neither does not all lie on the surface nor yet sink clear below it ?

7. What is necessary in order to drain a swamp ? Can you think why it is that all level ground is not swampy ?

8. What kind of ground is most favorable for the passage of underground waters ?

9. Would rocks be a help or a hindrance to it ? What part in spring making can clay perform ?

10. When the surface water sinks to a layer of clay or rock through which it cannot pass, what must then become of it ?

11. What circumstances would favor its reappearance at the surface ?

12. Can you think why it is that it appears at one point instead of being spread out ?

13. It is a rule that those springs whose flow is constant throughout the year are but little affected by wet or dry weather. What conditions can you imagine which will account for this ?

14. What conditions must exist underground which render the flow from a spring constant and uniform in amount ?

15. How must the conditions differ in those springs which flow for a few days only, after a heavy rain ?

16. There are springs which flow for a time and then cease for a while ; after a period of rest the flow is again resumed, which is again followed by a rest. These are called intermittent springs. Can you see any way of accounting for such a flow ?

17. The supposition has been made that such springs have an outlet through a siphon-shaped tube ; will such a supposition account for the facts? Make a diagram of such an underground basin, with an outlet of this kind.

18. Since rain water is soft, how does it happen that spring water is frequently hard ? What kinds of rock will make hard water ?

19. What would be the result if the soil did not absorb large quantities of water when it rains ? Of what value, aside from drinking purposes, are springs ?

20. How is it that water may be obtained by boring a deep hole in the ground ?

21. Sometimes, after boring a considerable depth, water is obtained and it rises even with, and often above the surface ; can you account for this when there is no gas in the well ? What must be the character of such an underground basin ?

22. Do springs ever deposit sediments about their out-lets ? Where are such materials obtained ?

23. Which would be more likely to deposit such sediments, cold or warm springs ? Why ?

24. The light, spongy material sometimes found about hot springs is called *tufa*.

25. Read some account of the geysers in Iceland and of those in Yellowstone Park.

Mineralogy.

STUDY OF SOILS.

Last month directions were given for finding out the mechanical constituents of soils. It will now be interesting to study some of the physical properties of the soils upon which their value to plant life depends.

1. Have you noticed any difference in soils as to the rate at which they allow water to pass through them? To test this, take several glass tubes, about half an inch in diameter and a foot long, and tie over one end a piece of linen. Argand lamp chimneys may be used for this purpose. Fill each one with a different specimen of soil which has been finely powdered and well dried. Set the tubes upright in a vessel having about an inch of water in it, and note the rate at which the water rises in the different tubes. Keep the water at a constant level in the pan by occasional additions.

2. Which soil would be best for plants ; that which allows the moisture to rise rapidly or slowly ? Why ?

3. Compare the sandy with clayey soils.

4. The *amount of water* which soil can hold will also affect the growth of plants. Illustrate the different capacities for water thus : Fold two filters and place them loosely, one inside the other, in a funnel. Carefully dry and place on the filter an ounce of finely powdered soil. Add to this cold water by drops until it begins to trickle

down the funnel tube. Continue to add until sure that the soil is perfectly saturated and then remove the filters to a piece of blotting paper or a cloth which will absorb the moisture from them. Then place the under filter in one scale pan and the other one, with the soil upon it, upon the other, and balance with weights. How much heavier is it now than the dry soil? What per cent. of its weight is water?

5. To get an idea of the *rate of evaporation* from soil, place the filter with the soil on it in the open air and weigh at regular intervals; what per cent. does it lose in an hour? Upon what conditions will the rate of evaporation depend?

6. Compare in the manner above described loam, sand, and clay.

7. The *power of soils to absorb water* from the atmosphere may be illustrated as follows : Spread out evenly half an ounce of carefully dried soil in a shallow tin box. The lid of a baking powder can will answer the purpose. Place it above a small cup of water (an individual salt or butter dish may be used) and invert a jar or large tumbler over both. Seal the tumbler around the edges so that it may be air tight. After standing a few days weigh the soil again ; has it gained any? To what is the increase due? What per cent. is it of the weight of dry earth?

8. Soils differ in their powers to *absorb and conduct the heat* that comes from the sun, and they may be tested in this respect in this way : Fill a large tomato can with finely powdered soil ; wrap the can with several thicknesses of paper and set it in the sunshine. After a little time test the temperature of the different parts with a thermometer. Compare sand with loam in this particular.

9. In what kinds of soils do plants thrive best ? In which the poorest ?

10. What are the qualities of good soil ? What are its constituents ? (See Mineralogy for May.)

11. How does abundance of rainfall affect the soil ?

12. Does the wind in any way affect the formation of soil ?

INDEX.

ABSORPTION, 109
Acetic acid, formation of, 46
Acid, effect of, upon marble, 117
Æolian harp, study of, 366
Africa, relief, drainage, climate, productions, 383
Air, 230; complemental, 390; elasticity of, 190; expansion of, 113; impure, 311; impurities of, 284; movements, 155; pressure of, 191, 195; residual, 310; study of, 189; supplemental, 310; tidal, 310
Alburnum, 271
Alcohol, boiling point, 84; formation of, 46; lamp, how to make a cheap, 115
Almanac, use of, 50
America, see North and South America
Amorphous bodies, 87
Amplitude of vibration, 369
Andes Mountains, 209
Animals, autumn influences upon, 29; coverings and warmth, 100; cruelty to, 345; habits of, after eating, 186; joints compared with man's 145; general observations on, for November, 99; movements of, 135; movements of, in eating, 224; winter studies of, 180
Angles, of incidence and reflection, 277; of sun's rays, how to measure, 62

Annuals, 107
Ants, how to keep, in confinement, 75; study of, 397
Apparatus, care in preparing, 108; for distillation, 84; for fermentation, 46; for measuring angle of sun's rays, 62; for measuring shadow, 61; for astronomy, 61; for study of light, 274; for study of refraction, 320
Appetite, 184
Aquarium, how to stock, 99; use of, and how to make, 98
Aqueous agencies, 172
Arms, their functions in man, 139
Areas, means for studying, 68
Astronomy, apparatus for, 61; charts to be used, 52–60; for April, 333; for December, 166; for February, 246; for January, 205; for June, 425; for March, 289; for May, 381; most important conception in, 62; for November, 122; for October, 90; problems in, 205; for September, 61
Atmospheric agencies, 172; movements, causes of, 429

BABY, helplessness of, in prehension, 221
Bark, study of, 272
Barometer, position of, 50; tube, 194

Batteries, 415–418
Bees, study of, 396
Beetles, 490
Berries, colors of, 39
Biennials, 107
Birds, flight of, 136–140; general observations, September, 32; migration of, 32–261; nests and eggs, 348; nests, robbing of, 345; return of, 307; study for October, 76; winter residents, 99; winter visitors, 99;
Blanks for minerals, 177
Bleaching process, 421
Blood, coagulation of, 265; circulation of, 267; constitution of, 265
Bloodvessels, 264
Blue flag, 318
Boats, pumping leaky, 232
Bogs, 339
Boiled egg, experiment with, 191
Boiling temperature, 84
Bone, study of, 78
Botany, for April, 312; for December, 146; drawings and paintings in, 36; for February, 228; for January, 188; for June, 403; for March, 269; for May, 357; mode of study, 36; use of key, 357; for September, 36; for October, 81; for November, 106
Brain, protection of, 143
Breadmaking, 184
Breathing, 309
Buds, classified, 317; development of, in spring, 315; freezing of, 228; unfolding of, 269–362
Bunsen burner, 115
Burning wood to illustrate chemical change, 115
Burrows of earthworms, 303; plugging by worms, 34
Buttercup, 319
Butterflies, habits of, 33

CALCAREOUS stones, 219
Calendar, natural history, 261
Cambrium layer, 409
Candle, study of, 375–377
Capillaries, 264
Capillarity, 232
Carbon dioxide, 243; from coal and wood, 239, 240; study of, 239
Carbonic acid gas, 46
Cardinal points, how to fix, 63
Cartilage, 80
Cat, movements of, 136
Centre of curvature, 279; of gravity, 150
Cereals, 411
Chapped hands, 102
Charcoal, 241
Charts, explanation of, 52–54; use of, in study of meteorology, 52
Chemical change, 47
Chemistry, for April, 326; for December, 159; for February, 239; for June, 420; for January, 197; for March, 282; for May, 375; for November, 115; for September, 46; for October, 86
Chicken, circulation in embryo, 267; development of, 349
Chlorine, 420
Cider, 46
Circulation, 262; affected by position and movements, 263; course of, 264; in chicken and frog, in embryo, 267
Clay, 220; amount in soils, 392; formation of, 97; models, burning of, 257
Climate, conditions of, affecting character of food, 181; effect of coast-lines on, 121; Euro-Asia, 293; relation of, to thrift of a people, 296; uniformity of, evidenced by certain plants, 269
Clocks, use of, 196

Clothing, change of, 105
Clouds, study of, 50, 84
Coagulation of blood, 265
Coal, history of, 340; origin of, 134-242; study of, 133-134.
Coast-lines, influence of, upon climate, 121
Cocoons, 262
Coke, 134
Colors, 324; natural mode of expression for, 22; relation to absorption of heat, 110; of fruits, 39; of spectrum, 43
Compass, 44
Concretions, 301
Condensation, 84
Conductors, 415; of heat, 154
Conjunction, superior and inferior, 292
Cooking, 183
Coral, study of, 298
Cortex, 272
Cow, movements of, 137
Crawfish, external parts of, 354; circulation of, 268; respiration of, 353; study of, 352
Cruelty, relation of science work to, 4; to animals, 345
Crystallization, 87
Culms, 410
Current, electric, direction of, 417
Cuticle, 105

DANDRUFF, 104
Day, length of, at different places compared, 247; variation in length of, 63
Dew, formation of, 153
Dip of magnetic needle, 44; of rocks, 70
Disinfectants, 421; charcoal, 241
Dissepiments, 40
Distillation, 84; apparatus for, 84; in nature, 327
Dog, movements of, 136
Drainage, 91
Drawing compared with paint-

ing, making, and modeling, 18; difficulties to be overcome, 19; function of, 18; use of, in science work, 19; when properly commenced, necessity for, 22
Duramen, 271
Dust in air, 285

EARTH, movements of the, 167
Earthworms, burrows of, 303; early appearance of, 303; casts of, 304; senses of, 305; respiration of, 314
Eating, number of times a day, 186
Ebullition, 83
Echo, 373
Egg-collecting, and directions for preserving and labeling, 346-348; study of the, 349
Electricity, 412 ; direction of currents of, 417
Embryo chick, 349; circulation shown, 267
Endocarp, 40
Endogens, 409
Envelopes, for seeds, 39; floral, 361
Epicarp, 40
Equatorial current, 432
Equilibrium of bodies, 150
Equinox, vernal, 290
Erosion, 94
Euro-Asia climate, 293; productions of, 336; relief and drainage, 248
Evaporation, 83
Evening star, 207
Exocarp, 40
Exogens, 409
Expansion of metals, liquids, and gases, 112-113, 154
Experiments, inaccuracy of, 108
Expression, 13; correspondence to modes of study, 14; function of, 14 ; inappropriate modes illustrated, 24; relation to art, 25; necessity of combin-

ing different modes, 20; later stimuli for, 21–25; modes of, enumerated, 14; order of development of the various modes, 21; peculiarity of each mode, 14; place of the various modes, 23; pupil to choose his own mode of, 24; relation to external stimuli, 21; relation to modes of study, 13; modes to be used in each lesson, 28; earliest stimuli for, 21

Extravagance in nature, 37

Eye, study of, 354

FAT, study of, 79

Fauces, pillars of, 227

Feathers, arrangement of, 100; study of, 395

Feet, position of, in walking, 138

Fermentation, conditions for, 47; apparatus for, 46; experiments in, 46

Ferns, 363

Fibrin, how to prepare, 265

Fibrous minerals, 302

Filtering with charcoal, 241

Fish, movements of, 140

Flame, singing, 199–372; study of, 375; tests for minerals, 341

Flames, characteristic, 342

Floral envelopes, 361

Flowers, adhesion and cohesion in, 362; complete and incomplete, 360; early, 319; essential organs of, 361; forms of, 362; function of parts, 360; habitat of, 359; habits of, 359; mode of study for children, 357; place for study of, in botany, 357; position of, 361; relation of, to fruit, 39; visits of insects to, 360

Focus, conjugate, 279

Fog, formation of, 84; study of, 88–9

Foliated mineral, 302

Food, amount needed, 184; cli-

mate affects character of, 181; cooking of, 183; of insects, 307; mastication of, 224; prehension of, 221; study of, 181; times of taking, 186; of young birds, 394

Form, modes of expression for, 24

Fossil plants, study of, 251; conditions of their production, 252–6

Fossils defined, 214; early ideas concerning, 212; meaning of, 212; a means for estimating ages, 217–218; picturing the necessary conditions for, 213; study of, 212–218; use of the study of, 213

Freezing, effects of, 173; on plants, 146

Friction, producing heat, 158

Frictional electricity, 412

Frog, circulation in, 267; development of, 308; eggs, 308

Frost, study of, 120

Frozen ground, 174

Fruits, colors of, 39; definition of, 39; dried, 82; function of, 37; parts developed by cultivation, 40; preyed upon by insects, 41; relation of, to the flower, 39; stone, 41; study of, 37

Frying meat, 184

Fur, hair, 82; use of, 101

GALVANOMETER, 416

Gas, mode of collecting, 160

Geese, migration of, 76

Geodes, 301

Geography, for April, 336; defined, 64; for December, 168; for February, 248; for January, 209; for June, 428; for March, 293; for May, 383; for November, 124; for October, 91; for September, 64; teach with history, 67

Geological collections, 27, 68, 69; key, 74; pictures, 297
Geology, for April, 339; for December, 172; dynamical, 69; for February, 251; for January, 212; for June, 433; for March, 297; for May, 386; conceptions of, 68; for November, 128; for October, 94; for September, 68; of surrounding country, 69
Germination in autumn, 38; of seeds, apparatus for, 312; study of, 313
Gesture, difficulties in teaching, 15
Geysers, 435
Glacial pebbles, 129
Glands, salivary, 226, 227
Glumes, 410
Great Dismal Swamp, 340
Grapes, color of, 40
Graphite, 134
Grasses, study of, 410
Gravel, amount in soils, 391
Gravity, force of, how to find center of, 150
Growing point, 316
Gypsum calcining, 257

HAIR, on the human body, 102-5; in the distribution of seeds, 82
Halos, 325
. Headache, causes of, 266
Heat, 108; capacity for experiments, 157; central thought of, to be developed, 109; conduction of, experiments, 154; conduction of, in liquids, 156; convection of, 155; expansion, 111; as a force in melting ice, 109; produced by friction, 158; radiation, absorption, and reflection, 109, 110; refraction of, 157; sources of, 158; study of, for December, 152

Hen's egg, study of, 349
Hepatica, 319; habitat of, 359
Hibernation, 100, 261
Horizon, 63
Horse, movements of, 137
House-fly, 399
Hunger, 184
Huxley, Prof., on science work, 6
Hydrogen, experiment with, 197-201

ICE, effects of, 172
Images, 278; studied, 323
Indian, mode of walking, 139
Inflorescence, varieties of, 359
Insalivation, 226
Insects, collections of, 307; coverings, 101; habits of, 32; how to collect, 31; how to mount, 307; movements of, 34; senses of, 34; visiting flowers, 360
Insulators, 415
Iron, filings combined with sulphur, 118; cast, uses of, 178; ore, varieties of, 176; pig, 178; pyrites, 343

JACK-IN-THE-PULPIT, 318
Joints, study of, 80; in man, 145
Jupiter, 382; study of, 291

LAKES, heating of water in, 150; effects on storms, 332
Language, 15; compared, 20; data for, 20; difficulties to be overcome, 20, 23; use of, in science work, 19
Latitude, 65
Larvæ, care of, 75
Leaves, compound, 403; the prey of insects, 38; study of, 406
Lenses, study of, 322
Lenticels, 272

Lessons, field, data gathered in, 388; directions for conducting, 386; plan for, 27

Lever, classes of, 147, 148; study of, 147

Levers found in the body, 149

Liber, 272

Life, plasticity of, 64

Ligaments, 80

Light, 42; apparatus for study of, 274; different rays of, 277; experiments with, 274; modes of darkening room for study of, 274; necessity for clear conceptions, 274; study of refraction, 320

Lightning, 415

Lily, 318

Limbs, relative strength of, 144

Lime-water, 116

Limestone, 219; calcining, 257

Liquefaction experiments, 153

Liquids, buoyancy of, 234; prehension of, 223; pressure of, 236; expansion of, 112

Litmus paper, 344

Locomotion, 136

Lodicules, 410

Longitude, 65

Luminous bodies, 276

Lyell's Principles of Geology, 213

MAGNET in study of minerals, 72

Magnetic needle, declination of, 44; dip of, 44; how to make, 43; pole, 44

Magnetism, 43–412

Magnum foramen, 142; making, 16; as a stimulus, 23; when properly commenced, 22

Map-making, 65

Maps, Signal Service, 52

Marble, effect of acid upon, 117

Marrow, 78

Marshes, study of, 70

Mastication of food, 224

Meal, full, before retiring, 187

Measurements in field lessons, 388

Meat, lean, 183

Medullary rays, 272

Mercury, a morning star, 427; capillarity of, 233; experiments with, 194; evening star, 335; compared with Venus, 246

Mesocarp, 40

Metals, expansion of, 112–154

Meteorology, for April, 330; charts, 52–60; for December, 163; for February, 244; general directions for, 48–54; for January, 202; for June, 422; for March, 286, for May, 378; for November, 120; for October, 88; for September, 48; times for observation, 49

Meteorological records, 48, 49, 205

Microscope, compound, 266

Minerals, blanks for, 177; forms of, 301; fusibility of, 342; of North America, 170; physical properties of, 71

Mineralogy, for April, 341; for December, 176; for February, 257; for January, 219; for June, 436; for March, 301; for May, 390; for November, 133; for October, 97; for September, 71

Mineralogical record, 73; how to make, 72

Mirrors, 277; axis of, 279

Mixture, illustrated by sulphur and iron filings, 118

Modeling, 17; necessity for, 22; use in science work, 17–18

Moon, the, 123; full, 90; phases of the, 50; rings of the, 325

Morning star, 207

Mosses, study of, 364

Mountain peaks, temperature of, 157

Mountains, effects of, on pro-

ductions, 337; effects on storms, 165; influence upon climate, 88
Muscle, study of, 77
Music, 15; and noise, 373

NAILS, care of, 104
Natural History Calendar, 261
Near-sightedness, 355
Negative electricity, 414
Nests, mounting birds', 346; preservation of, 346; for insects, 31
Neutral equilibrium, 151
Nitrogen, 282;
Nodes on plant stems, 317; on strings, vibrating, 371
Non-conductor, 415
Noon-marks, use of, 206
Normal, the, 277,321
North America and Europe, contrasts in climate, 432; climate of, 124; drainage of, 91; position of, etc., 67; rainfall of, 124–126; relation of its geography to history, 92–93; soil and productions of, 168
North pole, magnetic, 44; altitude of sun, 334

OIL on the skin, 102
Onion, 318
Oral sounds, 21
Organs, essential, 361
Organic agencies, 297
Oscillation, 195
Oxygen, experiments with, 160-161; preparation of, 159

PAINTING compared with modeling and making, 18
Pans for germination of seeds, 312
Papillæ of tongue, 182
Peat, 134; swamps, 340
Pebbles, study of, 128; formed by glaciers, 129

Pencil placed in water, 321
Pendulum, 195; arc of, 196; different forms of, 196
Penumbra, 281
Perennials, 107
Pericarp, 40
Perimysium, 77
Perspiration, 103
Phosphorus, 282
Physical change, 115, 116; properties of minerals, 71
Physics, for April, 320; for February, 230; interest in experiments, 42; for January, 189; most important conception of, 42; for March, 274; for November, 108; relation to other studies, 42; for December, 147; for June, 412; for May, 366; for October, 83; for September, 42
Pig-iron, 178
Pillars, clay-capped, 94
Pine trees, 229
Pistil, 361
Pith, 271
Placenta, 40
Planets, positions of, 292; relative distances from the sun, 61
Plant-life, cycle of, 36; changes in, 38; lice, 398; preparation for winter, 106; reproduction of, 106
Plant axis, underground forms of, 318
Plants, composition of, 403, geologic effects of, 339; growth of, 38; shapes of, 270; water-culture, 404; witnesses to uniformity of climate, 269
Plumbago, 134
Pneumatic trough, 159
Poison-bottles, 31, 306
Pole, balancing, 152
Poles of magnetic needle, 44
Pollen, 361
Polyps, coral, 299

Positive electricity, 414
Potato, 318
Pond life, 308
Prickles and hooks on seeds, 37
Prism, 324; mode of making, 43
Pulse at different ages, 266
Pump, how to make a, 230
Pumping leaky boats, 232
Pyrites, iron, 343

QUARRIES, 173
Quartz, 220

RABBIT, movements of, 137
Radiation, 109
Radiators and reflectors, 110
Rain, effects on surface, 94
Rainbow, 325
Raindrop, history of, 84
Rainfall, effects upon soils, 438
Rain-guage, 51
Rain-water, what becomes of it, 433
Rapids, how formed, 95
Rays of light, 277
Reading, 354
Reflection, 109; angle of, 277
Refraction of heat, 157; of light, 320
Region, how to study a, 69, 70
Reptiles, 400
Respiration, 309–314, 353
Rocks, dip of, 70
Root compared with stem, 319
Roots, 316; aerial, 319
Rope-walkers, 152

SALIVA, uses of, 226
Salivary glands, 226
Salt in water, tests for, 328
Sand in soils, 392; study of, 97
Sarcocarp, 40
Scales of fishes and reptiles, 101
Science record, 54; work, 23

Season, influence upon animals, 30
Sealing-wax, to electrify, 413
Sedimentation, 94
Sediment in stream's course, 95
Seeds, collections of, 81; distribution of, 82; effects of early growth on, 37; freezing of, 146; germination of, 37, 312; study of, 314
Seeing, 275–354
Sensation, 104
Shadow, how to measure, 61
Shadows, 280
Shoes, improper forms of, 139
Shrubs, 271
Signal service, for April, 331; for December, 164; for February, 244; instruction, 51; for January, 203; for June, 423; for March, 288; maps, 52; for May, 379; for November, 121; for October, 89; officer, 52; for September, 55
Silicious stones, 220; effects of burning, 258
Silver nitrate, 328
Simmering, 83
Singing flame, 199–372
Siphon, the, 231
Skeleton, the, 140
Skin, the, 102–104
Skull, human, 142
Slopes of South America, 126, 127
Smell, sense of, 181
Snakes, 401
Snowfall, 163
Soap solution, 327
Soft water, 327
Soils, absorption of heat, 437; adaptation to vegetation, 438; water held in, 436; effects of winds upon, 438; evaporation from, 437; formation of, 97; study of, 390–393; study of properties, 436

Solids, prehension of, 223
Solomon's seal, 318
Solstice, summer, 426; winter, 166
Solution, 86
Sori, 364
Sound, rate of speed, 373; reflection of, 373; location of, 374; study of, 366; vibrations, 374
South America, climate, 170; climatic conditions, 210; drainage, 126; forest area of, 210; productions of, 209; slopes of, 126, 127
Specific gravity, 133; how to find, 235
Spectrum, 43
Spiders, 398; circulation of, 268
Spike, 410
Spores, 364
Spring, early signs of, 289
Springs, 388; intermittent, 434; study of, 433
Squirrel, movements of, 138
Stable equilibrium, 151
Stalactite, 302
Stalagmite, 302
Stamens, 361
Steel, uses of, 179
Stem, compared with root, 319
Stems, forms of, 270; underground, 318
Stone fruits, 41
Stones, calcareous, 219; frost action, 175
Stratification 70
Stratified rocks, 302
Stream, its swiftness, 95
Strike of rocks, 70
Sublimation, 343
Suction, 189
Sulphur and iron filings, 118
Summer rains, 422; solstice, 426
Sun's rays, angle of, 62
Swallowing, 226

Swamp, Great Dismal, 340
Swamps, study of, 339
Symbols, function of, 333; use of, 122
Synovial fluid, 88

TADPOLES, 35, 308; circulation of, 267
Taproot, 319
Taste, sense of, 181
Tears, 356
Teeth, study of, 225
Temperature, contrasts, 124–126; mode of study of, 111; region of lowest, 121; sense, 109
Tendon, 77
Tests for carbon dioxide, 47; flame for minerals, 341; for impure air, 311; for purity of water, 326; for salt in water, 328; for temperature, 111
Thawing, effects of, 173
Thermometer, position of, 50
Thunderstorms, 422
Time, estimates of, 217, 218; for observations, 49; of day, 62; importance of, 130
Tissue, adipose, 79; connective, 78; material for study of, 76, 77
Tongue, 186–226
Tones, study of, 368; pitch of, 370
Tonsils, 227
Touch, sense of, 105
Trade-winds, 429, 430
Training, importance of, 222
Trunk, the, 140; the flexibility of, 143
Tufa, 302; formation of, 435
Turtles, 400, 402; hibernation of, 100
Twigs, changes of, 38; growth of, 313
Twilight, 382

UMBRA, 281
Units of measurement, 68

Unstable equilibrium, 151

VALVES in veins, 264
Vapor, 84
Variation, of day's length, 206
Veins, 264
Venation of leaves, 407
Venus, 207, 382; compared with Mercury, 246
Ventilation, 153; 311
Vernation of leaves, 363
Vertical rays, effects of, 429
Vibrations, study of, 369–377; time of, 195
Vinegar, 118
Voltaic electricity, 415

WALKING, habit of Indian in, 139; position of feet in, 138
Water, hard and soft, 327; impurities in, 326; effect of boiling, 327, 328; effects of, in pebble-making, 128; study of, 326; contains sand and silt, 128
Waterfalls, how formed, 95
Water-newts, 267
Weathering of rock, 97

Weather, effects on plants, 39
Webs of spiders, 398
Wells, study of, 433
Wind, determining direction of, 44; effects upon soils, 438; effects upon land and water, 430; study of, 428; variable, 430
Winter, condition of plants in, 188; condition of living things in, 135
Wood, burning of, 115; formed in one year, 81; rings in, 271; study of, 271
Worms, burrows of, 303; habits of, 34

YEAST, 46
Yellowstone Park, 435

ZERO isotherm, 245
Zoölogy, for April, 303; for December, 135; for February, 221; for January, 180; for June, 394; for March, 259; for May, 345; for November, 98; for October, 75; for September, 29